Issues in Art and Design Teaching

Issues in Art and Design Teaching draws together a range of pedagogical and ethical issues for trainee and newly qualified teachers of art and design, and their mentors in art and design education. Arguing for a critical approach to the art and design curriculum, the collection encourages students and teachers to consider and reflect on issues in order that they can make reasoned and informed judgements about their teaching of art and design.

Among the key issues addressed include:

- Challenging orthodoxies and exploring contemporary practices;
- Measuring artistic performance – art and design education and the assessment debate;
- Art history and multicultural education;
- Research in art and design education;
- Transitions in art and design education: primary/secondary and secondary/ tertiary;
- The role of art and design in citizenship education.

Newly qualified and trainee teachers will find *Issues in Art and Design Teaching* invaluable for its thoughtful and stimulating coverage of the central concerns in this subject.

Nicholas Addison and **Lesley Burgess** are both lecturers in Art, Design and Museology at the Institute of Education, University of London.

Issues in Subject Teaching series
Series edited by Susal Capel, Jon Davison,
James Arthur and John Moss

Other titles in the series:

Issues in English Teaching
Edited by Jon Davison and John Moss

Issues in Geography Teaching
Edited by Chris Fisher and Tony Binns

Issues in History Teaching
Edited by James Arthur and Robert Phillips

Issues in Physical Education Teaching
Edited by Sue Capel and Sue Pietrowski

Issues in Mathematics Teaching
Edited by Peter Gates

Issues in Modern Foreign Language Teaching
Edited by Kit Field

Issues in Music Teaching
Edited by Chris Philpott and Charles Plummeridge

Issues in Science Teaching
Edited by John Sears and Pete Sorensen

Issues in Teaching Using ICT
Edited by Marilyn Leask

Issues in Design and Technology Teaching
Edited by Su Sayers, Jim Morley and Bob Barnes

Issues in Religious Education
Edited by Lynne Broadbent and Alan Brown

Issues in Art and Design Teaching
Edited by Nicholas Addison and Lesley Burgess

Issues in Art and Design Teaching

Edited by Nicholas Addison and
Lesley Burgess

RoutledgeFalmer
Taylor & Francis Group

LONDON AND NEW YORK

First published 2003
by RoutledgeFalmer
11 New Fetter Lane, London EC4P 4EE

Simultaneously published in the USA and Canada
by RoutledgeFalmer
29 West 35th Street, New York, NY 10001

RoutledgeFalmer is an imprint of the Taylor & Francis Group

Typeset in Goudy by
BOOK NOW Ltd
Printed and bound in Great Britain by
Biddles Ltd, Guildford and King's Lynn

British Library Cataloguing in Publication Data
A catalogue record for this book is available from the British Library

Library of Congress Cataloging in Publication Data
A catalog record for this book has been requested

ISBN 0-415-26668-8 (hbk)
ISBN 0-415-26669-6 (pbk)

Contents

Figures

Contributors

Nicholas Addison is a lecturer in art, design and museology at the Institute of Education, University of London and teaches on the PGCE (postgraduate certificate of education), MA and EdD courses. For sixteen years he taught art and design and art history at a comprehensive school and a sixth form college in London. He has lectured in art history on BA courses and is chair of the Association of Art Historians Schools Group. He co-edited with Lesley Burgess *Learning to Teach Art and Design in the Secondary School* (RoutledgeFalmer 2000). His educational research investigates the place of interpretation in the art and design curriculum: he has recently directed an Arts and Humanities Research Board (AHRB)-funded research project, Art Critics and Art Historians in Schools.

Dave Allen lectures in the School of Computer Sciences and Mathematics, Portsmouth University. Since 1998 he has been the external examiner for the MA in Art and Design in education at the Institute of Education, University of London and is currently the external examiner for the part-time PGCE 14–19 Art and Design course. He began his professional life as an art and design teacher in secondary schools although he really wanted to be a musician (and before that a cricketer). He no longer has any formal involvement in teaching art and design: it feels like a country he once inhabited which gave him many good friends and an enormous number of stimulating and important experiences but was ultimately too restrictive and frustrating. Now he has moved to a foreign country called computer science. The natives are delightful and they get on very well, although they are often as mystified by him as he is by them (and their strange machines). He now teaches the course which is closest to his epistemological, technical, aesthetic and pedagogical interests – it's called entertainment technology – so he is unlikely to come home. At least there is still cricket.

Dennis Atkinson is a senior lecturer in the Department of Educational Studies, Goldsmiths University of London. He taught for seventeen years in secondary school and was head of art for twelve years. He gained his PhD from the University of Southampton in 1988. He was course leader for the PGCE art and design secondary course at Goldsmiths for ten years and still contributes to this programme. He is MA tutor for modules in art and design, visual culture and culture pedagogy and curriculum, and also supervises MPhil and PhD research students. His research interests include art and design in education and initial teacher education. He has a particular interest in employing hermeneutic, post-structural and psychoanalytic theory to explore the formation of pedagogised identities and practices within educational contexts. He is currently principal editor of the *International Journal of Art and Design Education* and has published regularly in academic journals since 1991. His forthcoming book, *Art in Education: Identity and Practice*, is published by Kluwer Academic Press.

Lesley Burgess is a lecturer in art, design and museology at the Institute of Education, University of London. She is course leader for the PGCE course in art and design and teaches on two MA courses in Art and Design in education and museums and galleries in education; between 1992 and 2001 she was co-director of the Artists in Schools Training Programme. Before moving to the Institute in 1990 she taught for fifteen years in London comprehensive schools. She is a member of the Teacher Education Board for the National Society for Education in Art and Design (NSEAD) and is a trustee of Camden Arts Centre. She co-edited with Nicholas Addison *Learning to Teach Art and Design in the Secondary School* (RoutledgeFalmer 2000). Her main research interests are curriculum development and resource-based learning and contemporary art and artists in education. She has recently co-directed with the Victoria and Albert Museum a DfEE-funded research project Creative Connections.

Tom Davies is head of the School of Art and Design Education, Birmingham Institute of Art and Design (BIAD), University of Central England, Birmingham. He is also chair of Art and Design Research Group (BIAD); director of Initial Teacher Education: Postgraduate Teacher Training – Qualified Teachers Status (QTS); founder member of the Teacher Education Board for NSEAD; member of the Advisers and Art Inspectors for Art and Design (AAIAD); adviser to HMI/Ofsted, Teacher Education Agency (TTA), Qualifications and Curriculum Authority (QCA) and a Fellow of the Royal Society of Arts (FRSA).

Gen Doy is professor and reader in the history and theory of visual culture at De Montfort University, formerly Leicester Polytechnic. She writes on and teaches issues concerning class, gender and 'race' in relation to visual culture. Her books include: *Materializing Art History* (Berg 1998), *Black Visual Culture: Modernity and Postmodernity* (I. B. Tauris 2000) and, most recently, *Drapery: Classicism and Barbarism in Visual Culture* (I. B. Tauris 2002).

Elliot Eisner is the Lee Jacks Professor and professor of art and education at Stanford University, California and is widely known for his scholarship in three fields: arts education, curriculum studies and qualitative research methodology. His research interests focus on the ways that the arts expand awareness and advance human understanding, and the improvement of school as educative institutions. He has published many books and received numerous awards for his work in the USA and elsewhere. His commitment to arts education is reflected in numerous prestigious awards, and his serving on a number of influential bodies and acting as president of the National Art Education Association, the International Society for Education through Art, and the American Educational Research Association. He is president of the John Dewey Society.

Anton Franks was a teacher of drama and English in London schools and now teaches, researches and writes on drama and English in education at the Institute of Education, University of London. Recent publications include 'Lessons from Brecht' written with Ken Jones in *Research in Drama Education*, 4(2), 'Drama, Desire and Schooling' in *Changing English*, 4(1) and 'The Meaning of Action in Learning and Teaching' in *British Educational Research Journal*, 27(2).

Kerry Freedman is a professor of art education at Northern Illinois University (NIU). She recently moved to NIU after teaching for fifteen years at the University of Minnesota. She received her PhD in curriculum and instruction in 1985 from the University of Wisconsin-Madison. She has taught art at all levels and for over twenty-five years. Her research concerns the relationship of curriculum to technology and culture. Recently, she has particularly focused on questions concerning student engagement with visual culture and the post-modern conditions of education. She is on several editorial boards, including the *Journal of Art and Design Education*, and is the incoming senior editor of *Studies in Art Education*. She is member of the Council for Policy Studies in Art Education and a distinguished fellow of the National Art Education Association. She currently has a book in press with Teachers College Press titled *Teaching Visual Culture*.

Henry A. Giroux holds the Waterbury Chair Professorship at Pennsylvania State University and is the Director of the Waterbury Forum in Education and Cultural Studies. His most recent books include: *Fugitive Cultures: Race, Violence and Youth* (Routledge 1996), *Channel Surfing: Race Talk and the Destruction of Today's Youth* (St Martin's Press 1997), *Pedagogy and the Politics of Hope* (Westview 1997), *The Mouse that Roared: Disney and the End of Innocence* (Rowman and Littlefield 1999) and *Stealing Innocence: Youth, Corporate Power, and Cultural Politics* (St Martin's Press 2000).

Tom Gretton is senior lecturer in the Department of History of Art, University College London. He has recently published essays on the relationship between fine art and illustrated magazine pictures in late-nineteenth-century France and is completing a book on the images made by José Guadalupe Posada, a 'popular' printmaker, in Mexico in the generation before the Mexican revolution of 1910–17. In 2000–1 he was chair of the group that wrote the QAA Bench-marking Statement for History of Art, Architecture and Design.

Neil Hall is presently Director of Research, School of Education and Training, University of Greenwich, London. His interest in art is that of an informed amateur, but relates also to his belief that mathematics provides a powerful tool for understanding and explaining the world: art is a highly mathematical medium. His research, though, is more often concerned with the cognitive processes associated with learning school-level mathematics, and the use of information technologies to support learning.

Richard Hickman is senior lecturer in education at the University of Cambridge. He has coordinated the PGCE art and design course at Cambridge since 1997 when he moved from the School of Education, University of Reading. His secondary art teaching career began in Leicester and subsequently in Leicestershire and Berkshire. He has been actively involved in the training of art teachers since 1985, at the University of Reading, National Institute of Education (Nanyang Technological University), Singapore, and Faculty of Education, University of Cambridge. He has exhibited widely and is editor of *Art Education 11–18: Meaning, Purpose and Direction* (Continuum).

David Hulks is an independent art historian with a strong interest in art education in England and Wales. He first worked in Hertfordshire schools as an art and design teacher then progressed to curriculum management in further education colleges in London and Bristol. He has recently completed a PhD in art history at the University of Reading and is currently engaged in research for the Henry Moore Institute.

Pam Meecham is research tutor in the School of Arts and Humanities, Institute of Education, University of London, with special interest in art and design education and museum studies. She writes on art history and has co-authored with Julie Sheldon, *Modern Art: A Critical Introduction* (Routledge 2000). Her PhD was on US art history in the 1950s.

Roy Prentice is head of art, design and museology at the Institute of Education, University of London. Formerly he was the art adviser for East Sussex Education Authority and a teacher of art and design in London. Currently he is responsible for the Institute's MA programme in the fields of art and design and museum and gallery education. He has gained wide experience as an art and design educator working with children, teachers, student-teachers, research students and museums and gallery staff. His main research interest is the role of practical studio-based work in art and design in the training of teachers. He is a practising painter.

Claire Robins is a part-time lecturer in art, design and museology at the Institute of Education, University of London. She is a PGCE tutor and the artefacts module tutor for the MA in museums and galleries in education. She also teaches on the foundation course at Camberwell College of Arts. She has worked extensively in further education, teaching both contextual studies and studio practice. Her research interests are contemporary theory and practice and their assimilation into educational contexts. Since 2000 she has been working on a DfEE-funded research that investigates art and design teachers' use of museums and galleries as a learning resource.

Kate Schofield has been working since April 2001 as a freelance tutor in art, design and museology and as principal examiner for the new AS and A2 examination; she is a consultant for QCA. Prior to April 2001 she was a part-time lecturer in art, design and museology at the Institute of Education, University of London working as a PGCE art and design tutor and an MA module tutor on the MA in museums and galleries in education. After training as a textile designer, she gained extensive teaching experience in further education in Nottinghamshire before studying for an MA degree at the University of London.

John Steers was appointed general secretary of the National Society for Art Education (now NSEAD) in 1981 after fourteen years teaching art and design in secondary schools in London and Bristol. He was the 1993–6 president of the International Society for Education through Art and served on its executive committee in several capacities between 1983 and 1999. He has served on many national committees and as a consultant to government agencies including the QCA. He is a trustee of the Higher Education in Art and Design Trust and the chair of the Trustees of the National Arts Education Archive, Bretton Hall. He is also a senior research fellow at the University of Surrey Rochampton, London.

Pete Worrall is a senior lecturer and ICT coordinator at the Birmingham Institute of Art and Design, University of Central England, Birmingham. He is also a member of the Advisers and Art Inspectors for Art and Design, founder member (AAIAD) New Media Group; first chair of Teacher Education Board, NSEAD; Art and Design Development in Information and Communications Technologies (ADDICT); UK Representative in Virtual School Art Department (EUN) coordination group; Curriculum Consultancy Group Member, BECTa; Steering Group Member for Creation Project (Special Needs and ICT) Wolverhampton Museum and Art Gallery and a board member of International Advisory Board for Child Art Foundation, USA.

Introduction to the series

This book, *Issues in Art and Design Teaching*, is one of a series of books entitled *Issues in Subject Teaching*. The series has been designed to engage with a wide range of issues related to subject teaching. Types of issues vary among subjects, but may include, for example: issues that impact on initial teacher education in the subject; issues addressed in the classroom through the teaching of the subject; issues to do with the content of the subject and its definition, issues to do with subject pedagogy; issues to do with the relationship between the subject and broader educational aims and objectives in society, and the philosophy and sociology of education; and issues to do with the development of the subject and its future in the twenty-first century.

Each book consequently presents key debates that subject teachers will need to understand, reflect on and engage in as part of their professional development. Chapters have been designed to highlight major questions, to consider the evidence from research and practice and to arrive at possible answers. Some subject books or chapters offer at least one solution or a view of the ways forward, whereas others provide alternative views and leave readers to identify their own solution or view of the ways forward. The editors expect readers of the series to want to pursue the issues raised, and so chapters include suggestions for further reading, and questions for further debate. The chapters and questions could be used as stimuli for debate in subject seminars or department meetings, or as topics for assignments or classroom research. The books are targeted at all those with a professional interest in the subject, and in particular: student teachers learning to teach the subject in the primary or secondary school; newly qualified teachers; teachers with a subject coordination or leadership role, and those preparing for such responsibility; mentors, tutors, trainers and advisers of the groups mentioned above.

Each book in the series has a cross-phase dimension. This is because the editors believe it is important for teachers in the primary and secondary phases to look at subject teaching holistically, particularly in order to provide for continuity and progression, but also to increase their understanding of how children learn. The balance of chapters that have a cross-phase relevance, chapters that focus on issues which are of particular concern to primary teachers and chapters that focus on issues which secondary teachers are more likely to need to address, varies according to the issues relevant to different subjects. However, no matter where the emphasis is, authors have drawn out the relevance of their topic to the whole of each book's intended audience.

Because of the range of the series, both in terms of the issues covered and its cross-phase concern, each book is an edited collection. Editors have commissioned new writing from experts on particular issues who, collectively, will represent many different perspectives on subject teaching, as well as including some previously published papers. Readers should not expect a book in this series to cover a full range of issues relevant to the subject, or to offer a completely unified view of subject teaching, or that every issue will be dealt with discretely, or that all aspects of an issue will be covered. Part of what each book in this series offers to readers is the opportunity to explore the interrelationships between positions in debates and, indeed, among the debates themselves, by identifying the overlapping concerns and competing arguments that are woven through the text.

The editors are aware that many initiatives in subject teaching currently originate from the centre, and that teachers have decreasing control of subject content, pedagogy and assessment strategies. The editors strongly believe that for teaching to remain properly a vocation and a profession, teachers must be invited to be part of a creative and critical dialogue about subject teaching, and encouraged to reflect, criticise, problem-solve and innovate. This series is intended to provide teachers with a stimulus for democratic involvement in the development of subject teaching.

Susan Capel
Jon Davison
James Arthur and
John Moss
October 2002

Introduction

Core debates and issues

Nicholas Addison and Lesley Burgess

Art educationalists have argued for a critical curriculum in the school subject Art and Design for many years (Field 1970; Eisner 1972). Since then, and following endless discussion and debate, a 'critical' dimension has found its way into legislation. If Ofsted (the government inspectorate for schools) is to be believed, this dimension is practised satisfactorily in secondary schools in England (Jones 1998). But we wish to challenge this judgement. Is the inclusion of this 'critical' dimension tokenistic, merely lip service to diverging canons, the western and the multicultural, a parade of signs of the critical that is neither critical nor ethical in conception and practice? However, if it does exist, where can it be found? Is it a fixed phenomenon or should it be subject to ongoing revision?

In our advice to postgraduate student teachers (Addison and Burgess 2000) we recommended that entrants to the profession needed to see themselves as agents of change, teachers who would question the orthodoxies that privilege the subject as uniquely creative, a distinct and autonomous realm divorced from other forms of social and cultural production. What student teachers find when they get into schools is a subject squeezed of resources: human, material, spatial and temporal. They meet resistance both from pupils, who prize the subject as an escape from the logocentric curriculum, and teachers, who use the prevailing orthodoxies to maintain high grades in external examinations. This is an inevitable strategy in the present audit climate where it is necessary to demonstrate each subject's contribution to the school's position in national league tables. Why question what is working?

Well, we believe there are questions beyond implementing simple instrumental solutions; meeting expectations is not a recipe for survival. Judged as professionally competent only if they achieve the standards set and evaluated by others, teachers are denied any real agency. Contributors to this book identify not only how existing practice is reproduced and maintained but also how it can be transformed.

Transitions and shifts in teaching and learning

If teachers are to achieve agency then it is necessary that they recognise and engage with the *paradigm shifts* of the late twentieth century, transformations that are determining the changing place of education in a postcolonial, postindustrial, post-patriarchal, global context. From the USA, Freedman (Chapter 1) provides seven conditions necessary to reshape art education within the expanding field of visual culture, relocating student practice within contemporary realities. From the UK, Steers (Chapter 2) insists that such a reshaping is possible only if teachers abandon pragmatism and adopt a more theorised and energised position both in relation to subject knowledge and pedagogy.

One difficulty is the lack of continuity between the different phases of art education, the disjunctions between primary and secondary, secondary and further/higher education. Prentice (Chapter 3) and Robins (Chapter 4) look at the implications of *cross-phase transitions* and discuss the need for 'dialogue' and 'mutuality'.

Curriculum issues

Eisner (Chapter 5) reasserts the need to underpin theory and practice with meaningful *research in art education*. For him this entails questioning the ready acceptance of quantitative data because it obscures what is vivid in art. The subtleties and nuances of practice in the subject can be recoded and evaluated only by employing qualitative methodologies and he provides insights into this process. Addison (Chapter 6) suggests that such methodologies are not without their tensions. However, by analysing a collaborative and interventionist, action research project involving art critics and historians in schools, he argues that the dialectical relationship between parallel discourses can in practice be productive.

One way in which the curriculum can be reshaped is through the changes brought about by revision of the old and recognition of the new, a process that requires an acknowledgment of other voices and the growing importance of *interdisciplinarity*. Franks (Chapter 7) reconsiders the role of language in art and design by examining its function within a multimodal theory of meaning-making. He visits an art room as a sympathetic and 'intimate outsider' to record the everyday interactions that are often overlooked by those following other teaching agendas, including a critical one. Hickman (Chapter 8) recognises what might be described as the political imperatives of 'the Third Way' and explores some of the rationales behind the introduction of Citizenship in English schools. He argues that Art and Design has a significant role to play in developing this new 'literacy'. A similar imperative informs the UK government's move to digitalisation. Within the teaching of new technologies Davies and Worrall (Chapter 9) reconsider the emphasis on technical and transferable skills; they argue instead for the potentiality of the new technologies as a research tool and as a way to promote electronic collaboration, suggesting the possibility of more reciprocal modes of learning and teaching. Allen (Chapter 10) reminds the reader that art within modernity has always to recognise its place alongside other forms of visual culture. In an autobiographical account of his own practice as a teacher he recounts his shift from fine art modernism to a multisensory, multimedia, interdisciplinary pluralism and argues for the recognition of other perspectives through disciplinary exchange.

Periods of change always produce anxiety, and this is manifest in *doubts and fears*.

Burgess (Chapter 11) highlights the continuing reluctance on the part of art teachers to acknowledge 'difficult' contemporary practice. Such practice is absent because schooling reinforces and reproduces dominant forms of cultural identity, ones that in a modern nation-state have been essentialised and fixed. In this context much contemporary practice appears difficult because it challenges these identities, and is therefore outlawed as monstrous. Addison (Chapter 12) suggests that absences are much wider and are predicated on modernist myths about what matters. He unearths a climate of iconoscepticism in which the value of the image is contested within a curriculum that privileges the word in the form of writing. He argues that the status of the logocentric curriculum can be questioned only if art teachers and their allies forgo the historical opposition between word and image and develop more discursive environments in which simple reproductive strategies are replaced by interpretative ones. Hulks (Chapter 13) recognises that assessment has been perceived negatively by art teachers, who, holding on to modernist myths, see it as an assault on aesthetic freedom and self-expression. He suggests ways by which art teachers might use assessment both to inform practice through teacher feedback and provide credibility and parity with other curriculum subjects.

The *principle of collaboration* has already been noted in other sections and it too has the quality of a mantra in government directives. All contributors to this section suggest that productive collaborations require participants to define their identities and clarify roles. Schofield's collaboration (Chapter 14) is at the level of institution and her example works because the partnership is based on intervention rather than consensus. Hall and Meecham (Chapter 15) warn against the rhetoric of collaboration revealing how 'creative partnerships' can easily be reduced to the celebratory and the acritical. Addison and Burgess (Chapter 16) examine ways in which student teachers can bridge the differences between institutional aims and philosophies and reinforce the need for critique both in the form of reflective dialogue and in student teachers' own practice as makers.

Towards an ethical pedagogy

In earlier sections this book suggests parallels between the USA and the UK in which common issues and transformative strategies are identified. In this way the book is framed by a transatlantic exchange, which, in the context of globalisation, may be seen as overly parochial. However, this dialogue, situated as it is within dominant and dominating educational debates, is neither exhausted nor resolved and is therefore worth revisiting. Giroux (Chapter 17) argues that educators should remember their previous engagement with the political field. He exposes the empty rhetoric of neoliberalism which, allied to the disengaged, consumerist agendas of corporate capitalism, produces a culture of selfishness. However, rather than locate revision solely within academe he hopes for the rebuilding of public arenas to enable debate and make possible the practice of democracy.

Gretton (Chapter 18) is suspicious of radical strategies in mainstream education and argues for 'critical pragmatism'. He reminds the reader that the canon is one means by which a culture reproduces itself. He recognises that this reproductive process may reinforce exclusive hierarchies, positioning the identities of many students outside the official curriculum. Gretton claims, nonetheless, that without access to dominant discourses the socially excluded will always remain marginalised and disempowered. He therefore recommends that, despite the dangers, art teachers should work from within the canon using it as a point of critical departure. Doy (Chapter 20) too wishes to go beyond the easy solutions offered by an acritical celebration of multiculturalism. She points out that all too often faith is used to provide a limited definition of culture, a restriction that denies the complexity of identity politics. By looking at the work of contemporary Black artists she identifies ways in which common assumptions about class, gender and 'race' can be questioned through studio practice. Here, *making* is far from neutral, neither is it a celebration of the 'natural' creativity of individuals, rather it is both critical and public.

Atkinson (Chapter 19) realises that the ethical conflicts first encountered by teachers entering the profession are formed in relation to a disjunction between the normative standards imposed from above and the contingencies and compromises of their experience in and outside the school. He recognises that it is important for them to question their motivations and sense of responsibility by understanding the social and psychic dimensions of teaching. With reference to Lacanian theory he suggests a way to move beyond a culture of blame.

Pedagogy in art education might be seen to lack an ethical dimension because it valorises the individual and promotes art as separate from other forms of social practice. This is not surprising when some educationalists claim that ethical questions, among others, can be addressed only within those privileged subjects that are based on inquiry: 'English is the only site which can deal with questions of individuality and responsibility in a moral, ethical, public, social sense' (Kress 1995: 32). Art it seems does not belong within a critical curriculum but within something other, within this equation, a 'creative' curriculum. If this is to be believed then the myths of modernism are still intact. This book is in part an attempt to question such assumptions but it is also an attempt to understand how they have arisen, why they are sustained and most importantly how they can be challenged.

Part 1
Transitions and shifts in teaching and learning

Paradigm shifts

1   Recent shifts in US art education

Kerry Freedman

Introduction

This chapter focuses on a transformation that is currently underway in art education in the United States of America. The professional field is changing in response to the new landscape of the visual arts and general educational reforms. The new perspective on art education involves an understanding of the curriculum as a conceptual space in which students develop their ideas with the aid of teachers who do not act merely as guides, but as critical partners. Curriculum is newly becoming understood as a form of mediation between and among students, teachers, and a wide range of texts and images from inside and outside of school.

In part, the change in art education is a response to the elitism and formalism of high modernism reflected in, for example, discipline-based art education. It is a broadly sociocultural approach that seeks to put back into art education the diverse meanings of art to human existence, and aid student understanding of the power of visual culture (including fine and popular arts and their interactions). It focuses on the complex and critical interaction between making and viewing that is at the root of learning in and through the visual arts.

Art education and the state

The public art education that has grown up over the past hundred and fifty years has had a profound effect in the US. Much more is generally known about art than in the past. Museum attendance has continually increased, becoming a major form of 'edutainment', and children's artistic expression is generally considered part of healthy growth and development.

At the same time, however, US art educators have been forced to struggle to keep art in the schools and are constantly threatened with reductions in programming, personnel, materials, and so on. This is the case even now, when it is likely that students learn more from visual culture than from texts, because people are still not convinced that the visual arts are as important as literacy and numeracy. Each state in the US has different requirements for the amount of art offered in schools and site-based management has resulted in an increase in art education in some and its elimination in others. At colleges and universities, art programmes are often those with the least financial support and political clout although student numbers are high.

These conflicting values and disagreements about the importance of art education have fuelled debates concerning how much or how little the central government should control curriculum and assessment. The debates are similar to those in other countries, but unlike many other countries, the US has no single, government-controlled curriculum.

However, other forms of national curriculum exist. For example, state and national standards have been developed and testing in the arts has become prevalent. Teachers are expected to teach to tests intended to assess students' memory of sometimes arbitrary and trivial art historical information and limited applications of elements and principles of design. In contrast to the flux and contradictions of actual knowledge and production in the arts, centralized curriculum standards and testing are based on what is hoped to be a consensus about the criteria and indicators of academic, including aesthetic, quality. The standards and testing suggest that curriculum can be made static and that change in the arts can be limited by putting regulated boundaries around it. The idea of an agreed national knowledge reflects the expectation that 'local' knowledge (of, for example, community and popular culture) is deficient and nationally defined borders delimit cultural (and epistemological) boundaries.

The conceptual horizons for state-controlled curriculum discourse and student assessment in art have been provided by scientific rhetoric, also promoting an implied national curriculum (Freedman 1995). Scientific rhetoric is not science *per se* and does not only apply to the study of scientific skills and concepts. Rather, it is an element of educational discourse that exemplifies common beliefs about the structure, certainty and applicability of science in all school subjects. Scientific rhetoric carries with it the assumption that social life may be systematically tested like the physical world. It reflects a belief that through testing, objective truths will be discovered and measured (or at least untruths will be revealed). It further reflects the assumption that science progressively moves towards a single truth by achieving better methods, technologies, and data. Scientific rhetoric is considered universally applicable, not only to the physical world it was intended to describe, but also to the social world, where it is used to prescribe. It does not carry with it a representation of the play of scientific ideas against a structural background of time and place. Rather, this rhetoric is considered neutral and self-contained, based on synthetic propositions, and unattached to historical crises and social transformations.

In part, the scientific rhetoric in US art education has resulted from the understandable, but misguided, conviction in the professional community that standards and high-stakes testing are needed to legitimize the field. It is also a result of the influence of the discipline-based art education of the 1980s and 1990s (Smith 1987). As a result, nationally published curriculum packages available to teachers are based on a discipline-based format. They focus on the structure and content of a few fine arts disciplines that both reflect a modernist aesthetic and echo scientific rhetoric; art is thus represented in pseudo-scientific ways. In effect these packages act as a national curriculum because they are used across the US. Most of them encourage teachers to break art objects apart, leading to a formulaic analysis of media techniques, decontextualized uses of elements and principles of design, and the study of names and dates of historical fine artists and 'masterpieces'.

Such modernist responses to the postmodern challenges of contemporary life seem to ignore the pervasive and didactic influence of visual culture. What used to be considered 'local' and popular now functions at the national and even international levels and the boundaries between visual forms have broken down as new types of 'edutainment' have emerged. By means of mass production and newer technologies, students are now learning *through the visual arts* a curriculum that no one group controls. It is a seductive curriculum that provides important and enriching information while also teaching lessons of, for example, violence and stereotype. This curriculum may be particularly at issue in the US where more students watch a nationally broadcast television programme than are influenced by the same school curriculum. Visual culture has become the US national curriculum.

New directions in the professional field

The current educational reform in art education seeks to recapture the imagination and meaning of art, as well as respond to the increasingly profound influence of the visual arts in everyday life. This reform is, in part, a grassroots movement in contrast to the Getty Institute's promotion of discipline-based art education or the top-down emphasis on national and state standards and testing. Teachers' conceptual-izations of the curriculum packages discussed above as resources, rather than as plans for practice, illustrate the rejection of artificial structures for learning in the art education community. The shift in art education revolves around a desire to relocate student experience, and contemporary realities concerning the visual arts, to the centre of art education.

Unlike many of the educational reforms that have taken place in the past, the current change is not just a shift in curriculum content or methods. It is a fundamental change in ways of thinking about teaching and learning in the visual arts and it is happening in schools, universities, museums, and other cultural institutions. At least seven new conditions of art education are shaping this change:

1   The domain of art education has expanded to embrace all forms of *visual culture*.
2   Research on *interactive cognition* is an important basis for educational planning.
3   *Social perspectives* to art education are paramount.
4   The realities of *pervasive technologies* are addressed.
5   Art education is understood as *cultural identity* formation.
6   The importance of *contextualizing form* is emphasized in both the analysis and making of art work.
7   Greater attention is given to *constructive critique*.

I shall briefly describe and explain each of these new conditions. Of course, some teachers have been attending to these conditions for a long time, but in the following I include related changes in practice that are receiving increased attention in the US.

Visual culture

The new domain of art education is visual culture. The forms of visual culture include all of the visual arts and design, historical and contemporary: the fine arts, advertising, popular film and video, folk art, television and other performance, the built environment, computer graphics and other forms of visual production and communication. Teaching visual culture is not just teaching about popular culture, nor is it a process of uncritical acceptance. It is a reasonable response to contemporary realities in which the visual arts from past and present, and from multiple cultures, are infinitely recycled, juxtaposed, co-mingled, and reproduced. Today, art education must have less to do with information distribution and more to do with ideas, analysis, and appraisal. Teaching visual culture is about students making and viewing the visual arts to understand their meanings, purposes, relationships, and influences.

Distinguishing among visual forms of culture is becoming increasingly difficult, in part, because the distinctions are no longer based on the quality of form *per se*. In the past, types of media, levels of technical skill, and compositional sophistication played a large part in determining whether an object was considered a work of art. However, such qualitative differences between visual forms have become less discrete. The old argument that fine art was the only art worthy of academic study because of its aesthetic qualities simply does not stand up any more because the same formal qualities can now be found in things both profound and mundane; what was once considered mundane, has become profound in its effects.

In postindustrial, advanced democracies the visual arts are increasingly understood as infused into daily life. Elite aspects of visual culture, such as the purchase of fine art objects have been historically linked to education, refinement, and good taste. Now, however, the ownership of these objects might be considered one relatively minor avenue of access to the visual arts among many, as geographical and institutional borders are crossed and boundaries between the visual arts blur. Fashion designers market scaled-down copies of their own haute couture to increase their visibility. Commercial and graffiti artists become fine artists who are then hired to make advertisements. The *Mona Lisa* has become a pop icon and the *Star Wars* exhibition has been shown in fine art museums.

Practices

Rather than struggle against this proliferation of the visual arts, we should embrace it because it means that the job of art educators has now truly become critical to students' everyday lives. As a part of their education, students are being encouraged to develop a critical awareness of the visual culture they encounter every day. For example, they are beginning to use the methods of feminism to investigate representations of gender, investigating the ways in which men and women have been depicted in fine art and advertising. Through these investigations, students are beginning to understand the immense power of the visual arts in their capacity to seduce, suggest, and educate.

Teachers are addressing the changing visual world by developing educational strategies that focus on the wide range of visual culture and interactions between various cultural forms. Rather than starting with the belief that students cannot make art until they have representational skills, teachers are now planning lessons to promote expression through *imaginative* and *communicative* work. Teachers are beginning with students' visual culture rather than the structure of the fine art disciplines.

Interactive cognition

The historical separation of knowledge from feeling as a foundation of western philosophy has devalued the importance of emotion to cognition and resulted in a lack of serious consideration of the arts in education (Eisner 1998a). Emotion in most school subjects other than art is considered best left at the classroom door, where cognition without ties to emotion, supposedly takes over. However, as Eisner (1994: 33–4) argues, the separation of the ' cognitive and intelligent' from the 'affective or emotional' is absurd because our experience of the world is largely qualitative.

Since the early 1990s, cognitive scientists have become interested in the realm of the arts and the relationship of the arts to learning (e.g. Gardner 1991; Solso 1994, 1997). The connection between form, feeling, and knowing is becoming understood as an important part of cognitive processing, as in the role of expectation to the perception and interpretation of form. Expectation is an emotional state tied to knowledge, for example when a person one knows well is not immediately recognized when seen out of context. Emotion is a form of knowing and it shapes, even determines, the construction of other aspects of knowledge.

The importance of (emotional) relationships between people and objects to learning is becoming increasingly apparent as a result of the new cognitive research. Learning takes place based on cognitive connections, including those that relate to emotion, and more connections mean greater learning. To some extent, each individual constructs knowledge in their own way, based on their own interactions with and interpretations of information, building on previous knowledge.

Differences in *individual* constructions of knowledge must now be taken into account, but at the same time, *group* cognition and situated cognition studies tell us that people come to know in relation to human and environmental contexts (e.g. Prawat 1989; Cole and Engestrom 1993; Kincheloe and Steinberg 1993). For example, computers and other visual technologies have changed both what we know and how we come to know. When we learn through visual technologies that enable fictional images to look real, our thinking about the world is transformed.

Practices

In schools throughout the US, students are making and analysing videos and other time art works to understand the ways in which group meanings are embodied by form. In art classrooms where individualized learning has traditionally been emphasized, cooperative learning activities have increased, reflecting the importance of creative partnerships in contemporary visual culture.

The shift in thinking about learning includes a rethinking about the ways that some common art lessons have appeared to tear emotion from cognition. High school teachers are beginning to move away from, for example, student hours spent making colour wheels and doing other formal and technical exercises, towards lessons that enrich and extend meaning through narrative and other complex concepts. In these lessons colour is investigated by students in order to give form to their ideas. The colour wheel can be seen on the wall, but the students do visual research that demonstrates their own intellectual path, making emotional aspects of cognition transparent. Part of the art learning process is revealed in student writing and other types of reflection that leave cognitive footprints.

Social perspectives

The vast and complex social life of art is important as an educational topic because separating art from its intents and purposes, its interpretations and influences, and its power, can lead to a lack of understanding about the centrality of art to human existence. The task of describing social perspectives on art education is difficult because so many exist. These perspectives include attention to issues of gender, race, ethnicity, sexual orientation, special ability, and other body identities and cultures; socio-economics, political conditions, communities, and natural and human-made environments, including virtual environments. The common ground among these perspectives is that they are based on the conviction that the visual arts are vital to all societies and that representations of art in education should be investigated to reveal their complexity, diversity and integral cultural location. Social perspectives on art education are not, as some have suggested, 'just political'; they represent the lived meanings of visual culture and communities.

Art education has always been important for social reasons. For those of us who were brought up in the period of 'art for art's sake' (which also has its social roots) the historical and social purposes of art might seem inappropriate. But what are the purposes of art if not to reflect and contribute to the life of the social animals who make, view, and use it? Art is, after all, for people's sake. Admittedly, the particular purposes of the past are not those I would wish to support now; but art is a form of social production. For art education to represent art from a social perspective is simply to admit its profound social meaning.

Today, artists often make comments about various social issues and crossover the boundaries of form to perform socially responsible acts. For example, the performance art of Dominique Mazeud and her collaborating volunteers has become a monthly process of clearing garbage away along the Rio Grande that began in 1987.

The art of Peggy Diggs includes the Hartford Grandmothers' Project, which began through the artist's concern about the impact of gang violence on the lives of elderly women living in inner city Hartford, Connecticut, but ended as a dialogue between these women and local teenagers. Art educators perform socially responsible service every day in their work with students.

Practices

Even before students reach adolescence, they become increasingly aware of social issues and take part in an increasingly sophisticated analysis of them. They learn from social interactions, are influenced by local and media culture, and are immersed in the culture of their peers. They begin to place a greater emphasis on social rules and mores, and in the process, question as well as accept social boundaries. Teachers are beginning to deploy many methods of investigation to enable students to understand social aspects of art such as interviewing members of the community and researching local forms. At the secondary level, instruction in social issues and purposes of visual culture, as well as group forms of production, help to ensure that students do not lose interest in the visual arts in what may be their last, formal art course. Teachers are integrating more of the social meanings of art through activities that range from discussions about the look of toys, to analyses of the socio-economic conditions of museum exhibition, to online performances about students' favourite television shows.

Pervasive technologies

The new global technology and unstable borders of culture have made popular culture pedagogical, as well as political (Giroux and Simon 1989). The fragmented, often contradictory, multidisciplinary and intercultural images that students interact with daily may have more to do with student understanding of art than does a curriculum based on the structure of the disciplines. An essential problem for educators is to help students engage with an increasingly influential visual culture in meaningful ways consistent with its increasing complexity, rather than to fit such new forms of experience with the visual arts into old curriculum frameworks. In order to solve this problem, art education must be thought of as including issues, concepts, and skills related to visual technologies.

As a result, the use of visual technologies and the analysis of technological visual culture are important parts of the shift in art education. The imagery in computer games, in feature-length films, and on the web will continue to increase in sophistication. It is already a major part of students' visual culture and will have an increasing effect on all the visual arts.

Every day, outside school, people experience the various and multiple effects of imagery created through visual technologies. These effects are physical as well as psychological in their influence on people's attitudes, behaviours, even body-weight. The imagery of most popular visual technologies is particularly designed around the interests of secondary level students and has visual qualities intended to capture their attention. Visual culture aimed at secondary students, such as rock videos, are becoming less about music and storylines than about visual effects used to quickly and efficiently convey suggestions of beauty, sex, and violence that make people want to look.

Practices

Inside school, art educators are helping students use, analyse, and criticize the technologies that are now providing an art education outside school through both their forms and contents. Teachers are using technology to take students beyond traditional production and viewing processes to real-time global connections. The Internet provides powerful possibilities for student learning. The interactive capabilities of computer technology coupled with the vast amount of imagery and information available on the net give students a wide range of resources that they can download, print out, and cut-and-paste into their own files. Several virtual exhibitions of student art have already been established on the net and teachers are using the web to connect students for group learning experiences.

Artistic production through the use of computers and related newer tech nologies is an important part of helping students to understand the power of contemporary visual culture. As teaching about the use of traditional art media did in the past, the use of computer technology in art classrooms to generate interactive graphics with paint programs, digital image capture devices, and animation soft-ware gives the power of visual culture to students. For example, students can test images, animate objects, and recycle pictures quickly and easily enabling them to interact with each other's work in ways that are unlike traditional media. Students can best understand the effects of visual technologies by using them and analysing their use.

Cultural identity

One of the roots of the new approach to art education is the importance of considering student identity in art curriculum planning and implementation. The visual arts are expressions of people's ideas, beliefs, and attitudes that reveal the identities of individuals and groups, while at the same time, working to produce identities. Cultural differences and identities are profoundly illustrated and supported through the visual arts while at the same time they cross cultural boundaries and comment on those boundaries. Visual identities are defined by a range of conditions, from how people dress, to where they go, to what they watch and the multiplicity of these indentities illustrates the ways that cultures clash, overlap and become fused.

The difficulty for contemporary art educators is to fairly interpret and represent visual cultural forms and their meanings. The struggle is over the representation of culture in the curriculum. Anthropologist James Clifford (1988) speaks of culture as a collage of many cultural identities that are selected and translated on a continuing basis. Far from being a unified whole, any particular culture is a combination of others, with its resulting contradictions and incongruities. The curriculum is similar; it is made of multiple contributions, from various sources, with competing interests. It involves a cut-and-pasted construction of the ideas of individuals and groups that promotes learning through suggestion and connection. The ideas are selected and brought together, with care and a sense of unease.

Practices

As art educators work to meet the challenge of representing cultural diversity within the limitations of educational institutions, we must keep these conditions of curriculum in mind.

As part of the change in art education, the term *expression* is being redefined from a therapeutic notion of self-revelation to a process of identity construction. Many contemporary artists give attention to struggles of identity and cultural traditions in contemporary contexts. For example, Ruth Cuthand's work *Living Post-Oka Kind of Woman* is a drawing of a paper doll with various outfits that raises issues of being Plains Cree and female in contemporary society.

Cultural questions, such as 'What is art?', 'What is good art?', and 'Whose art?', often do not have a single answer. Such questions are professionally debated and personally lived throughout decades, even centuries. As a result, teaching methods concerning issues of diversity and identity often focus on differences of opinion and conflicts. The emerging practice seeks to promote debate and negotiation through various discursive forms that can reveal and respond to cultural difference.

Contextualizing form

The results of the US *NAEP 1997* (Persky *et al.* 1999) indicate that education generally has not attended very well to helping students make meaning. In this study, most students had a basic knowledge of form and media, but had difficulty connecting meaning to form. The results of this study question the way in which the relationship between form and meaning is typically taught: that is divorced from ideas.

Of course, form is critical to the visual arts and it is the immediacy and seductiveness of form that makes art so powerful. The problem is not form *per se*, it is an over-reliance on formalism. Formalism is reductive, pseudo-scientific and primarily concerned with the physical and perceptual characteristics of art objects. It does not involve serious consideration of the relationship between makers and viewers and the ways in which mediation occurs.

To conceptualize aesthetics as only formalistic does not do justice to the complexity of the visual arts. For example, postmodern artists often reject formalistic uses of the elements and principles of design in favour of symbolic uses that suggest multiple and extended meanings; formalistic analyses do not go very far in helping viewers to understand much contemporary art.

Practices

The contexts of both production and viewing should be taken into account. Teaching visual culture includes past contexts that help to maintain the integrity of artists and cultures, but is also grounded in the understanding that art of the past is mediated by conditions of the present. In a sense, all art is contemporary art because, although contexts of production are important, art is always represented in new contexts (institutional conditions, media contexts etc.) which become part of the story of art.

When context is taught *as a type of narrative* attached to the physical art works, just as a story is portrayed by its image, art is presented as an integral part of human existence. As a result, some teachers are giving up their value-scales and contrast exercises in favour of lessons, for example, that start with student interpretation and end with painted, personal metaphors or computerized self-portraits. This is not to say that such formal elements do not matter. They do, but they learn it in a narrative context.

Constructive critique

Many of the conflicts now faced by art educators are a result of attempts to address postmodern problems with modern solutions. As the curriculum changes to take postmodern experience into account, greater attention is being given to critical analyses of visual culture and to the types of assessments appropriate to the visual arts.

One of my graduate students describes a new course she was developing which illustrates well the importance of changing assessment in relation to changes in curriculum. She explains:

> Both the written committee reviews and the large group discussions proved essential for assessing the success of the students' art products . . . Sometimes students drew associations between materials and images with which I had no experience. For example two students constructed an assemblage based on their childhood memories. They brought in a wide selection of toys and games, glued and plastered them together in a somewhat random fashion, and attached working Christmas lights. The work was titled 'Childhood Pinball Machine.' At first glance, the work had little order to it. It was not unified, had no center of attention, and did not follow most of the formal 'rules' of art. In contrast, two other students . . . constructed an assemblage based on a trip to Niagara Falls [which] had a wonderful unity of color and texture and a Monet-esque painting of a waterfall. Initially, I regarded 'Niagra Falls' to be the more successful assemblage. I, having been trained in a formalist tradition, responded to it using this lens. Yet, in the discussions and committee reviews of the artworks, the students had little to say about 'Niagra Falls' and were overflowing with things to say about 'Childhood Pinball Machine.' They recalled all the times they have played with pogs, collected baseball cards, and

played arcade games. They were excited about the addition of an old car headlight which reminded them of stadium lights . . . what I discovered from this discussion was that 'Childhood Pinball Machine' was rife with associative power, while 'Niagra Falls' was simply beautifully painted and carefully arranged. From a postmodern standpoint, then, 'Childhood Pinball Machine' was a more successful artwork.

(Pereira 1999: 20)

Through this experience, this teacher became aware that change must take place in her means of assessing student work as she broadened her curriculum to include postmodern concepts.

Practices

Assessments should be related to the concepts and skills that students are intended to learn, but should also allow for those student intentions that go beyond 'the box' of instructional objectives. When teaching postmodern concepts and skills, such as suggestiveness, which demand multiple, varied and extended responses, alternative forms of assessment are needed. As the example illustrates individual educators may not always be the best determiners of success. Student response may help teachers to judge whether individual works are successful and collaborative assessment done by peer educators tends to strengthen student work overall (Boughton 1997). Also, the form of work may indicate alternative forms of assessment. For example, installations, performances, and community projects may be most effectively assessed through the inclusion of audience/community response.

Conclusion

Changing the direction of art education has not been easy nor will it be quick to succeed. Frankly, it is harder to teach this way. But we are in a new artistic renaissance in which art educators must take part. Images are becoming more pervasive than texts, the visual arts are being seen by new audiences in new ways, and artistic methods, such as portfolio assessment, have gained currency even in general education. If we want students to understand the new world, art education must change in relation to the visual arts now.

2   Art and design in the UK
The theory gap

John Steers

The problem

At the start of the twenty-first century, any theoretical stance underpinning art education in English state-maintained schools is profoundly confused and, to an unnecessary degree, defined by incoherent political and bureaucratic imperatives. The control exercised by bodies such as the Qualifications and Curriculum Authority (QCA) is driven by a spurious belief that curriculum and assessment developments can simply build upon examples of assorted existing good practice in schools. But what is said to constitute 'good practice' – by Ofsted (1998) for example – is seldom contested or debated, and rarely, if ever, defined theoretically. Rather, there is an assumption that such practice is self-evidently 'good' and should therefore provide the basis for development. The problem with such pragmatism is that at best it leads to uninspiring and slow evolutionary development and, at worst, to atrophy. Practice in art education has reached the point where the subject is in danger of becoming an anachronism. The vital energy required to jolt it forward is lacking so that the subject neither meets the needs of students nor keeps pace with professional practice.

Recent history

The introduction in the mid-1980s of the General Certificate of Secondary Education (GCSE) marked the beginning of the 'reforms' that have continued unabated to the present time. For many art teachers the GCSE was welcome and overdue, moreover, the rationale for its introduction was clear enough: the old system was incompatible with comprehensive education and, according to Her Majesty's Inspectors of Schools (HMI), work in secondary schools was dominated by examinations which governed the type and length of classroom activities. The reliability of inter-examination board standards then, as now, was considered questionable, so the new GCSE was administered by just four regional examining groups in England, one examination board in Northern Ireland and another in Wales. At the core of the proposals was a requirement that common national assessment criteria must be established for all syllabuses to ensure that all those with the same subject title had sufficient content in common, and that all boards applied the same performance standards to the award of grades. To this end, 'draft grade criteria' working parties were established for some subjects as early as 1981. However, in a pattern that was to become familiar in the following years, the working party for art was not convened until 1984 when the template for such assessment criteria had been firmly established.

The members of the Secondary Examinations Council (SEC) GCSE Grade Criteria Working Party for Art & Design (SEC 1986) – of which I was one – recognised that the key to the whole exercise was how to define candidates' achievements through explicit criteria while not overly restricting the methods by which those criteria might be achieved. The working party accepted that this approach involved many compromises and these included tacit agreement that it might not be possible adequately or equally to assess all curriculum objectives because the evidence for some would be too ephemeral. Lengthy consideration led to the identification of three equally weighted, closely interdependent and interrelated domains:

- A *conceptual domain* concerned with the formation and development of ideas and concepts.
- A *productive domain* concerned with the abilities to select, control and use the formal and technical aspects of art and design in the realisation of ideas, feelings and intentions.
- A *critical and contextual domain* concerned with those aspects of art and design which enable candidates to express ideas and insights which reflect a developing awareness of their own work and that of others.

I now recognise that this model is only one among many that could have been adopted (Secondary Examinations Council 1986). In retrospect it can now be seen as the thin end of a wedge leading towards a state where, as Eisner (1985) warns:

> Infatuation with performance objectives, criterion referenced testing, competency based education, and the so-called basics lends itself to standardization, operationalism, and behaviorism, as the virtually exclusive concern of schooling. Such a focus is . . . far too narrow and not in the best interests of students, teachers, or the society within which students live.
>
> (Eisner 1985: 367)

From the mid-1980s, through successive agencies such as the School Curriculum Development Committee (SCDC) to the present QCA, governments have sought once and for all to 'nail the jelly to the wall' through repeated attempts to define the content, aims, objectives and assessment parameters and criteria for art and design. But there has been little new thinking and in reality much of this relentless process has consisted of 're-packaging' by means of repeated editing and precis of documents to make them fit the current template for all subjects. Thus the publication of Curriculum 2000 and the latest specifications for qualifications give the false impression that, at last, all questions of what constitutes good practice in schools have been resolved. Of course this is just an illusion; before long another perceived change of circumstances or belated admission of inherent problems will require another round of reductionist tinkering. In my view there is more than enough evidence that the control exercised by government agencies has acted as a drag anchor, stifling open debate and real progress.

To anybody who takes a long or international perspective it will be clear that in visual arts education conflicting aims and values have always been in evidence. Thistlewood (1992) reminds us that when histories of art and design education over the past hundred years are reviewed:

> It is difficult to ignore the obvious fact that fundamental, irreconcilable disagreements about policies, rationales and justifications have been usual. Revolution versus convention; child-centrality versus subject centrality; the expressive versus the utilitarian.
>
> (Thistlewood 1992: 8)

It needs to be recognised that these debates are the lifeblood of art education. They should be encouraged rather than suppressed and, most importantly, they need to be informed by theory and research rather than the traditional, but unsatisfactory, English approach, a *post-hoc* rationalisation of gut instinct.

For example, consider the compelling *economic* argument for an enhanced place for the arts in the curriculum at the end of the twentieth century. Recent research work by the Department of Culture, Media and Sport (DCMS) estimates the value of the creative industries to the UK economy as £112 billion, and concludes that this sector of the economy is growing in output three times faster than the rest of the economy, creating new jobs faster than any other sector. Professor Frayling, chair of the Design Council and Rector of the Royal College of Art, makes the point that underpinning the collation of such statistics by the DCMS

> was and is the argument that in a post-industrial economy – especially in a country like Britain where labour is not cheap, raw materials not plentiful, and where the manufacturing sector is struggling – the work of creative individuals and multidisciplinary teams has become one of the most important engines of wealth creation; in fact it has increasingly played this role over the last quarter of a century, only for some reason no-one has been noticing – at least not at the policy level.
>
> (Frayling 2001: 2)

Where is this research recognised in Curriculum 2000 with its water-tight and hierarchical subject boundaries and structure? Certainly there is evidence that most school managers are unaware of the very significant shift described by Frayling – accommodation and resources for art and design in schools are in a state of decline and extremely variable across the UK to a point where the average spend per secondary pupil is £2.68 per year, while some schools spent as little as 60p.

The curriculum

Perhaps the key question is whether a National Curriculum (NC) for Art is necessary? In England and Wales, much of the initial support for the statutory Art Order was predicated on two views that with the benefit of hindsight seem over optimistic. First, that it would be the best art and design curriculum the world had ever seen; and second, such an Order would secure proper time and resources for all pupils aged 5–16. It is now obvious that these assumptions were naive; a secure and well-resourced place in the curriculum remains a primary goal, but art educators need to look to other means to achieve it.

Since national curricula, *per se*, are designed to define what knowledge should be transmitted (although not necessarily how things should be taught) there has been an obvious concern by politicians, if not the wider community, to make teaching, learning and assessment increasingly teacher-proof. Eisner has argued convincingly that trying to produce teacher-proof materials is a mistake and 'teachers need materials that stimulate their ingenuity rather than materials to which they are subservient' (Eisner 1985: 372). The NC Art Order and associated documents tend to fragment subjects by failing to distinguish between outcomes of greater and lesser importance. They concentrate on what is to be *taught* rather than *learnt* and on relatively easily defined and assessed competencies. Little or no attempt is made to accommodate more challenging postmodern perspectives, instead everything is forced into a modernist or formalist framework. Ross makes a resonant and damning assertion that an overwhelming feature of the NC Orders for Art and Music is that 'they only make sense to specialist teachers who know something about progression and development in the arts already' (Ross 1995: 273).

Arguably, however, the introduction of the NC has done little to change practice in secondary schools. Hughes (1998) described the art curriculum as an arbitrary set of practices passed down over years in need of radical reconceptualisation:

> It is a curriculum which has been arrived at by a process of accretion which the National Curriculum has done little to resolve. The result is a set of procedures, processes and practices which are a kind of historical trace of past theories of art education, child development or art, craft and design practice, all existing simultaneously and each exemplified by activities which jockey for time and space.
>
> (Hughes 1998: 45)

While I believe that art and design should be a statutory *entitlement* for all pupils during their years of compulsory schooling, I am by no means convinced that the subject is best served by a statutory Order; one prescribed curriculum restricts choice. 'Multiple visions' of the curriculum need to be developed – a series of curricula with identifiable differences, for example, of approach, content, medium or type, and/or a series of shorter curricula that could be built up as learning modules. Such curricula need not be idiosyncratic. Documenting exemplary case studies could inform a continuing and rigorous debate in the profession (a much under-utilised resource in art and design). At the same time, an associated range and variety of assessment procedures would need to be developed for clearly identified and different purposes.

Assessment

Can a wholly objective standardised system of assessment be designed for art and design? Do attempts to achieve this affect course content for better or for worse? Who is qualified to make such judgements?

For many years concerns have been expressed about an increasing orthodoxy of approach and lack of experimentation in art and design. In 1982, Price, an experienced chief examiner, expressed concerns about the effect of the examination system on classroom practice and prophesied problems with standardised assessment criteria:

> The existing relationship between curriculum and examination syllabuses is a 'dog and tail' affair. The influence of external examinations has, to some extent, bred a species within the genus of 'School Art' . . . The question of whether the 'tail wagging the dog' is a satisfactory state of affairs must be linked with the possibility that the existing dog is a mongrel that defies simple definition. This is not to say that some mongrels are not more healthy than some more easily categorised pedigrees, but it does make the establishment of national criteria guidelines more difficult – more difficult in the sense that criteria will necessarily be based upon generalisation of a plethora of objectives and practices – generalisation which will undoubtedly influence the future of art education.
>
> (Price 1982: 399)

Binch, at one time chair of the art and design panel of the biggest examination board, reflected on how the examination system introduced into England and Wales in the mid-1980s, with its strong emphasis on 'process', influenced the type of work produced in secondary schools. He claimed that this led frequently to a single, linear classroom methodology where:

> The starting point is usually investigation and research, followed by the development of ideas and some experimental activities, and the completion of a 'finished' piece of work. Whilst the investigation and research can be into any relevant matters, including the work of artists, craftspeople and designers, or into concepts, issues and ideas, it is most commonly based upon objective drawing and visual analysis. The predominant sources of reference are collections of objects set up in the art room. The model reinforces the insular nature of 'school-art' and, even when reference is made to external sources, it is usually based on the same methodology of objective drawing and visual analysis.
>
> (Binch 1994: 124)

Over subsequent years this approach has proved very reliable, producing 'safe' work, which of its kind is often of high quality and secures predictably good grades. Today, examination pressures are overwhelming and influence all aspects of the classroom. In this high-stakes education system it should be no surprise that teachers are adept at finding an effective prescription for their pupils, one that satisfies the various demands of the awarding bodies and, in turn, league tables, inspection and threshold payments (a form of payment by results). But whether such a dominant conventional approach is in the best interests of pupils is another question.

Of particular significance has been a marked trend away from an optional formal art and design history element towards a general requirement for a critical and contextual studies component. This shift has been largely uncontentious but it is not unproblematic. Pragmatism has played a part in the widespread acceptance of critical studies in secondary schools because the 'old' art history was very demanding of teaching time and was suited only to academic pupils. In contrast, critical studies at examination level is often dependent on pupils researching 'personal studies' in their own time. The outcomes of this approach are varied with some exceptional projects in evidence. More generally, however, 'descriptive and non-contextual studies' might be a more accurate title and questions need to be asked about what coherent knowledge of art practice pupils gain from 'research' with a narrow focus that often encourages plagiarism accompanied by 'unproblematic' pastiches of 'style'. There is a need to develop a clear rationale for the inclusion of critical studies based on a coherent view of content and cultural transmission; real critical thought and reaction, and articulate debate.

Since the early 1980s there has been a trend away from holistic assessment without published criteria, to a schematic process in which marks are aggregated based on published assessment criteria. It is becoming evident that this leads to fragmentation. Teachers now teach to specific criteria in the knowledge that if pupils provide evidence of engagement with these criteria they will be rewarded regardless to some extent of the actual quality of their work. Of necessity, assessment criteria are drafted to be generic, applicable to a wide range of specialisms and activities. As a consequence they are not easy to apply to unorthodox outcomes and tend to inhibit those responses that engage with contemporary practice.

Although coursework was not generally a component of the GCE O level examination, it was a valued element of the GCSE from the outset. However, from the early 1990s onwards the government has sought to reduce the importance of coursework in all subjects in favour of the terminal test (in art and design the permitted ratio of coursework to terminal examination is presently 60:40). What constitutes a 'unit' of coursework is generally ill-defined, the best and most committed candidates continue to select from a considerable body of work.

Most change has been ostensibly in the interests of increasing examination reliability. However, art and design examination reliability remains an issue, particularly given the much-increased size of the entry for GCSE now that there are fewer awarding bodies. In the past, smaller examination boards with relatively small entries employed small teams of examiners. Although not dependent on formal mark schemes or assessment criteria, it seems reasonable to assume that a good level of consensus could be reached on standards, especially as one examiner often assessed all the work for a particular component. In 2000 at least one awarding body employed over 200 art and design moderators. Reliability is totally dependent on effective moderator standardisation procedures – a very considerable challenge.

Achieving accurate standardisation presents a considerable challenge to the awarding bodies and ever-tighter drafting of assessment criteria and their rigid application is not the answer. Boughton (1995) succinctly identifies the inherent problem:

> Any attempt to use written statements intended to describe the range of complex and subtle characteristics of visual expressive work at any level of schooling will be less than adequate . . . The qualitative nature of the arts . . . cannot be effectively captured in words alone. Linguistic representation of the arts is at best reductionist, and at worst misleading.
>
> (Boughton 1995: 146)

In September 2000, the government introduced reformed GCE A levels, together with new vocational A levels and a Key Skills qualification. The introduction of modularity into the examination system created new problems for art and design. One concern was greatly increased workload for teachers while the other was more philosophical and concerned with the effect of the examination on teaching and learning. It was clear that the government perceived that the first year of the old A level had been a time for relaxation therefore it was necessary to prescribe student productivity. However, they were mistaken: in art and design, that first year was often a time for student experimentation, a time to try out new ideas and for teachers to support individual creativity by making students less dependent on teacher-led projects. This is threatened by the new exam because, in effect, every project, every piece of work from the start of the course needs to be fully realised and of the required standard. In effect, the message is don't bother being creative, avoid risks, play safe, do what is expected. This is damaging to students and the discipline.

I have no doubt that, over time, teachers will as usual shoulder the additional burden of the new examinations rather than disadvantage their students. But is it worth it, given the likely damage to the subject? There seem to be few advantages and it seems this format was imposed because once again QCA saw no compelling reasons for art and design to be different from other subjects. But it is different and it needs to be recognised as such.

Creativity and cultural transmission

Developing individual creativity and imagination on the one hand, and knowledge and understanding of cultural heritage (however this is defined) on the other, are core aims in just about every art and design curriculum and Curriculum 2000 is no exception. However, I have suggested that in practice art education is often devoid of any coherent transmission of cultural heritage and a pervasive orthodoxy threatens real creativity.

In an era of increasing and sometimes dangerous awareness of national, ethnic and religious identity, the transmission of cultural values seems to be high on the political and educational agenda. There are those who argue that arts education should be concerned *principally* with the business of cultural heritage and the transmission of cultural values. For example, Tate (1997), a former chief executive of the QCA, has stated this position clearly. He said that matters of taste in culture and morals were not to be equated trivially with questions of taste in food and clothes because these things are not just a matter of personal preference. He advocated the need to define a literary and artistic canon and the need to introduce pupils first and foremost to high culture and, moreover, he said that those things English should be central to the curriculum in England. He maintained that the roots of British culture can be found in what he identified as the classical, Christian, European tradition and that the best hope for the many minority cultures in Britain was recognition of this strong dominant culture (Tate 1997).

But many art educators espouse a radically opposite view and have a more liberal, progressive vision of the curriculum. They claim that teachers must avoid an ethnocentric, culture-bound view of the arts, emphasising the need to draw on a *range* of cultures in a search for a truly humanistic arts education. Cultural relativism (Chalmers 1995) (i.e. 'the co-equality of fundamentally different frames of thought and action characteristic of diverse cultures': Pancratz 1993: 14) might be anathema to many conservatives, but I would argue that in our multiracial, multi-faith country – or multinational, multiracial, multi-faith Europe – the curriculum must represent the sociocultural diversity. Some, like Chalmers, have consistently argued that the curriculum must be designed to be both multiethnic and multicultural and that it needs to be reformulated: 'so that it emphasizes the unity within our diversity, showing all humans make and use art for fairly similar purposes' (Chalmers 1996: 45). Chalmers goes further by stressing that 'unfortunately, there are issues, such as racism and sexism, that absolutely require us to implement approaches in which art making and learning become ways to participate in social reconstruction' (Chalmers 1996: 45).

If art and design teachers make a more conscious and systematic attempt both to transmit cultural heritage and celebrate cultural diversity through their teaching, would this imply less emphasis on individual making and creating? Another crucial question teachers need to answer, of course, is not only *whose* cultural values should they transmit, but *who* determines the priorities? There are huge issues at stake here.

Arts education should not in my view be concerned solely with cultural trans-mission: the other key concern is developing the creative potential of students. In England, following the report of the National Advisory Committee on Creative and Cultural Education (NACCCE 1999), a working party has been convened by QCA to advise on guidance for schools about ways to promote pupils' creativity. Is there, I wonder, some chance of progress? As the curriculum is already boxed in by attainment targets, programmes of study and closely linked assessment procedures, it will be profoundly depressing if the 'solution' is to present schools with exemplary 'creative' projects and yet another template or framework to assess and report on the supposed competencies associated with creative behaviours.

The pitfalls should be obvious. In his anatomy of creativity *Creating Minds*, Gardner (1993) points out that creativity is not the same as intelligence: that while these two traits are correlated, an individual may be far more creative than he or she is intelligent, or far more intelligent than creative. He states that while it has proved possible to devise highly *reliable* tests for creativity there is little evidence that such tests have much *validity*.

Clearly creativity is not the exclusive prerogative of the arts, rather it is shorthand for a raft of multifaceted abilities and predispositions that need to be fostered throughout the curriculum. Creative individuals may display a range of characteristics that extend beyond some assumed general capacity for divergent thinking. For example these might include: a tolerance for ambiguity and a certain playfulness with ideas, materials or processes; an ability to concentrate and persist, to keep on teasing and worrying away at a problem rather than seeking premature closure. They are likely to recognise, or have a willingness to explore, unlikely connections. They may be particularly self-aware and have the courage (or plain stubbornness) to pursue their ideas in the face of opposition. Most of all, creative individuals must have the confidence, the self-belief, to take intellectual and intuitive *risks* in the cause of innovation, breaking or pushing back the boundaries of what is known or thought possible, or in achieving new aesthetic conjunctions.

But does the education system allow such characteristics to be properly valued? Politicians' rhetoric may emphasise the creative imperative – 'Our aim must be to create a nation where the creative talents of all the people are used to build a true enterprise economy for the twenty-first century – where we compete on brains, not brawn', says Tony Blair, the British prime minister (NACCCE 1999: 6). But Ken Robinson, chair of the NACCCE, responds, 'If the government were to design an education system to inhibit creativity, it could hardly do better' (Cornwell 2001: 23).

The problem is that it is possible to run an ostensibly effective and efficient art department and achieve excellent examination results by means of assiduous teacher *prescription and direction*, where students are coached to replicate safe and reliable projects year after year. In this case, activities may be more re-creative than genuinely creative and often typify what has been described as 'School Art'. By contrast, creativity is allied with the pursuit of ideas that are the antithesis of such orthodoxy, ideas that may be innovative, radical and sometimes heretical or revolutionary. Is it this that so worries the politicians and civil servants? In a recent discussion an examination board spokesperson blithely told me that creativity in schools was a good thing – provided, he said, it is '*controlled*'. And controlled it often is, not just in art and design. A *Sunday Times* feature proclaimed: 'Forget creativity, imagination and play. For children at school in Britain, life is tests, tests and more tests'. 'But', the writer asks, 'if stamping out their individuality is designed to get better results, why isn't it working?' (Cornwell 2001: 22).

Towards a reconceptualised art education

Whether art education is seen as a way of protecting and nurturing the autonomous, imaginative life of pupils, a form of instruction with the potential to transform individuals and society, or as a distinct discipline with its own methods for conducting enquiry and forming judgements, there should be no doubt about its continuing importance in general education. It is precisely this variety of potential function that should encourage us to challenge the monolithic vision enshrined in the NC and its assessment. 'A Manifesto for Art in Schools' (Swift and Steers 1999), co-authored by John Swift and myself, was intended to do just that.

The manifesto based its proposals on a postmodern view of art and design in education with an emphasis on three fundamental principles: *difference*, *plurality* and *independent thought*:

> Through their application in art [and design] practice and theory, knowledge and knowing will become understood as a negotiation of ideas which arise from asking pertinent questions, and testing provisional answers rather than seeking predetermined ones. The emphasis is on the learner and learning, negotiating what they learn, learning how to learn, and understanding knowledge as a multiplicity of changing hypotheses or theories which are subject to evidence, proof, argument and embodiment. As such *difference* becomes a locus for action and discussion at a personal and social level, *plurality* points to a variety of methods, means, solutions and awareness for any issue, and *independent thought* develops individuality, the capacity to challenge, and creativity through introspection into the nature of learning and teaching in art. These abilities are as vital for teachers as they are for learners.
>
> (Swift and Steers 1999: 7)

The essential content of art activity should be what it has always been – exploring what it is to be human. The universal themes of birth, death, love, war, gender, disease, spirituality and identity can be re-examined in the context of our rich and varied postmodern, postcolonial, multiethnic and multi-faith societies. It is also about how educators make and shape the environment and the world. I believe the approach to cultural education is too often hierarchically ordered, based on received opinion. Educators need to open up a rich variety of cultural forms, past and present, near and far, for interrogation, appraisal and evaluation, and should be prepared to debate, rather than reiterate, such concepts as superior/ inferior, fine art/popular art, etc. Educators should do more to address contemporary issues, current debates and practices, art's changing role in changing societies and the way art can shape society.

How do we persuade pupils to take more responsibility for their own learning and encourage them to engage with issues of real personal concern through their artwork? In art and design, teachers need to be more prepared to challenge 'typical' student responses with innovative ideas and examples of different forms of representation, for example, in perception, identity, cultural grouping, and so on.

Students should be given a real opportunity to question and influence their education by negotiating a variety of approaches, with more or less emphasis on theory or practice according to need, age, development, ability, and through curricula and assessment procedures that exercise choice by definition.

Merely modifying or replacing the curriculum Order or various national guidelines for art will not in itself resolve the problems I have identified, given the interconnectedness of teaching, learning, subject knowledge, assessment, and the preparation and development of teachers. All these factors need addressing if education (and within it art education) is to become a more meaningful and high quality experience for teachers and learners, and create the artists, craftspeople, designers and discerning consumers of art that Britain needs.

There are several prerequisites to the implementation of the three principles of difference, plurality and independence of mind:

- The preparation and development of teachers should be redesigned in order to give them the confidence and ability to embody and promote risk-taking, personal inquiry, creative action and thought, both before and during their teaching career.
- More opportunities need to be created for learners to understand art as something that actually matters in their lives and has relevance to their present and future actions.
- More choice, autonomy and empowerment needs to be offered through the development of a more critical, inquiring, reflexive and creative mindset, assisting self-generated and self-aware learning.
- The range of choice and type of study available across all forms of art needs to be broadened without any implied hierarchy.
- There should be more opportunities for different types of study through a greater range of media in order to raise consciousness of current personal and social issues, their representation in past and present art forms, and their representation in different cultures. This requires the development of a diversity of curricula where the various aims, practices and purposes would be designed to raise difference, plurality and independence. This can be achieved either through modules related to age, ability and intention, or through specific areas of, and approaches to, study, or a mixture of both. Educators should additionally reconsider the values implicit in current evaluation, assessment and examination practices, who and what they are addressing and why.

In sum, the proposals call for more decision-making powers and authority for teachers and learners within a climate of inquiry, risk-taking and creative opportunity. If cultural studies and creative practice are to become properly complementary in art education, this will require roundly educated, dynamic and creative teachers. We need creative teachers with the confidence to take creative risks, teachers who are themselves creative and reflective practitioners. At present this takes exceptional commitment and vision in an increasingly high-stakes education system, with heavy workloads and the pressures to conform created by ever-increasing accountability. The concept of high-reliability schools, analogous to air traffic control, where any failure of the system is potentially disastrous, severely limits the scope for individual teachers to innovate or push the boundaries. Instead, subjugated to successive governments' vain search for a 'teacher-proof' education system, teachers are too often reduced to the role of curriculum delivery automatons.

Far greater flexibility is needed than the present statutory Order and assessment instruments allow. Investment is essential for an innovative and creative curriculum development that seeks to develop philosophically sound, varied and rigorous new approaches and effective teaching and learning strategies. Above all, governments have to learn to trust teachers and give them 'permission' to practise the 'risky thinking' that brings cultural education to life. The prevailing Gradgrind ethos in schools needs to change and it needs to be recognised, in Eisner's words, that 'Empathy, playfulness, surprise, ingenuity, curiosity, and individuality must count for something in schools that aim to contribute to a social democracy' (Eisner 1985: 167).

Questions for discussion

1   How can we persuade pupils to take more responsibility for their own learning and encourage them to engage with issues of real personal concern through their art work?
2   How would you describe and justify the key components of your vision of the art and design curriculum?
3   Can a wholly objective standardised system of assessment be designed for art and design? Do attempts to achieve this affect course content for better or for worse?

Further reading

Chalmers, G. (1996) *Celebrating Pluralism: Art, Education and Cultural Diversity*, Los Angeles: Getty Education Institute for the Arts.

NACCCE (1999) *All Our Futures: Creativity, Culture and Education*, London: Department for Education and Employment.

Swift, J. and Steers, J. (1999) 'A Manifesto for Art in Schools', *Journal of Art & Design Education*, 18(1): 7–14. Oxford: Blackwell.

Cross-phase transitions

3   Changing places?

Roy Prentice

> To view what we ordinarily call deviance from a different perspective is one way in which to see the limits, and the arbitrariness, of our usual portrayal of proper kinds of life course.
>
> (Salmon 1985: 125)

Introduction

In this chapter a number of issues are raised about the process that is commonly referred to as 'moving' from one stage of education to another. The purpose of the present discussion is to examine the impact of this process on learning in art and design. The particular focus of attention here is the 'move' from primary to secondary education that most children in the UK experience at the age of 11. This significant event is layered with both general and subject-specific expectations. An image is conjured up of a child who has climbed one curriculum ladder, being required to switch to a different (extension) ladder, to begin another ascent, rung-by-rung, guided by what Schostak (2000: 42) calls the 'safety rail' of a 'paranoid curriculum', with a promise of loftier, government-imposed standards being reached.

Within a system of education based on an age-stage model, the ladder metaphor is predictable. Getting a grip on the first rung can be physically and psychologically harrowing for very young children who require the sensitive support of knowledge-able and caring adults. The complex range of variables that determine how well 3 to 5 year olds adjust to the change from informal learning in a domestic setting to formal learning in an institutional setting is well documented in the specialist research literature (Yeboah 2002). However, it would be a mistake to assume either that the high levels of disruption and distress experienced by many children on starting school are automatically repeated at later stages of transition or that disturbances are always negative.

Learners soon learn that they are required to 'move' at a regular pace, in step with their peer group, onwards and upwards. Such an arrangement is invested with an artificial age-stage appropriateness. While some decisions about curriculum, pedagogy and institutional organisation are informed by a genuine understanding of intellectual, emotional and physical development, others owe more to long-established custom (ritual) and unchallenged practice (routine). Inevitably any age-stage approach has built into it a degree of potentially damaging disruption to learning at each point of transfer. Policy makers are aware of this perceived shortcoming and much effort has been directed towards ways of reducing this problem. Indeed, it was to minimise such disruption that the National Curriculum in England provided a framework 'designed to promote continuity in the curriculum and in pupils' progress' (School Curriculum and Assessment Authority (SCAA) 1996: 3). However, concern continues to be expressed about the 'loss of momentum in pupils' progress' between the final year of primary education and the early stage of secondary education. The point is often made by primary teachers that during their first year in a secondary school insufficient value is attached to, and use made of, children's earlier achievements. In response, secondary teachers draw attention to the unenviable reality of having to teach a class of children recruited from a large number of diverse primary schools.

Ongoing efforts to make the transition between successive stages of education as smooth as possible tend to emphasise the importance of general administrative procedures and professional links between primary and secondary teachers. Based on an assumption that all change can, and should, flow smoothly, the government's attention has focused on two heavyweight concepts, continuity and progression. Unfortunately, the widespread adoption of lightweight interpretations of these concepts has resulted in a reinforcement of a predictably narrow and linear view of learning. Driven by rather superficial notions of continuity and progression, a curriculum conceived as an unbroken, logical sequence of pre-specified encounters, intended to span different stages of education, runs counter to fundamental features of learning in art. In contrast, art educationalists reaffirm that 'Learning is messy. We rarely learn anything by proceeding along a single path to predetermined outcomes' (Scottish Consultative Council on the Curriculum (SCCC) 1996: 9).

It is argued that for learning in art and design to develop and sustain its integrity across the primary–secondary divide it is necessary to embrace alternative ways of making connections between earlier and later experiences. A freshness of vision is required to see beyond stereotyped views of continuity and progression in order to extend the scope of the debate about transition.

Images of art and design

Deep-seated and widespread stereotyped expectations of art and design operate in different ways at both primary and secondary levels. They promote a kind of age-stage appropriateness in relation to subject content, organisation and pedagogy, that reinforces a 'school-art' style in many schools (Efland 1976). Writing in 1970, Field makes the point that 'Ideas in art education change, develop and become modified in response to pressure and needs from inside and outside' (Field 1970: 47). It is acknowledged that most changes in art and design have tended to be superficial, reflecting interests in new imagery and media, rather than fundamental shifts in purpose, content and ways of teaching (Prentice 1999: 148). The recent history of developments and dislocations in the subject within each stage, and between successive stages, is well documented (Prentice and Dyson 2000). However, it is useful to draw attention to some significant differences between the nature of art and design in primary and secondary schools, in an attempt to highlight the transitional shortcomings of a curriculum conceived as a fixed sequence of key stages.

A familiar scenario for many children between 7 and 11 years of age is a curriculum that emphasises the teaching of practical skills and the formal elements of a visual vocabulary, through a range of traditionally defined, predominantly two-dimensional activities. Rarely is sufficient time available to enable children to sustain a level of engagement necessary to gain competence and confidence in their handling of ideas, materials, processes and tools. Also, when work involves little more than isolated exercises to explore the qualities of the formal elements of a visual world it is easy to mistakenly assume such exercises are an end in themselves. Traditionally, primary teachers have viewed art and design as a practical subject. Justifications for children's engagements in the art-making process in order to develop aesthetic awareness, imagination and creativity are firmly rooted in the liberal tradition of primary education (and underpinned by a belief in the value of play). This justification is encapsulated in the Plowden Report's definition of art: 'a form of communication and a means of expression of feelings which ought to permeate the whole curriculum and the whole life of the school' (Central Advisory Council for Education (CACE) 1967: 247).

In recent years most generalist primary teachers have agonised about how they might satisfy the demands of a National Curriculum that requires them to address an additional dimension of art experience – ways of responding to the work of historically, stylistically and culturally diverse artists, craftspeople and designers. Unsurprisingly, given the limited subject-knowledge in art that most primary teachers bring to this task, and the lack of appropriate visual resource material available to support them, in most schools the outcome is reduced to a reliance on a restricted range of accessible reproductions of Impressionist and Post-Impressionist paintings as a basis for highly derivative work. Hence a proliferation of pastiche!

Between 1998 and 2001 the UK government's pressure on primary teachers to raise standards of literacy and numeracy peaked with the introduction in 1998 of the National Literacy Strategy (NLS) and in 1999 of the National Numeracy Strategy (NNS). The impact of these strategies on art and design in primary schools has been enormous. As the curriculum became increasingly narrow and prescriptive, art and design lost ground. Visual modes of representation were relegated to the margins of the curriculum and reduced to an instrumental role in a large number of schools (for a more detailed analysis of these issues see Rogers (1998) and Eisner (1998a) respectively). During this period, for high-status subjects the claim could still be made that 'As the child progresses through the later years of primary school, learning in the subject disciplines becomes more differentiated' (Riley 1999: 14). Curiously the dilution of learning in art and design that frequently occurred in the 1960s and 1970s within cross-curricular topic and project work has been replaced by equally diluted experiences as a result of tokenistic attempts to include the subject as a kind of illustrative device, to support learning in, say, history, science or English.

In secondary education art and design teaching is shaped by an equally complex and often conflicting set of beliefs and assumptions about art and design and art education. A growing number of influential art educators are challenging the status quo and articulating more relevant alternatives to 'a tradition formed over time' that is 'perceived as natural and fixed rather than cultural and subject to change' (Burgess and Addison 2000: 41).

Frustrated by the self-perpetuation of school-art orthodoxies and the ineffectiveness of successive attempts to develop or enrich the existing secondary curriculum, Hughes (1998), in a desperate bid to influence revision, claimed:

> We are still delivering art curricula in our schools predicated largely upon procedures and practices which reach back to the nineteenth century – processes and practices which cling to a comfortable and uncontentious view of art and its purposes. As a result, secondary Art and Design education . . . is in general static, safe and predictable.
>
> (Hughes 1998: 41)

Solutions informed by postmodern ideas are advanced by Swift and Steers (1999) in the form of a manifesto that proposes a rationale for a curriculum that has greater relevance for learners by favouring 'difference, plurality and independent thought'. Other advocates of change imaginatively explore interrelationships between alternative pedagogical approaches and contemporary art practices. For Burgess and Addison (2000: 18) 'contemporary art can usefully be defined as belonging to two contested critical spaces, the late modern and the postmodern'. They argue for a curriculum in which contemporary art and artists have greater prominence, and through which skills of critical inquiry become more highly developed to enable teachers and students to move fluidly in and between unfamiliar sites for learning with increasing confidence.

By drawing attention to some determining characteristics of art and design at different stages of education, differences between primary and secondary experiences are revealed in relation to the learning environment, curriculum content and organisation, teachers' subject knowledge and ideological positions.

Images of learners and learning

> We are used to thinking about the way a life unfolds in a deterministic fashion . . . a creative life is still determined but what determines it is a will moving across time – the fierce determination to succeed, to make sense of the world, to use whatever means to unravel some of the mysteries of the universe.
>
> (Csikszentmihalyi 1996: 182)

National education policies produce structures that often constrain rather than facilitate learning. It is strange that what is known about different ways of learning, including the relationship between deep learning and each learner's idiosyncratic, active participation in the process, seems to have little influence on the forms such structures take. The current National Curriculum for Art and design (Department for Education and Employment (DfEE) 1999b) is an example of this. Divided into separate key stages, with transfers at the ages of 7, 11, 14, each stage draws attention to a particular requirement to support the development of creativity and imagination. The rubric that accompanies the first stage highlights the importance of exploration and sensory qualities. At the second stage complexity and control in relation to ideas and media are promoted. The third stage stresses the need for activities to be sustained, for critical skills to be acquired and for contemporary practice in art, craft and design to be used as a resource for learning.

Presented in this way, as a linear progression from early childhood to adolescence and adulthood, through a succession of predetermined stages, each with declared priorities, the nature of art as a learning activity with personal meaning is distorted. At transitional points distortions become accentuated and teachers and learners alike become unnecessarily confused. For example, is it implied that with increasing age, exploratory activities and sensory qualities should be replaced with approaches that favour predetermined outcomes and received information? On what grounds are more complex ideas and solutions to problems considered to be more appropriate than simple ones? Is sustained engagement in art activity achievable only on reaching secondary education? Is it also assumed that 7 to 11 year olds are incapable of developing critical skills and of responding to the work of contemporary artists, craftspeople and designers? Taken further, such a structure accommodates unhelpful oppositional ways of thinking about, for example, play and work, art and non-art, exploration and intention, historical works and contemporary practice, information and understanding, concrete and abstract modes of thinking. The shortcomings of a curriculum conceived as a series of fixed relationships are encapsulated in Eisner's assertion that:

> The conduct of inquiry is seldom a series of single certain steps towards some unambiguous destination, except of course in its textbook version. In the real world, inquiry proceeds haltingly, uncertain about both means and ends, and displays the flexibility and the concern for pattern which enables the intelligent inquirer to create ideas or products that possess the elusive but precious quality we call coherence.
>
> (Eisner 1998a: 51–60)

It is necessary to have more than an agreed set of skills with which to make responses to experience if learning in art is to have personal significance throughout schooling. What is required is the development of a reflective dimension.

> In place of top-down knowledge, pupils must construct things for themselves. And what is learned must go beyond merely doing things; the learner must come to reflect on that practical experience, to articulate something of what it means.
>
> (Salmon 1995: 22)

Provision should be made for children to acquire, refine and apply their reflective skills at different stages in the development of their work and in their responses to the work of others. Previous ideas and actions are subject to scrutiny by being revisited and viewed afresh in a contemplative mode. The evidence of sense impressions and intuitive responses is an important part of this process. It is essential, therefore, throughout successive stages of education, to value and support insights into experience gained through ways of human functioning other than linear, logical, rational patterns of behaviour (Claxton 1997).

Three key issues emerge that are fundamental to the debate about transition. First, there is an acceptance that art has the power to change people, whatever their age or stage of development. Central to learning in art is the concept of lived-through experience. Understanding is created and recreated through a process of construction and reconstruction of events (not as a result of climbing another rung of a ladder). Second, learning of this transformational kind involves the whole person, it embraces in a holistic way thinking and feeling, perceiving and doing. Third, it is recognised that to function with confidence and competence in the field of art and design learners from their earliest age should be initiated into the various codes and conventions through which visual modes of communication and expression in diverse cultural contexts are made possible.

Making authentic connections

> Central to transition from one school to another is a capacity to adapt while retaining a sense of self.
>
> (Pollard 2002)

The focus of the discussion now shifts to consider some implications for art education of alternative ways of thinking about connections and transitions. The challenge is to find new ways of sustaining a sense of self in a rapidly changing society, and of developing an authentic sense of art and design in a rapidly changing, diverse, cultural landscape. As a result the aim of producing learners to fit a standardised ideal dependent on acquired specified skills, knowledge and understanding is punctured. As Schostak (2000) makes clear:

> There can be no grand narrative concerning what is 'good for all'. Standardisation and its surveillance techniques to create the curriculum are patently absurd in a context of change that is so fast, so diverse and so technologically and culturally creative. A forward-looking curriculum for personal and social development requires principles that facilitate diversity, dialogue and mutuality of relationship. Such a curriculum cannot have personal meaning unless time is brought into the ambit of an individual's lifetime, an individual's life course.
>
> (Schostak 2000: 48)

These references to 'diversity', 'dialogue' and 'mutuality' strike chords with the ideas of art educators such as Swift and Steers (1999) and, with particular reference to their commitment to critical pedagogy, the work of Addison and Burgess (2000: 320). The point is made by Elliott in his discussion of Schostak's position that he 'argues for a curriculum of "unstructured situations" which enables students to reflect on their life experiences and to experience education as a democratic process in which they are able to negotiate their own "agenda for learning"' (Elliott 2000: 191).

By grounding wider discussions about contemporary ideas related to curriculum change and pedagogy in a subject-specific debate about transition, it is possible to contextualise explorations of alternative ways of thinking about relationships between earlier learning and later learning in art and design.

The way forward is to develop a national framework of opportunities for newly qualified teachers to address issues central to the development of a critical pedagogy grounded in art activities. This could best be achieved through primary and secondary teachers working and reflecting on their shared experiences. The emphasis would be placed on how subject knowledge is transformed into subject-specific pedagogical knowledge in a variety of formal and informal settings. Further opportunities are needed to develop dynamic, reciprocal relationships between primary art coordinators, secondary art and design teachers and representatives from the cultural and creative 'industries'. The overriding purpose of such networks would be to develop the capacities of art and design educators to question orthodoxies and to encourage them to take risks. The outcomes may challenge the assumption that transition is about people changing places, rather than changing the places that enable people to change.

Questions for discussion

1   What shared strategies might be adopted by primary and secondary teachers to support their management of change in art and design teaching?
2   Should a case be made for the removal of art and design from the compulsory school curriculum in order to promote greater risk-taking by alternative providers of art and design experiences?
3   Why is 'transformation' such an important concept for art and design educators to understand?

Further reading

Csikszentmihalyi, M. (1996) *Creativity*, New York: HarperCollins.
Prentice, R. (1999) 'Art: Visual Thinking', in J. Riley and R. Prentice (eds) *The Curriculum for 7–11 Year Olds*, London: Paul Chapman.
Schostak, J. (2000) 'Developing under Developing Circumstances: the Personal and Social Development of Students and the Process of Schooling', in H. Altrichter and J. Elliott (eds) *Images of Educational Change*, Buckingham: Open University Press.

4　In and out of place

Cleansing rites in art education

Claire Robins

> Belief supports the fantasy which regulates social reality.
>
> (Zizek 1989: 36)

In this chapter I examine issues that circumscribe the transition between secondary and tertiary art education. Central to the issues discussed is the commonly held perception that during this phase students need to undergo a form of educational purging that requires them to reject many of the values about art that they have learnt in school. The implications of this are explored with reference to signs of difference contextualised within social and cultural networks.

Something out of place

The metaphor of purging may be helpful when looking at those objects which society deems 'dirty', those objects in need of cleansing. Mary Douglas' theory that whatever needs cleansing is in fact 'matter out of place' reveals that 'where there is dirt there is a system' (Douglas 1966: 35). Her anthropological stance draws attention away from the spot or mote in need of outing and steers the reader towards a consideration of the taxonomies that exist in order to differentiate between what is and what isn't 'pure' or 'dangerous'. Food is not considered dirty until it appears 'in the wrong place', for example, a bolognese stain on someone's tie, where it is embarrassing and takes on the status of dirt. Where something needs to be wiped away, it is not just the 'undesirable matter' that is brought into question but the construction of a system that categorises it as such. Likewise, various forms of art practice and theory and their adherents are unproblematic until they transgress a boundary and appear in an 'inappropriate' context, then they may be commensurate with the bolognese stain.

Within the particular sphere of culture known euphemistically as 'the art world' these boundaries are not clearly signposted but this does not mean that they do not exist or are about to collapse, far from it. If postmodern rhetoric cajoles people into believing that any[art]thing goes, then they must take care because they would be fooling themselves if they failed to understand that the production of artists and art works relies on a highly sophisticated set of culturally and socially framed conditions. Not all art practice is thought of as desirable in all contexts. Where irony and 'appropriation' (Foster 1996) may have recently let in some unusual suspects into the arena of legitimate culture, they are there with the caveat of Peter Berger's (1991: 4) speculations on the cultural status of a garden gnome: 'a quotation [to] testify to an artistic sensibility so sophisticated as to be perverse'.

When Becker (1994b) discusses the complexity of coming to terms with many contemporary works of art she acknowledges that their 'discourse is often hermetic and incomprehensible to those outside' (Becker 1994b: 104). She refers back to Dewey's (1934) notion that 'The Language of Art has to be acquired' and adds that: 'It is a learned discourse that may be accessed only through immersion in art and the art world' (Becker 1994b: 104). When works of art are not understood they don't make sense and are indecipherable; they are inaccessible. Bourdieu (1993) takes this further and defines works of art as existing:

> as symbolic objects *only* [my italics] if they are known and recognised, that is, socially instituted as works of art and received by spectators capable of knowing and recognising them as such, the sociology of art and literature has to take as its object not only the material production but also the symbolic production of the work or, which amounts to the same thing, belief in the work.
> (Bourdieu 1993: 37)

This provides some clues as to why, at a particular moment in students' art education, a significant shift in their understanding of the object of study appears to be necessary. In England, since the 1960s, a mandatory dip in the efficacious waters (baptismal or disinfectant) of a one-year art foundation course has been the place where this shift is realised. On embarking on this course of study, A level art work that some months previously looked so impressive (the same art work that young pupils may have gazed at in wonder and aspired to, with its copious 'preparatory sheets', annotated and mounted on black card) meets with a terrible fate; it is suddenly deemed 'inappropriate'. No longer desirable, it is now something the student must learn to reject.

There are many references to general educational ablutions, but Williams (1998), writing in the *Guardian*, refers specifically to the art and design foundation course as a 'compulsory creative cleansing between school and art school' and she is not alone in her portrayal of the course as a time when the rejected aspects of experience are wiped from the slate. Hollands (2001: 54) also remarks that 'progression from school art to art on a Foundation course has traditionally been based on an ethos of liberation'. He characterises this with the slightly ominous hypnotic incantation: 'We want you to forget everything you have done in school' (Hollands 2001: 54). Hollands is less sure that it is the content of what is learnt that is liberating suggesting that it is mainly the social context. However, for many students it will certainly be both. Williams' and Hollands' descriptions imply a rupture but simultaneously offer the promise of alternatives that are cleaner, truer, freer, or just plain different. Is it an act of sublimation that is promised? This clearly begs a question that concerns the worth of what is taught in many secondary schools especially if it needs to be forgotten in order for students to 'progress'; 'what is to replace that which must be forgotten?'

The right place for a change?

Although there are other stages when art education presents students with a set of oppositional experiences it is in this particular cross-phase transition that the continuum is most forcefully and consciously disrupted. When PGCE students, training to be teachers of art and design, are asked to reflect on their experiences of art education from primary school to BA or MA, they often identify their foundation course as the most significant moment; a time when a major shift in their understanding occurs. This juncture rarely seems to precipitate a traumatic or negative reaction, conversely words like *free, liberating, eye opening* and *exciting* are most frequently used to describe the experience. Students' understanding of the object of their study during this period often changes irrevocably, altering both their comprehension of what is relevant and by corollary how they now understand the art they produced at school.

The art and design foundation course has been something of an anomaly in an English education system that has been directed increasingly towards standardisation, consequently its death knell has been sounding since the late 1980s. In 1997 streamlining into the national qualifications framework (QCA 1997) saw the BTEC (Business and Technician Education Council) diploma course in art and design foundation studies, examined by Edexcel, sandwiched between the national diploma in forestry and arboriculture and the advanced certificate in front office operations in the listings of approved external qualifications. Homogenisation may have guaranteed a momentary reprise for the course but also brought about fundamental changes that affect its overarching philosophy.

The present-day art and design foundation course has its origins in Germany's Bauhaus foundation course or Vorkurs, and it has retained salient aspects of the course designed by Johannes Itten in 1919. Students are admitted for a similar limited period, usually one academic year (at the Bauhaus it was six months), with the aim to sample a range of art experiences. There are many reasons given as to why students need this experience. Ostensibly it offers an opportunity to experience a range of subject areas such as visual communication, three-dimensional design, fashion etc. that students are unlikely to have experienced at school, thus enabling them to make informed decisions when selecting BA courses. It also offers opportunities for students' interests and abilities to be tutored and developed by specialist members of staff who are often practising artists and designers contracted to teach for a limited number of days each year. Contemporary versions, like their predecessor, still aim to 'liberate students' creative powers' (Efland 1990: 216) and to determine, not so much, as was the case at in 1919, 'whether they have the aptitude to continue with further study' (Efland 1990: 216), but *what* they have the aptitude and inclination to study further. Itten reflected that at that time 'teaching was designed to guide the student in acquiring the means of artistic expression by appealing to his [*sic*] individual talents and to develop an atmosphere of creativity in which original works became possible' (Itten 1965: 8, quoted in Efland 1990: 216). Although this can be seen as symptomatic of the self-assured discourse of modernism in which the Bauhaus was conceived, it also points to a pedagogical stance of fostering independent learning and the aspiration for more than formulaic outcomes.

Signs of dissent

The lack of shared values between secondary and tertiary education is most publicly manifest by the refusal of foundation courses or BA courses to value A level art grades as an indication of a student's potential. Although this situation represents a cause for concern, perhaps surprisingly, it has not generated dialogue and there remains a lack of common values between secondary and tertiary art education. Foundation course candidates continue to be selected on 'portfolio interview' in which the interviewers are very often looking at the very same art work that will be graded for A level examination. That there may be two groups of art and design educators considering the merits of the same work and often making different pronouncements, says less about the educators themselves and more about their positioning in relation to institutional values and assessment methodologies.

Like two ends of a telescope, these separate viewpoints are shaped by institutional perspectives. The secondary school's final examination structures are looking for a form of closure in school student's art work at the very same time that foundation courses selectors will be looking for emergent signs of potential. So in effect, selection for foundation courses is dependent on qualities in students and their work that are different to those recognised by A level examinations. If the written evidence for this is thin on the ground, and a comparison between criteria for A level examinations and new foundation diplomas finds them replete with shared terminology, it cannot be assumed that this convergence in terminology precludes a disjunction in assessment. By simply reading from syllabi and course guidelines it may be hard to detect a new set of expectations but the act of interpretation within very different educational settings can generate contrasting meanings.

Embodied within both the school and the art college are powerful legitimising discourses that rarely seem to reflect one another. Bourdieu (1977) refers to these legitimating discourses as exerting *symbolic violence*, his term for the imposition of a cultural arbitrary by an arbitrary power. In other words he suggests a system of values that are not arbitrary in the sense of being random or haphazard, but that have been instituted as universally beneficial and accepted as quasi-natural structures that determine learning. These acts of symbolic violence are silent and invisible, acted upon agents with their consent. Schostak (2000) points out that this is part of the general condition of having a curriculum with a set of canonic values promoted to the exclusion of others, he too draws on the process of purification that results in displacement.

In this process of purifying – that is becoming a good representative of a given category – a waste product emerges and has to be dealt with in some way as a rejected aspect of experience which can find no acceptable place within the subjectivity of the individual.

(Schostak 2000: 42)

If it is obvious that art and design lecturers in tertiary education do not revere examination systems as a means to identify appropriate candidates for further study, it is perhaps less obvious that neither do many teachers of A level art and design. There are certainly many teachers who actively demonstrate an antimony between obtaining good grades at A level and satisfying entry requirements for further study by guiding their students to produce separate bodies of work: one to satisfy A level criteria and another to gain students a place on a foundation course. Although this does not apply to all teachers, it is a significant demonstration of the effects that different systems of external scrutiny exert on what is taught.

External testing informs institutional values and can exert a powerful influence on a teacher's or lecturer's relative autonomy to teach what they 'believe in', it can directly undermine conviction about what is taught, resulting in what could be termed a 'cynical curriculum'. To put this another way, teachers' belief in art, their belief in the symbolic network that constitutes the field, may be compromised by a set of educationally framed beliefs that determine what and how it is appropriate for students to study at particular stages in their development. They may not always believe in what they are teaching but they persist in teaching it, often very well, in order that their students will be successful. Here, students' success is seen solely in relation to verification by external testing. As Zizek points out, this is the 'paradox of false consciousness: one knows the falsehood very well, one is aware of a particular interest hidden behind a universality but one still does not renounce it' (Zizek 1989: 29). Not surprisingly, most teachers feel unable to renounce the clash of values without risking the guarantee of success in terms of good A level grades, which in turn affects school league table results and impacts on their reputation and position within the school. Zizek's position on belief draws on the Lacanian concept that:

contrary to the usual thesis, that belief is something interior and knowledge is something exterior (in the sense that it can be verified through an external procedure). Rather it is belief which is radically exterior, embodied in the practical, effective procedure of people.

(Zizek 1989: 34)

If belief is articulated in exteriorisation, then this would indicate that teachers of art act out their belief in the legitimacy of certain educational values knowing that this action eclipses belief in particular cultural values. There is a curious circularity about this that reveals transitions from secondary to tertiary and tertiary to secondary (in the case of those who return to teach in secondary schools) as moments when belief is problematised.

Recent government drives towards standardisation have resulted in an increased occurrence of external examinations and assessment procedures. Although secondary schools have traditionally sung to the tune of the external examining bodies, they are now facing ever increasing demands for this form of testing.

Swift and Steers (1999: 7) acknowledge the effects that increased standardisation in art and design education have had on 'decreasing variety' and 'increasing standardised responses' in pupils' work. They are referring to school curricula. Until very recently foundation courses have not had an external examination component. As a transitional year the emphasis was never towards standardised examination closure, rather emphasis was placed on a range of assessment objectives to enable students to progress towards diverse outcomes appropriate to their BA course selections. Students were internally assessed and externally moderated but these assessment processes were marginal to successfully gaining a place on a BA course that suited their abilities and interests. Risk taking and experimentation were encouraged right up to the final phase of the course which in many colleges was largely seen as celebratory and concluded with a final exhibition of work that was not assessed separately.

It is interesting that Swift and Steers (1999: 7) also advocate that the art curriculum for schools should 'reject testing in favor of procedures which require students to engage in long-term, complex and challenging projects reflecting real life situations'. This was once a clearly distinguishing feature of the foundation course that undoubtedly contributed to the descriptions of it as liberating and challenging. Sadly, Swift's and Steer's words have fallen on deaf ears, and since 1999 the emphasis on testing has increased with the addition of AS level examinations at the end of Year 12 and the implementation of Edexcel external examinations for foundation courses.

Into the field

> This idea of dirt takes us straight to the field of symbolism.
>
> (Douglas 1966: 35)

The rites of passage marking the transition from secondary to tertiary art education does not only describe the educational classification systems that determine what is in and what is out of place. More specifically, it implicates a significant moment, a coming of age when art practices and theories learnt in schools begin to be brought into question. This is precisely when they appear in the domain in which legitimate cultural production commences. By this I mean the moment at which students have elected, and been selected to follow the first stage in a course of study that prepares them to be art, craft and design professionals.

Bourdieu (1993) identifies the field of the cultural alongside that of the economic, the political, and the educational. He defines these fields as possessing their own structuring systems and relations that are relatively autonomous but structurally corresponding. The cross-phase transition from secondary to tertiary art education brings the *cultural field* as an ever more powerful influence on the *educational field*. The different structuring systems are revealed as the necessity for students to understand and engage in the ever changing sphere of contemporary art practice and in this way theory becomes established. The educational field both shapes and is shaped by the field of legitimate cultural production.

Students whose experience of art at school has included a substantial engage-ment with contemporary art work and who have benefited from independent learning and self-initiated projects may find the transition relatively smooth. Those whose experience of art at school included neither are likely to experience tensions as they struggle to reconcile previous understandings of art with new ones and come to terms with structuring and taking responsibility for aspects of their own learning. It is something of a cliché that students who have achieved the highest grades in A level examinations may often have the most difficult start to the course because they have the most 'unlearning' to do. These students, understandably, may be the least willing to relinquish the security blanket of a tried and tested route to success for less certain new demands that ask them to 'give up everything for nothing' (Leader 2002: 101). For as Leader points out in his Lacanian reading of our relationship with art, art requires us to believe not just in it, but in something beyond it. Leader suggests this is precisely the gap between 'the special sacred place that the artwork inhabits' and the work itself, the space that makes us question, 'Is this art?', he goes on to say, 'the problem, and the power, of this space is that we can't see it' (Leader 2002: 177). There are certain works of twentieth-century art that explicitly ask us to do this, Michael Craig-Martin's *An Oak Tree* (1973) or Duchamp's *Fountain* (1917) for example. These special demands for belief are also characterised by Bourdieu (1993: 76) as 'the charismatic ideology which is the ultimate basis of belief in the value of a work of art'.

Whatever it is at this moment that emerges as problematic for students at this time does so as a symptom of the truth about these cultural relationships, relationships between things that are normally taken for granted but that are momentarily exposed before they are once again properly disguised as a quasi-natural relationship between things. It is an initiation into a particular aspect of culture that relies on the impetus of an important moment or event. It means that things will never appear to be quite the same again. An alternative reading of the foundation course's *raison d'être* could be that it acts to manage and sublimate these problems, successfully reconfigures understanding and re-establishes order. Leader suggests that 'sublimation will be linked to precise historical moments, points at which there is a change in the way we see things, in the way that we experience reality' (Leader 2002: 62). In order for the symbolic network of cultural value to be reproduced, the inchoate art students must become inculcated as 'players in the field'. They must be like fish in water. Induction into the nuances of the field are as necessary for players as they are not necessary for non-players. Difference is essential for the reproduction of the symbolic networks that we see forming in this cross-phase transition.

Art in schools, as Addison (2001: 20) among others has pointed out, 'is not for the training of artists, craftspeople and designers'. This of course is true; however, the corollary appears to give credence to the notion that the subject content taught in schools can be very far removed from the concerns of twenty-first-century and late-twentieth-century art practice and theory. An essential dimension of the transitional phase from secondary to tertiary education centres on bridging the gap from the canonic models for art education in schools, typically situated in practices from the late nineteenth and early twentieth centuries, to those of the present day.

The process that students find themselves going through is reminiscent of a symbolic exchange in Paul Auster's book *Moon Palace* (1989). Here, the central character, Marco, is presented with his uncle's collection of over a thousand books when he leaves home for university. In his unfurnished flat he starts to use boxes of these books as improvised furniture – seven for a chair, twelve for a bed etc. Hereby a transitory illusion of reality is constructed where Marco's desire for what might be assumed as the potential contained by books is pragmatically negated or deferred by their ability to temporarily stand in as furniture. The books are unproblematic in their boxes, their potential to pose questions, challenge preconceptions or emotionally destabilise, is nullified. This compares with many students' experience of art at secondary school, like Marco's improvised furniture, art has a visible presence but it is often so effectively disguised it resembles something else. Most frequently it resembles itself 'school art', a particular genre of art production characterised by Hughes (1998) as akin to 'the conceptually unambitious work of a skilful amateur' (Hughes 1998).

Like bolognese on a plate this sort of work in the right place appears wholly desirable. It is strongly advocated by Sunday painters and believed in by many school pupils (although it is unlikely that it is believed in by all art and design teachers). Concepts of what constitutes art and art practice are constantly prey to different classification systems that have at their core a perpetuation of symbolic networks; Marco is about to find this out.

Marco's life is strongly affected by the event of his uncle's death. This precipitates both him, and his flat, into a difficult transitional period of grieving where the books that had remain untouched for eighteen months gradually enter into the hitherto concealed domain of the culturally symbolic and economic. Marco *reads* and *sells* the books and as he does so he becomes inevitably and inescapably entangled with the discourses of desire, taste and value. Many students who go on to study art after leaving school are confronted with a similar complex symbolic network of practices, processes, judgements and encounters, that have little to do with former understandings of the word and just like Marco's flat the furniture has to be taken apart for this to happen.

Marco agonises over the price the secondhand bookseller will pay for his inherited possessions: to him it is obvious why 'three volumes of Descartes were worth less than one by Pascal', why 'a dog eared Homer was worth more than a spanking Virgil'. For Chandler, the bookshop owner, these distinctions 'did not exist. A book was just an object for him a thing that belonged to the world of things and as such it was not radically different from a shoebox, a toilet plunger or a coffee pot' (Auster 1989: 24).

When Marco enters into the world of the symbolic, he accepts that his bedroom reality has been eclipsed by another more compelling version of reality which, from then on, will condition his social interactions with others. He now knows that there are things that are and things that aren't what they seem. That Marco knows this, sets him apart from the bookseller, it constitutes their difference, and if it is obvious to Marco why Pascal should be worth more than Descartes it begs the question, how has he come to understand this? How has he become such an assured player in the cultural field?

Marco inherited his cultural disposition in a way that more or less reflects Bourdieu's notions of habitus, from his family. The very fact that he was given a thousand books by a relative tells us something of his background, that in the collection were canonic texts of western philosophy, that these were the particular texts to which Marco is drawn tells us more, and should we be surprised that he defends these texts against the threat to the symbolic order posed by the suspect judgement of the bookseller, Chandler; no, it is all perfectly 'natural'. But this is not 'real', it is a story, a fiction concocted by Auster and a game is being played with the reader. Auster's choice of name for the bookseller is not random, and when we know that Raymond Chandler is his personal literary hero we may begin to wonder if he is not sticking two fingers up at Marco's conceits from the doyen of twentieth-century detective fiction and asking the reader to question what is in and out of place in this resolution of order.

This is at best what the first dip into the cultural field has permitted students to do. In a brief respite from the pressures of testing it could give them the chance to critically question the established order, to choose the popular over the seminal to lose naivety but not yet to gain cynicism, or perhaps, as John Thompson says, to embrace the 'part that desire plays in this game of chance encounters, intuition, and unsystematic knowledge that we call art education' (Thompson 1991: 46).

The vast majority of secondary school pupils will not, of course, experience this initiation into the nuances of the cultural field nor be given an opportunity to critically engage with the discourses of artistic production. So if this transitionary stage calls for a reconceptualisation of art through baptism or ritual cleansing, then it is part of a system that reproduces the conditions for most secondary school pupils to become the 'great cultural unwashed'.

Questions for discussion

1   There is rarely an opportunity for discussion between secondary school art teachers and their colleagues in tertiary education. Would students benefit from increased collaboration between these two groups of art educators?

2   Currently many art and design foundation courses are being squeezed of their original identities in an attempt to achieve standardisation. Is it important to retain phases in art education that many graduates find particularly significant?

3   What are the implications, for the majority of school students, of an education system that promotes different values about art in secondary and tertiary education?

Further reading

Bourdieu, P. (1993) *The Field of Cultural Production*, Cambridge: Polity.
Leader, D. (2002) *Stealing the Mona Lisa: What Art Stops us from Seeing*, London: Faber and
    Faber.
Zizek, S. (1989) *The Sublime Object of Ideology*, London and New York: Verso.

Part 2

Curriculum issues

Research in art education

5 Concerns and aspirations for qualitative research in the new millennium

Elliot Eisner

This chapter describes some of my concerns and aspirations for qualitative research as we moved into the new millennium. The exploration and promotion of qualitative research have been an important focus of my intellectual life. In fact, it has been a part of my intellectual life long before I became a doctoral student at the University of Chicago in the late 1950s. My interest in qualitative matters started in elementary school when I discovered that I had developed a love affair with art. That love affair eventually led me to a part-time position working with inner-city children as a teacher of arts and crafts, and from there to the study of education and art's role in its promotion. In this transition, the arts and other qualitative considerations were deeply integrated into my way of thinking about education.

The Department of Education at the University of Chicago, at the time I enrolled, did not offer courses in qualitative methods. I can't remember ever hearing the term 'qualitative research'. The department at Chicago was a part of the division of the social sciences and its relationship with the social science division of the university was cherished and protected by the faculty. Research was what the faculty was to do and research meant doing the kind of work that real social scientists did. This meant doing work that used statistical methods to measure the effects of experiments, correlational studies to determine the magnitude of association among variables, and that employed assumptions about the 'discovery of knowledge' that were standard fare in the social sciences. Indeed, my own doctoral dissertation was a factor analytic study that used a Univac computer the size of a small room to perform varimax rotations and to calculate eigenvectors in order to discover types of creativity elementary school students displayed in their drawings and sculptures (Eisner 1965). The university socialized me in social science methods, but alas, that socialization could not really compete with the inclinations of my heart or with the intellectual convictions that my immersion in the visual arts had generated, first as a painter and later as a teacher of art. That brief personal history is, as they say, to let you know where I am coming from.

To describe my aspirations and concerns about the future of qualitative research I begin with the visual arts and the parallels that can be drawn between the visual arts and qualitative research.

If the visual arts are focused on anything, they are focused on the creation, selection and organization of visual qualities. By 'qualities' I mean phenomena that can be experienced by the senses; for example, the unique quality of experience that a particular shade of blue engenders, or the relationship between that shade of blue and, say, a field of gray on which it is situated. Artists in general and visual artists in particular pay attention to the nuanced qualities of the particular to create work having aesthetic value. This interest is revealed in the way in which a painter like Pierre Bonnard treats a sunlit interior, the way Mark Rothko creates the particular ethereal qualities of light that seems to radiate from behind his canvas, or Edward Hopper captures the loneliness of a rural roadside garage. Artists concern themselves with such nuances because in doing so they draw attention to particulars. In doing so they slow down perception and invite exploration (Dewey 1934).

Another feature of the visual arts is that they are used to communicate the way something feels, that is, its emotional character. Picasso's *Guernica* (1937), one of the great visual achievements of the twentieth century, doesn't merely tell us about the bombing of a small Basque town by the Nazis on 26 April 1937, it shows it and in showing it, it makes empathy possible. *Guernica* conveys to the competent percipient what destruction feels like. Rembrandt does the same to reveal the feel and character of the sitter in his portraits. In literature Hemingway does this with his novels, Tennyson with his poems. Artists convey the sense of a situation, they create and organize qualities that make those situations palpable.

But that's not all that artists do. Artists also invent fresh ways to show us aspects of the world we had not noticed; they release us from the stupor of the familiar. The process they employ is called defamiliarization. In ethnography it's called making the familiar strange and the strange familiar. As Dewey put it, 'The arts remove the veils that keep the eyes from seeing and in that sense', he added, 'the arts are more moral than morality' (Dewey 1934: 348).

The practice and products of qualitative research have much in common with the practices used in the arts. Consider the features I have already mentioned: qualitative researchers pay careful attention to highly nuanced qualities in both their uptake and their output; they are focused on cases, that is, on the particular; they use forms of communication that are intended to do more than tell, but to show, that is, to convey a sense or feeling of person or place. Qualitative research has much to do with making vivid what had been obscure. Like the arts themselves, good qualitative research contributes to what Maxine Greene calls 'wide awakeness' (Greene 1995). Nuance, particularity, emotion and perceptual freshness characteristic of the arts are also critically important features of good qualitative research.

It seems odd to talk about research as having parallels with the arts. Research is thought to belong to science, and art and science are usually believed to reside in different worlds (Snow and Collini 1993). The sciences deal with abstraction, truth, the literal and the quantitative. The arts deal with the concrete, the persuasive, the metaphorical and the qualitative. The pursuit of truth belongs to science, the pursuit of the good to morality and the creation of the beautiful to the arts. It is best that we don't confound their functions. Research is a scientific enterprise, art is something else entirely. This is what I was led to believe as a graduate student, if not in so many words, by example and by being introduced to unexamined assumptions about what was regarded as legitimate method.

As we all know, times have changed. The separation between the arts and sciences is nowhere near as wide as it once was. Of course, there are still places where the division is kept tidy, places where graduate students are discouraged from building connections, exploring alternatives, or even 'blurring the genres' as Clifford Geertz (2000) might say. And, if truth be told, there are still editorial boards and proposal review committees that look at all forms of qualitative research as reconnaissance efforts that precede 'real' research. But on the whole the movement over the past thirty years has been to problematize, gradually to be sure, the old unexamined assumptions about research and to push into new ways of thinking about how to do research, and who will do it. Why the change?

One of the reasons for change is that scholars have become attracted to the idea of getting close to practice, to getting a first-hand sense of what actually goes on in classrooms, schools, hospitals and communities. That kind of knowledge takes time. The one-shot commando raid as a way to get the data and get out no longer seems attractive. You need to be there. A clean research design with tight experimental controls might be right for some kinds of research, but not for all kinds.

Two early examples of research that got close to practice are found in Philip Jackson's book *Life in Classrooms* (1968) and Lou Smith's *The Complexities of an Urban Classroom* (1968). These books (published in the same year) provided powerful models of what such research might look like. Indeed, even though the first half of Jackson's book presented conventional quantitative research data collected during his year-long stay in classrooms, it was his narrative that was most revealing. Jackson and Smith's books broke new ground for those of us in education.

Jackson and Smith were not alone. Joseph Schwab (1969) also called for the study of practice and, following Aristotle's lead, built his argument on epistemological grounds; practical knowledge, Schwab argued, required attention to particulars, to contingencies, and to moral virtues. It was a form of knowledge different in kind from that produced by testing hypotheses. Schwab was followed by scholars such as Lee J. Cronbach (1975), Robert Stake (1975) and Geon Guba (1978), all three quantitatively oriented psychologists who discovered other stars to guide them on the road to Damascus. These scholars, and others too numerous for me to name here, made a difference in the historical course of qualitative research.

Second, since the early 1970s there has been a growing interest in, and acceptance of, pluralism in our social life. We are less certain about the virtues of homogeneity that we once were. Feminists have taught us about the multiple ways in which the world can be experienced and have uncovered assumptions and values in our so-called value-neutral research practices that make them seem less neutral than we once believed they were. Put another way, the politics of method became visible (Eisner 1988).

Third, traditional research practices have been less of a stunning success than we hoped for and some of the disappointment has motivated some scholars to seek other models of inquiry. Qualitative research is one of the alternatives. It is an alternative that has commanded greater interest year after year. Although I haven't taken a count, I would estimate that at least half of all the dissertations done in the School of Education at Stanford are qualitative. The paper topic categories listed in the index of the American Educational Research Association (AERA) annual meeting programme indicates that papers in qualitative methods are the fifth or sixth largest category. There are now five journals, two handbooks, and I can't count the number of books and articles on qualitative research methods. This is a domain that is vibrant and growing.

Fourth, we have come to realize that research predicated on a problem-solving model of practice is, at best, itself problematic. Researchers concerned with human relationships do not solve problems, they cope with situations. Sometimes we resolve situations – and then only temporarily. What this means is that our situations are in a dynamic state and that while the actions we take may temporarily resolve them – if we are lucky – almost assuredly, our resolutions will generate other situations that will need further resolution. In addition, in the context of practice we cannot hold conditions constant. Qualitative research deals more easily with such dynamics than its traditional counterpart. We are not trying to invent the equivalent of space ship *Discovery* nor are we going to capture reality in a bag. We are trying to develop some insights we can work with.

Fifth, there has been a growing realization among researchers of something that artists have long known in their bones; namely, that forms matter, that content and form cannot be separated, that how one says something is part and parcel of what is said. This idea in wider terms was the core idea in my presidential address to the AERA in 1992 (Eisner 1993). The title of that address was 'Forms of Understanding and the Future of Educational Research'. My aim was to convey the idea that the form of representation one uses has something to do with the form of understanding one secures. Once this idea penetrated the research community the form used to inquire and to express what one had learned was no minor consideration. This idea, the idea that different forms could convey different meanings, that form and content cannot be separated, has led to the exploration of new modes of research (Barone and Eisner 1997). This exploration has been the most daring and difficult part of the research picture in the qualitative research community for it eventually leads to basic questions as to what will count as research. In fact, it reminds me of Cole Porter's lyric,

> In olden days a hint of stocking was looked on as something shocking, now heaven knows, anything goes.
> Good authors too who once knew better words now only use four letter words – writing prose. Anything goes.

I doubt that anyone really believes that anything goes, but we often find it difficult to define the standards – if standards is the right term – to determine what does go (Dewey 1934). And this brings me to another part of my remarks, on my concerns about some of the efforts I have encountered to invent new approaches to educational research.

One of those concerns pertains to the connection or lack thereof between the form a research project takes and the degree to which it informs someone about something. One of the virtues of prepositional discourse is that it has the capacity, when well used, to describe situations in reasonably precise terms. To be sure, it is not free from ambiguity, but it can be used to communicate in ways that promote mutual understanding. I regard that as a virtue. By contrast, I have seen at conferences presentations conceived of as examples of the new wave in qualitative research that appeared to me to have more to do with novelty than with an effort to inform. One presentation I saw used a coffin accompanied by a bevy of pallbearers to illustrate a theme whose point escaped me. The presentation was novel, the image vivid, but in the end uninformative. It is critical that there be sufficient clarity to render a work useful to someone. Put another way, researchers who employ inventive ways of presenting what has been learned have the obligation to create something that a reader or viewer will find meaningful.

In the arts two sources are called upon to evoke meaning. One is what is called *sense*, the other *reference* (Jackson 1998). Sense refers to the feel a form evokes, the emotional state or quality of experience the work engenders. For example, the form of the visual qualities Picasso employed in *Guernica* engenders in most a particular sense of horror. *Guernica*'s black, grey and white newspaper-like colours, its sharp flat shapes, its oblique composition express such feeling.

Reference refers to something the work refers to; the scream of a wounded horse or the cry of a mother holding her dead child have reference to destruction and pain. The integration of sense and reference is used by artists to communicate. In the arts the scope for ambiguity may be wider than in the research community. Mind you I am not implying that we fall back to literal word or number, only that we should not become so enchanted with novelty that we forget about matters of meaning and the need to communicate.

The tension between ambiguity and precision with respect to reference may be very difficult to alleviate. We have cultural expectations regarding how reliable information is to be secured and provided. Science is the paradigm. Will people accept forms of research that are non-scientific for making consequential decisions? If they will not, does this mean that we will be limited to what scientific forms of representation can describe or explain? I have no issue to take with science, social or otherwise, but scientific frameworks do not exhaust the ways in which we experience the world or render our experience of it public. Bias, ironically, comes not only from commission, but also from omission. Science, like the arts, omits as well as includes. In that sense, all forms of representation are biased.

At the same time in our ordinary life we do use novels, films and exhibitions to learn about matters we care about. The film *Hoop Dreams*, for example, is a stunning example of what can be revealed through film, in this case a film about two African American adolescents, about their families, about competitive sports, about ambition, about failure and success. What it presents through both sense and reference informs in distinctive and powerful ways.

To make such a film requires skills that most researchers do not have. That lack is an impediment, but not an unmoveable one. It is a problem that can be addressed. The more critical question is whether people who see the educational equivalent of *Hoop Dreams* treat it as fiction or as fact? Will it be seen as a source of insight and understanding or only as entertainment?

In making the distinction between fact and fiction I know I'm on slippery ice. I am reminded of an interview with the important American writer, Wallace Stegner, that I heard on national public radio. Near the end of the interview, the interviewer asked, 'Mr Stegner, we have been talking a lot about writing fiction. Before we close can you tell us what a work of fiction must have to be really great.' Stegner paused and then said, 'To be great, fiction has to be true'. What an oxymoronic idea! Fiction had to be true to be great. I don't think I will ever forget that line. That's why I said I'm on slippery ice in making the distinction between fact and fiction. Yet, while there is a sense in which great fiction is true – the way in which the work of Chekhov is true, or Mark Twain, or Charlotte Brontë, or Wallace Stegner – true in the way it displays the universal in the particular, there is a sense in which fiction is not true. It's not true in the literal sense. Can fiction count as a genre of research? I believe it can *if* it is true in the former sense. Whether people will regard it as such will depend on the quality of their education. Can we provide that kind of education in our schools?

Another concern I have pertains to the role of theory in qualitative research, especially arts-based research. Some argue that the arts need no theoretical accoutrements, that they were made to stand alone, no screen, no confessor, only direct contact with the work. By analogy the same argument is made by some when it comes to qualitative research. Theory, for some, is an interloper. I don't see it that way. I believe not only that qualitative researchers should use theory when they can to account for what they have described, but also they ought to use the careful attention they pay to particular situations to generate concepts and to formulate, if not theories, then theorets: theorets are small theories!

Theory is important not only because it satisfies aspects of our rationality, but also because it distils particulars in ways that foster generalizability. Although theory loses some local colour when particulars are left behind, theory makes distinctions and packages thematic relationships so that they will travel well; when we distil, we come away from a research site with ideas that can sensitize us to situations and events like the ones from which theory was derived. For example, if I know that teachers and students in a high school I have studied often engage in a form of collusion in order to survive the unrealistic demands the particular school imposes upon them, I can look in other situations to determine if the collusion I discovered in one school can be found elsewhere (Powell *et al.* 1985). This anticipatory schemata is a form of generalization. The generalizations derived from qualitative case studies are essentially heuristic devices intended to sharpen perception so that our patterns of seeking and seeing are more acute. We don't use the generalizations drawn from the specific case to draw conclusions about other situations but, rather, we use them to search those situations more efficiently.

Another concern emanates from one of qualitative research's strengths, its capacity to particularize. As we get better and better at making vivid the distinctive features of the situations we wish to understand and improve, we may diminish our ability to make meaningful comparisons among them. To the extent to which qualitative researchers reveal what is distinctive, we distance ourselves from the comparative. That is why Dewey once commented that nowhere are comparisons more odious than in the arts (Dewey 1934). Qualitative research, like the arts, gives a premium to the distinctive. We don't really put works of art on a comparative scale. We try to see them in their own terms.

Yet we live in a culture that is predicated upon comparison: we rate people, we rank them, we assign them to league tables, we put them into stanines, quartiles, we apply cut-off levels, we run them down the same track and see who wins. All of these practices depend upon comparison. We are a meritocracy (or aspire to be one) and we determine merit comparatively. In the process, as my colleague Ray McDermott points out, we not only create successes, we produce failures (McDermott and Hervé 1998).

Will the kind of work that, at its best, qualitative research yields satisfy our culturally voracious appetite for comparisons? If not, will it be seen as useful?

There is a way to think about the productive, if somewhat ironic, functions of comparison that can give us comfort. The comparative analysis of student work can awaken us to what is distinctive about any individual's work. It can do this *if* the tasks that students are asked to engage in are sufficiently open-ended to allow their individuality to be expressed *and* if the appraisal of their performance employs criteria that suit the work to be assessed. Let me illustrate what I mean through examples of assessment in sports.

In a mile race all runners run the same track from the same start line. The assessment task is to measure the time it takes to complete the race. Given this criterion, and as long as runners break no rules, how this is accomplished is irrelevant. Differences among runners are represented by performance on a single dimension: time. Consider now high diving. If the divers are to perform a half-gainer with a full twist, the assessment task is to determine the extent to which the performance matches a standardized model of perfection in the minds of the judges. Judges look for discrepancies and assign a score based on an approximation to an ideal. The point of the assessment is to determine which diver comes closest to the model. Again, the criterion is held constant, but a larger array of differences in the way approximation to criterion is achieved is taken into account than in the mile race. In a third example, say improvisational ice dancing, there is a special interest in the individual character of each performance. Time is not a consideration nor is approximation to a fixed model. Comparisons among performers can illuminate the differences among them and, if asked, judges may be expected to justify their judgements by referring to these distinctive features. In this third example, the task for the performer is wide open, and the distinctive qualities of each performance are sought by judges.

This comparative process promotes fine-grained attention to distinctive features. Through comparative analysis, qualities that constitute uniqueness can be identified, bringing us to what is, paradoxically, non-comparable. Attention to what is distinctive is complex, subtle, and time-consuming, but it is also central to educational purposes. My concern is that these purposes may be undermined by our desire to put students and schools on a common scale and in the process lose sight of what is special about them.

But what about the future? Let me turn to my hopes rather than to matters of prediction. Let the wish be the parent of the deed.

What do I hope for? These are my hopes. I hope that educational policy makers and others who shape policies impacting the lives of people use qualitative research to understand the impact of those policies on the people and institutions they are trying to influence. I emphasize this point because so much policy in education is based upon a desire to increase test scores and utterly neglects their side-effects. The cost to student health, the increased incidence of cheating, the displacement of intrinsic satisfactions of learning for extrinsic rewards, the kinds of compromises that students and teachers are forced to make in order to survive: these consequences need to be known. Horace Smith in *Horace's Compromise* (Sizer 1992) really did have to compromise. Policy makers need to know about the side-effects of their policies. At present they do not.

I hope that the experience students have in school becomes a major subject of study. Experience is the medium of education but, surprisingly, studies of student experience in school are rare (Pope 1998). What do students make of their school experience? What *is* their school experience? Where do their epiphanies come from? Do they have any? Where do their frustrations reside? How do they deal with them? What kinds of relationships do they have with their teachers? Have they learned to adapt to the pressures of schooling without being changed? What are the deep lessons they are learning? In short, we need to know much more about the meaning schooling has for students. We operate now largely in the blind.

I hope that increasingly qualitative research is seen as one of the legitimate ways of studying the people and institutions we care about. Since the early 1970s there has been enormous progress in developing and strengthening qualitative research. But I receive enough letters and email from graduate students in the United States and Canada seeking advice and comfort to know that we still have a way to go. There is still a good deal of prejudice out there, especially for forms of qualitative research that do not look like conventional ethnography. We need to walk the line between the risks inherent in innovation and the need to do work that has the quality it needs to be persuasive.

I hope that somehow the public's understanding of education becomes sufficiently complex to realize that many of the most important outcomes and features of schooling will require what only qualitative research is likely to provide. I speak here of dispositional outcomes – the desire to want to continue to learn about what schooling has introduced, for example, the kind of place the school is, the values that it covertly promulgates, the intellectual courage that it promotes, what the school as an institution takes pride in, the range and variety of what it acknowledges as important. When you consider that students spend more time with their teachers than with their parents, these matters matter. Qualitative research can inform us here.

I hope that graduate students wishing to pursue new ways of studying education are given the support and guidance they need to do it well. As I said, I receive many requests for guidance and support from graduate students I never meet; their problem is usually related to their adviser or to the difficulty of putting a committee together. In too many universities there seems to be too little support. Yet we are moving along. I wish the trip was faster and that the rails went to more destinations.

I hope that in universities there will be opportunities for students to develop the skills needed to use new forms of representation to conduct qualitative research. To work effectively in the arts at least four human abilities are critical. You need refined sensibilities, you need an idea, you need imagination, and you need technical skills. Without refined sensibilities the ability to read the subtleties of the world, including the subtleties of one's own work, is impaired. Without an idea of importance whatever is created is likely to be trivial. Without imagination the work produced will be pedestrian, unable to catch and hold the reader's interest. Without technical skills all the sensibility, ideas and imagination in the world will remain hopeless aspiration. While these qualities are critical in the arts, they are also important for doing good qualitative research.

If we cannot see the situations we look at, we will have nothing to say about them. If we don't have an idea that matters, what we say will not be worth reading. If we can't use our imagination to give it form, it will not capture the reader's attention, and if we don't have the technical skills to work within the constraints and affordances of a medium, our intentions will go unrealized. The good news is that these abilities can be developed. Universities need the appetite to do so.

Finally, I hope that the outlets for qualitative research expand so that it is not confined to the limits of the print media. Currently we are largely restricted to what publishers and journals can print. This format is too limiting. Here I have hopes for the computer. It will make sound and images possible in ways that now exist only for commercial media. That realm needs to expand so that it includes the results of scholarly inquiry. Someday it will. Think about what this will mean for teaching research methods, for working with students, for reviewing work for publication and tenure. The prospects are, from a technical perspective, endless. The new millennium may very well bring them in.

6 Productive tensions

Residencies in research

Nicholas Addison

Introduction

This chapter is an analysis of the tensions arising between participants during an interventionist and collaborative action research project ACHiS (Art Critics and Art Historians in Schools). Such tensions are a necessary and productive component of interdisciplinary research despite the discomfort and destabilisation they engender. The simple premise of ACHiS was to place art critics and art historians in secondary schools to work alongside art and design teachers to develop critical studies (critical, contextual and historical studies) in studio education. Critical studies is theorised as an integral component of all courses in art and design but research suggests that it is a 'fragile' one (Davies 1995); ACHiS was thus partly conceived to address a perceived need. The primary aim of the project was formulated to test and evaluate the significance of recent art historical methods for the analysis and interpretation of visual and material culture in secondary schools. It was hypothesised that this would both inform modes of investigation and contextualisation and provide reflective tools for the evaluation of studio practice.

The school-based collaboration took the form of ten five-day residencies (or equivalent) over two academic years. Most of the residencies could be characterised as interventionist, that is, through them, critical, contextual and historical investigation took place that had either not been present or not present in that form.

To help me make sense of a complex, multifaceted research project I have drawn on the work of Basil Bernstein, in particular his last book *Pedagogy, Symbolic Control and Identity* (2000), to help analyse an elusive but highly generative site of cultural reproduction, those uncertain spaces *in between* the varying discourses and practices within and outside the school. These spaces fluctuate over time as they are defined by shifting boundaries, boundaries that are being continuously eroded, shored up and reconstituted. Such movement destabilises the means of control whereby power is maintained, in this case the power invested in the curriculum subject art and design. In analysing these spaces it becomes apparent that the 'in between' is a place where the relationship between control and power, the dependency of the latter on the former, is most vulnerable. It might be said that the school is a notable instance of social and cultural in-betweenness, a peculiar microcosm in which the in-between of discourses is regulated and maintained. It became evident as ACHiS developed that art and design is a subject where very different discourses meet, confront one another and are contested. Inevitably these discourses are multiple and each is layered by interdependencies and contradictions. But three discourses (which here includes practices) dominated the ACHiS dynamic, two professional: art criticism–history and secondary art and design, the third demotic, popular assumptions about the nature of art and art education. None of these three has absolute boundaries but the second, that is pedagogical practice, sits uneasily between the extremes of the first and last and is thus a fascinating site for the analysis of the production and reproduction of cultural consciousness.

Singularities and regionalisations

In recent years art history and history of art have rapidly formed alliances with alternative disciplinary positions (or, as some might say, invaded their territories) in order to answer new questions and sustain relevance; an interdisciplinarity that has increasingly become theoretical in orientation. Art history's expansion towards, or subsumation within, cultural studies, rather than within say history or philosophy, is partly determined by its geographical location within the art college, the theoretical wing of the theory–practice continuum that characterises the academic profile of these institutions. Almost everywhere in education, and at all levels, legislative and institutional, the filial pact between theory and practice is assumed (Peters 2001).

In secondary schools history of art appears as an autonomous subject only at A level (AS/A2) and is largely followed by students from the independent sector; it has always been and remains a minority subject. However, all practical courses in art and design have critical studies written into their syllabuses. How this is to be managed has been a topic of heated debate particularly since the advent of the National Curriculum for Art (Department of Education and Science (DES) 1991; see also Thistlewood 1989; Dawtrey *et al.* 1996). Some have argued for a parallel, complementary course, others for an integrated model, but whichever way the pact is delivered, its 'fragility' (with isolated exceptions) is determined by a sense that such study sits uncomfortably alongside the production of art, craft and design; such study seems, from the point of view of many school teachers and most students, entirely other. Why should this be so?

Art and design in schools is what Bernstein (2000) would call a 'singular', that is:

> A discourse which has appropriated a space to give itself a unique name. So for example physics, chemistry, sociology, psychology are, for me, singulars. And the structure of knowledge in the nineteenth century was, in fact, the birth and development of singulars. These singulars produced a discourse that was about themselves.
>
> (Bernstein 2000: 9)

The traditional subjects of the school curriculum are a typical example of such 'singularity'.

For Bernstein (2000: 5–11) a central concept for the understanding of pedagogic practice is the principle of classification, a principle that enables the analyst to focus on the spaces between categories. It is this space, a space he calls a 'region of silence', that preserves the 'insulation' and 'dislocations' that determine a singular's particular rules and specialised voice. So, for example, art and design is regulated by a regime of 'making', that is the making of art, craft and design. Thus art-specific discussion is usually front and/or end loaded leaving as much time within the limited time available for what is deemed 'productive' work. Although pupil discussion does take place within the classroom, it tends to ignore the stuff of art; that which relates the subject to the wider field, its external contexts. At those points where the teacher is in contact with the pupils, one-to-one or in small groups, attention, of course, is given to the internal matter in hand, but pupils can be very protective of the socialising 'chatter' which the 'liberal' environment of the art room makes available. The tradition of talking about art is the tradition of art history; discussion of art is singularly what art and design is not.

Despite the nineteenth-century foundation of subjects, the school has not been totally immune to what Bernstein terms 'regionalisations': 'a region is created by a recontextualising of singulars . . . Singulars are intrinsic to the production of knowledge in the intellectual field. Regions are the interface between the field of production of knowledge and any field of practice' (Bernstein 2000: 9); art and design has to contend with design and technology throughout every key stage (KS) and media studies from KS4. Both the latter subjects are characterised by their 'interface': the former meeting changing social and environmental needs, the latter focusing on mass communications and thus explicitly the relationship between power and control in contemporary society; if the first subject is 'productive' the latter is 'critical'. Art and design, however, must preserve its singularity if it is to maintain its power: quite where that power is located is one of the questions that the ACHiS project attempted to clarify. As will be evident popularity is the key to its power, to its insularity, for a strong principle of classification ensures that its boundaries are not breached. As Bernstein insists:

> If that insulation is broken, then a category is in danger of losing its identity . . . Whatever maintains the strengths of the insulation, maintains the relations between the categories and their distinct voices . . . If this insulation changes its strength, then the principles of the social division of labour – that is, its classification – changes.
>
> (Bernstein 2000: 6)

What ACHiS shows most clearly is that the existing power of art and design does not reside in critical discussion of art and certainly not critical discussion of craft and design.

Nonetheless, critique is what the researchers were about, both as art critics/ historians and as educational researchers. However, because the research project took the form of action research, the critique was directed as much at their own actions as on practice in schools. Yet the critics/historians presumed that this critical interventionist position was likely to create some tension within the research team, as, ever since the introduction of regulating bodies (QCA, Ofsted) and their regime of scrutiny and accountability, teachers have tended to take up defensive rather than reflective positions when being observed (inspected). There is also evidence to suggest that schooling in the UK is primarily concerned with cultural reproduction rather than cultural critique. By cultural reproduction I mean, in this instance, the maintenance and replication of a dominant cultural identity predicated on the cohesive and unifying effect of a humanist, universalist yet nationalist rhetoric (this is evidently much closer to the aims of classical art history than to the new). Thus practice in schools, despite democratic aims, remains predominantly celebratory rather than critical. But art and design in its singularity avoids overt critique other than that based on formalist criticism. Art criticism–history is not art and design education, this is a strong classificatory principle; the power of each is based on seemingly antithetical oppositions: objectivity/subjectivity; fact/feeling; structure/appearance, the list, albeit a caricature, could go on. In describing the ways in which each discipline regulates and maintains its classification it is necessary to introduce a further concept of Bernstein's that of 'framing'.

> The principle of classification provides us with the limits of any discourse, whereas framing provides us with the form of realisation of that discourse; that is, framing regulates the realisation rules for the production of the discourse. Classification refers to *what*, framing is concerned with *how* meanings are to be put together, the forms by which they are to be made public, and the nature of the social relationships that go with it.
>
> (Bernstein 2000: 12, original emphases)

To reiterate: ACHiS was an attempt to find ways of integrating social and cultural critique within the art and design curriculum; the interventionist, critical residency was the form of its realisation, collaboration the mode of its social relations.

For at least one researcher, Jane Trowell, the principle of collaboration also characterised her relationship with students. Drawing on the theory of engaged pedagogy (hooks 1994) she was determined that her residency would not be a pre-formed, if negotiated, intervention. Rather she sought to develop a project in dialogue with students, albeit in relation to a perceived problem within the realisation of the A level course. I wish to quote extensively from her report in order to examine Bernstein's concept of 'framing' as it relates to the ACHiS project.

The main aim of Trowell's residency was to investigate the possibilities of the 'critical studies diary', one 'realisation rule' by which students could provide evidence of critical thinking in the Edexcel A level for the year 2000. The dialogic tenor of the residency could be seen to constitute a prolongation of the diagnostic period of all the residencies, two half-days in conversation with the collaborating teacher and at least one day's observation with them in the department. For various reasons Trowell was able to spend significant time alone with the students and she believes this elicited more open responses to questions because the hierarchical power relation that can limit discussion between teacher and students was reduced. Bernstein refers to these power relations as the 'social order'; censorship is employed by the student, Bernstein's 'acquirer', because: 'an acquirer can be seen as a potential for labels. Which labels are selected is a function of framing' (Bernstein 2000: 13). Through such interchanges and the extent to which students can accommodate themselves to the 'regulative discourse' (that is the extent to which they behave appropriately within the codes of the discourse and its 'distributive rules') they can develop an understanding of 'recognition rules' (the means by which they can regulate their own behaviours to determine which labels a teacher chooses). Trowell made it clear to students that her initial role would not be judgemental, that nowhere would their statements be referenced in any formal assessment. Evidently students trusted her:

> When asked for their associations with the word 'critical', students brainstormed 'pessimism', 'something wrong' (S), 'tell you what's bad about it' (C). Pushed further, H said 'I don't think you can be critical in a good way'. H and N expressed great discomfort about 'being critical': it's 'rude to criticise' (H – diagnostic session), 'imposing my thoughts' (N); 'it's down to my taste and their taste' (N). Given this, it is not surprising that these students might feel resistant to behaving in a way they don't approve.
>
> (Trowell in ACHiS 2002: 12)

The place of language in the art and design classroom tends to be situated in the domain of *regulative discourse* that is as a part of the social order. The social organisation of complex practical activities – spatial, temporal and technical – is largely responsible for this orientation, so any lesson is liable to consist of vocal and gestural directions, timings and reminders; it is within this domain that students must be aurally attentive. The other side of the dual but embedded discourses that constitute Bernstein's concept of framing is the *instructional discourse*; this determines the discursive rules of a subject. As has already been noted, art and design teachers frequently bypass discursive instruction (in the form of language) in favour of instruction by demonstration and exemplification both of which demand visual and kinaesthetic attention before aural. The framing of art and design's discursivity is weak, so it is no wonder that sixth form students, habituated to the recognition rules of the subject, have problems deciding how to use language in what is for them a dislocated context. However, another researcher, David Hulks, noted that with Year 7, where the subject-specific recognition rules had had little time to become established, pupils appeared to enjoy the discursive environment despite the criticism of the collaborating teacher who saw the activity as inappropriate.

Trowell categorises student responses to the critical studies diary into types of recognition or misrecognition of purpose:

> E alluded to the issue of progression, and stated that the Critical Studies Diary was a 'jump from GCSE', that they 'never did this before', and that she had thought '"critically analyse" – what's that?!' (all verbatim notes, 2.2.00). One

could deduce from this that if students had not previously been asked to participate in such an endeavour, or been asked to use such a term as 'critical', and yet had been 'successful' in art, that it was reasonable that the new activity of the Critical Studies Diary could seem additional, and inessential, and therefore without a central purpose.

(Trowell in ACHiS 2002: 14)

For these students the singularity of art and design is self-evidently its visuality. Up to the sixth form success has been measured entirely in relation to the look of realisations and the criteria for assessing this look are frequently mimetic and formalist despite a rhetoric of self-expressivity. Success is celebrated by the display of exemplary student work which pupils from Year 7 onwards admire and to which they aspire; in other words pupils/students are immersed in the look of school art and it is usually at odds with the visual environments of the home, the mass media and the gallery/museum. If, for students, the home is a visual and material given, a mute receptacle rather than a site for the production of visual and material meaning (with, in some instances, leeway to stake a personal claim to a bedroom) the gallery/museum is a place where the visually and materially privileged is mediated by a professional language, a language encountered mostly in the context of formal education and often perceived as alien (Robins and Woollard 2001). However, the mass media is characterised by its overt multimodality, its easy marriage of recorded image, sound and movement. Here the relationship between word and image is not perceived as problematic, whether the word is in the form of speech or writing. Thus art and design is somewhat unique, for elsewhere in the curriculum the interrelatedness of different modes of learning is well established (Kress and van Leeuwen 2001). The art and design classroom is of course eminently a site of multimodal discourse, but the status of the word within that mix, and particularly the status of writing, the most privileged mode in the academic curriculum, is contested.

The findings of the first year residencies confirm the singularity of art and design although the teachers' questionnaire would indicate otherwise. Using Bernstein's concepts of classifications and framings, the place of critical studies within this singularity can be summarised as follows. I have acknowledged in parentheses the source of a statement when it is drawn from the researchers' first year findings. Those without a name or letter are generic, although they do not apply to each and every department collaborating in ACHiS.

Classification

- Art and design is often a hermetically sealed practice which, other than in relation to some notion of interiority or cultural identity, rarely refers to the lives of students, the wider curriculum, nor indeed broader social and cultural issues. Students are encouraged to follow either a perceptualist model, recording the appearance of things, or an expressive model, finding equivalents for feelings.

- Few students realise that they can deploy skills developed elsewhere in the curriculum: without explicit guidance most are either unwilling or unable to do so.
- In current academic discourse, craft's relationship to design and to fine art is often expressed in a structurally oppositional way despite the fact that art in schools supposedly accommodates art, craft and design as some sort of creative continuum; thus the crafts are suffocating within their allocated non-space of unattainable coexistence (Georgaki in ACHiS 2002: 50).

Framing

Instructional discourse

- The 'critical' dimension of courses tends to be based on formal and mimetic analysis and appreciation in support of practices reproduced by demonstration and exemplification.
- The historical and contextual dimension tends to be either didactic; taking the form of a short illustrated introduction and/or directed, taking the form of student 'research'; constituting biographical information, some formal analysis, personal preferences and copious transcriptions.
- Although art educationalists advise an integrated, investigative approach to critical studies, advisory documents, despite disclaimers, invite it to be taught on the model of transmission, i.e. information-led, supplementary to practical work (DfEE 1999b: 20–1); e.g. 'Pupils will be taught *about*' (Papazafiriou in ACHiS 2002: 17).

Regulative discourse

- The perceptual model (with various 'expressive' alternatives) privileges the mimetic paradigm of the picture; through this paradigm students develop an aversion to abstraction and other forms of modernist and postmodern practice.
- The historical artist is imagined almost exclusively as a white male although students are exposed to a range of gendered, historical, cultural practices (Asbury in ACHiS 2002: 17).
- The hierarchical distinctions between art, craft and design are historical and social constructs which are replicated in the structures of art education and are thus invisible to its participants (both teachers and students). One of the most pernicious aspects of this hierarchy is a distinction based on gender bias (Georgaki in ACHiS 2002: 17).
- Teachers are not provided with the reflective space necessary to develop pedagogic practice, that is the opportunity, as classroom practitioners, to research and assimilate within their teaching complex theory (e.g. semiotics) so that it can be applied to learning in the classroom (De Souza in ACHiS 2002: 17).

I believe it is fair to say that such a profile characterises the singularity of many secondary school art and design courses at KS3 and GCSE, although by no means all of the departments in partnership with the ACHiS team. It must be remembered that all participating schools welcomed an opportunity to develop critical studies, in addition all the departments are seen as successful both in terms of Ofsted and public examinations. It can only be assumed that student perceptions about the problematic status of writing would be magnified in departments less receptive to the notion of a critical curriculum. Sixth form courses can be more investigative and critical and, in their specialisations such as ceramics, graphics, photography, textiles, there is the opportunity to move outside the school fine art model. But increasingly schools do not include a sixth form and therefore younger pupils do not see this type of work. From the point of view of a critical curriculum, a discursive curriculum that would enable students to contribute to a democratic society, such singularity appears neglectful. Yet the subject retains its immense popularity and herein lies its power. Quite how that power is maintained requires an examination of the systems of control through which its singularity is communicated and naturalised. As Bernstein asserts:

> The principle of classification comes to have the force of the natural order and the identities that it constructs are taken as real, as authentic, as integral, as the source of integrity. Thus a change in the principle of classification here is a threat to the principle of integrity, of coherence of the individual.
>
> (Bernstein 2000: 7)

ACHiS, by intervening at the point of classification, the territories in between discourses, was one such threat. It arrived offering solutions through participation, changing the values of pedagogic practice at the level of framing (in part something it achieved), but also further problematised the situation through critique and classificatory destabilisation. After the experience of the first year, and with this in mind, the researchers decided to increase the level of collaboration in the second. Based on interim findings the art and design profile appears overtly negative, and in relation to the place of critical studies, it is; the strength of the subject's classification is in direct relationship to the weakness of its discursive potential, an aspect of its framing. But before a more collaborative model could be developed it was necessary to reconsider the framing of art and design by establishing its internal strengths. These became more apparent at the beginning of the second year, when, during a research meeting at which the collaborating teachers were not present, various doubts were raised concerning a basic assumption of ACHiS: namely that existing models of critical studies, largely discursive and or logocentric in orientation, are appropriate for learning in art and design. The ensuing discussion noted practices that the researchers and I had observed and evaluated positively in the participating schools. It is paraphrased by the following description.

Art and design framings

Instructional

- Isolates and develops modalities of meaning-making unrecognised (if utilised) by other curriculum subjects, e.g. the visual, haptic, spatial.
- At best promotes experiential rather than information-driven learning.

Regulative

- Admits that learning may be pleasurable and might possess a therapeutic component.
- Encourages a degree of absorbtion and sustained activity.
- Reconciles students to the agency of their bodies by foregrounding the sensory dimension of learning.

Bernstein argues:

> Although classification translates power into the voice to be reproduced, we have seen that the contradictions, cleavages and dilemmas which inhere in the principle of classification are never entirely suppressed, either at the social or individual level . . .
>
> I suggest the following: if a value changes from strong to weak, or vice versa, if framing changes from strong to weak or the classification changes from strong to weak, there are two basic questions we should always ask:
>
> - Which group is responsible for initiating change? Is the change initiated by a dominant group or a dominated group?
> - If values are weakening, what values still remain strong?
>
> (Bernstein 2000: 15)

The second profile is an attempt to answer the second question. In response to the first, it must be acknowledged that ACHiS was initiated from a higher education institution responding to the overwhelming demand voiced by art and design educationalists, usually no longer teachers in schools, to reconceptualise the curriculum along critical lines. In this way the initiators might be seen to belong to a privileged and dominant group. The project did, however, have the blessing of participating teachers. Interest from art critics and art historians was encouraging in principle, however there was little interest from either group to participate as researchers; it was difficult to recruit for ACHiS, although those who were proved to be highly motivated and committed.

The second profile also goes some way to acknowledge the difference in values between the participating groups. Within it there is recognition of a pedagogic code perhaps at odds with the critical model being promoted, but nonetheless valid. This seemed a good starting point from which to develop a model of collaboration. When stated in this way art and design's insularity might be seen to offer an alternative to the logocentric curriculum. Its popularity would suggest that many students find its difference empowering or find in its singularity a place of solace or sanctuary.

Conclusion

Bernstein is most interested in those processes that unite the material and immaterial worlds, in terms of knowledge, the 'thinkable' and the 'unthinkable' (Bernstein 2000: 28–30). The gap between these worlds is for him a potential, 'the meeting point of order and disorder, of coherence and incoherence. It is the crucial site of *the yet to be thought*' (Bernstein 2000: 30, original emphasis). The unnameable in art, its affectivity, in combination with its ability to refer, is its power. It is not that visual culture does not have its histories, its grammars, its semantic equivalents, but its material bases, its modalities, have a peculiarity in the way they make meaning possible. This is because the material base is foregrounded in most art. Material and visual artefacts induce visceral arousals and emotional states of a different quality to words, and these cannot be contained by analysis, indeed these meanings may be experienced and understood outside language. Mediated by language, such experiences may appear precious, but experientially they can be profound. The problem for the school subject, art and design, is that to enable students to explore this potential is threatening, transgressive. The affective/referential potential of visual and material culture suggests an alternative order, one at odds with the logocentric curriculum and the 'rules of the father'.

But there is a danger in the unnameable, for when art and design attempts to tame the affective and limit referentiality, when it is reduced to formal exercises, when even its powers of representation, its ability to refer to the experiential world, are limited to the picturing of artefacts chosen for their formal qualities alone, then school art is at its most hermetic and stultifying. As Bernstein claims:

> These meanings are so embedded in the context that they have no reference outside that context. These meanings are not simply context dependent, they are necessarily context bound: and meanings which are context bound cannot unite anything other than themselves.
>
> (Bernstein 2000: 30)

If art and design retains its hermetic singularity, if it reproduces school art *ad nauseam*, it will ultimately petrify. If it ignores language it fails to control the force that would dominate it. In the era of multimedia and multimodality the need for visual and material culture to come under the orbit of a critical curriculum is incontestable; art and design is not empowered to do this alone, it is not given the resources, particularly in relation to time. In the current iconosceptic climate of UK education (see Addison, Chapter 12 in this volume) art critics and art historians could undoubtedly find a constructive place within the curriculum even as it stands, whether contributing to art and design, citizenship, English, history, media studies, philosophy, the list could go on. But because their pedagogic devices are at odds with those of art and design, because any intervention is recognised as an attempt at further logocentric regionalisation, in the immediate future the strengths of art criticism–history would find a more sympathetic home within the logocentric curriculum. Located here the art critic–historian in residence would be able to mediate between the critical and the celebratory, the affective and the logocentric, the past and the present, the reflective and the productive, the social and the institutional, they would enable students, if not to act other, at least to think other. In the mean time art and design needs to develop its discursivity, it must recognise and celebrate the power of its affectivity and referentiality, but in the context of developing technologies and media, it must attempt to name the unnameable.

Questions for discussion

1   Is the insularity of art and design a strength or a weakness?
2   What are the power relations between the participants in the subject art and design (art educationalists, art teachers, examination boards, Ofsted, pupils/students)?
3   Is it possible to find a place for pedagogic critique in a climate of inspection and accountability?

Further reading

Bernstein, B. (2000) *Pedagogy, Symbolic Control and Identity*, Oxford: Rowan and Littlefield.

Interdisciplinarity

7 The role of language within a multimodal curriculum

Anton Franks

Here my interest is in exploring the role that language has to play in the teaching and learning of art and design in schools. For this purpose I look in some detail at instances of language in use within the context of the complex meaning-making processes that play out in an art lesson. This raises issues about the place of language in the teaching and learning of the subject. There are, though, wider contexts and perspectives that underlie my particular approach to issues of language and its role in learning, and these frame my discussion.

My own concerns are shaped by a spirit of inquiry into the relation between language and learning represented in the Bullock Report (1975). However, I cannot ignore the context created by the somewhat instrumental requirements of current policy as outlined by government agents in the National Literacy Strategy (DfEE 2001). I therefore want to emphasise the *agency* of teachers and learners as makers of learning situations through action and interaction. To talk of agency is to speak of people who have choices to make. Yet teachers' choices are constrained by relations of power and authority in classrooms and by curriculum and policy frameworks. I am therefore also concerned to take into account reflexive views of the ways teachers think of themselves as professional subject specialists; this allegiance determines their perspective on the role of language in their teaching.

As a teacher of drama and English, I have a close interest in the role of language and learning, but it is an interest tinged with certain feelings of ambivalence. The interest in language, spoken, written, printed and now digitised, is central to the study of all aspects of the English curriculum. The drama specialist in me, however, wants to place verbal language firmly *alongside* other ways of communicating in and through drama: gesture, posture, arrangement in space, movement and so forth. All these things work together with language in drama to make meaning and I want to help students make dramatic meaning, choosing and using various modes of communication alongside words. I am conscious that language is heavily privileged in education. Not only that at the most basic structural level, the history of educational policy and practice, the structure of schools, teaching and assessment are bound up with written words, laid out in printed codes and bulleted documents, but also that students' 'ability' is most often measured by their competence with (written) language. In drama, though, learners might be offered access and the opportunity to succeed by communicating meaning in other modes alongside, or beyond words. Here, I might assume or deduce a certain affinity with teachers of art and design, who are concerned more with visual and material culture than they are with the centrality of language.

Language is a problematic issue in relation to teaching and learning in art and design; its role may be resisted, downplayed or not considered at all. The notional and practical divide between the disciplines and practices of art and design and art history might give some evidence of ambivalence and discomfort with the role of language and its relation to the cultural field of art (see Addison, Chapter 6 in this volume). If no attention is given to the role that language has to play in art and design, an important component of the whole picture is missing.

In thinking about how language works in relation to other modes of communicating and making meaning, it is important to shift from the located perspective of individual teachers towards broader theoretical perspectives on communication and meaning-making in the curriculum. The term 'multimodal curriculum' derives in the main from the work in the area of social semiotics associated with Gunther Kress and colleagues. Starting in the area of linguistics, he has moved towards an interest in ways that different ways of communication: the visual, the architectural, the gestural, the musical etc., work together to make meaning (see Hodge and Kress 1993; Kress and van Leeuwen 2001). With the expansion in contemporary culture of digital and broadcast media, for example, there is greater choice in ways of communication and so people choose the mode that best expresses their purposes. Now, more than ever, educators need to move beyond preoccupations with verbal language to explore the ways in which people make particular choices of specific ways of communicating that fit different social purposes and contexts. Although multimodal semioticians respond to developments in broad cultural domains, they also investigate ways that groups and individuals use communicative resources to make meaning at home and in school. Kress and van Leeuwen (1996) use the language of semiotics to explore the ways that young children make meaning from the representational resources available to them at any one time. In their homes children use costume, marked sheets of paper, chairs and other furniture to make a car, for example, for the setting of their dramatic playing. Nursery schools provide playhouses, sandpits, discarded cardboard boxes, paint and paper to enable children to make 'texts' and communicate meanings. Often their play incorporates aspects of books that have been read to them, things viewed on television or everyday interactions. For the small child, there is a continuum between things on a page or screen and tangible things in the here and now. These are *meaningful* things that can be called signs, and there appears to be a strong relation between signs as various objects in the world and the signs in the head called imagination and thought. Imagination for Kress involves the ability to range freely across modes.

In the domain of formal education Kress recognises that particular curricular formations and teaching practices, especially in an emphasis on the written word, might engender dispositions that constrain or inhibit the development of particular modes of thinking. There are two aspects of teaching practice and curriculum that point to the development of an increasingly multimodal curriculum. Looking at the teaching and learning of science, recent research shows how teachers and learners move between images, words, diagrams, gestures, bodily actions, objects and materials in explaining and making sense of science (Kress *et al.* 2001). Teaching and learning in this 'traditional' curriculum subject is necessarily multimodal. At the same time, the continued and developing presence of arts and media subjects in the curriculum offer different modes of engaging with the world (Kress *et al.* 2001). For my purpose, the idea of the multimodal curriculum shifts my perspective wider than language, but it still retains the notion that verbal language is an important resource for making meaning.

Kress moves through his interest in signs and meanings towards learning and schooling. The cultural psychology developed by Vygotsky (1978) has learning and the development of mind as its main focus but moves from this interest towards the role that sign-making in general, and language in particular, have in learning processes. There is vast literature in this area, and so my explanation here is indicative and related to my particular focus. Broadly speaking, Vygotskian approaches to the psychology of learning emphasise that individual learning always takes place in specific social, cultural and historical contexts. In looking at children in the early years, Vygotsky (1978: 92–120) noted there is a continuum between imaginative play, drawing and the development of writing. A small child might, for example, put a stick between her knees and 'gallop' around pretending to be a 'horse'. The child gets the 'idea' of the horse from immediate experience of horses, or pictures seen in a book. She connects these with the word horse that she gets from her involvement in social and cultural life, reading, watching TV, conversations and play with others. Later, she may draw a horse and after that she may be able to write the word. In this kind of progression, Vygotsky traces the ways that participation in social life, involvement in patterned activity, and the trade of signs in cultural domains (including, especially, words) relate to the development of conceptual thought.

In the art lesson observed, the teacher introduces and works with the term 'vessel'. In one way, the word 'vessel' is an 'internal' sign given form in some kind of mental representation that holds a network of associations. In this instance the teacher uses questioning to get the pupils to 'fill out' the sense of the word vessel by relating the art and design concept of 'vessel' to their everyday experience. A vessel may be a jar, a jug, a domestic implement. It could also be a boat. When the teacher introduces the term, she asks pupils to draw a vessel for homework and then directs them through the stages of making a vessel in the classroom. Pupils are the linking agents in these moves between words, actions and the socially and culturally organised settings of home and classroom. Through this activity the sense and concept of vessel is 'filled' with meaning. The pupils could do this alone or with their peers, but there is an important role here for the teacher as a more experienced 'other', exploiting and enhancing the potential the pupils have for the development of conceptual thinking. To aid learning, the teacher as instructor enters a pupil's *zone of proximal development*, thus the potential of what a learner might achieve independently is enhanced through the intervention of a 'more experienced other' (Vygotsky 1978: 84–91). Understanding patterns of learning, especially in relation to those that include a view on the role of language, may help to review and modify teaching.

Lessons are highly complex social occasions in which the parameters of description are broad and deep. There are social, cultural, historical, psychological and semiotic aspects to every lesson and issues of content and form, both in terms of knowledge and social organisation. This description is not intended to be 'representative' of all art and design lessons. It stands solely as an 'interpretative device', a kind of fixed point, a measure. The transcript has been edited to concentrate on the beginning and the end of the lesson. The format conventions follow those of a playscript rather than more conventional linguistic formats.

Let me take you first through the school setting as a multimodal environment. From the reception area, where we might see neat displays of art and craft objects around the walls, we move through corridors. As we approach the art classrooms, we might note a thickening of art stuff displayed on the walls. There is smell here too, of tempera paint, clay and pencil shavings. We have a kind of 'funnelling process' towards the subject area, whereby we gain some sense of the school as it is regionalised and mapped in spatial terms. The setting for art and design, the location, architecture and layout of its rooms, makes it a particular setting and the 'discourse' of the subject includes its spaces, layout and decoration. When meeting the art teachers, we might see how they signal their subjectivity in their person; they wear aprons spattered with paint and clay. When they speak they use particular words and in particular ways connected with the subject. In quite specific ways, art teachers embody the art curriculum through their patterns of action and interaction with learners. Art and design as a field of operation is established partly in this complex layering of setting, actors (among whom the teacher is the leading player) and patterns of action.

From the point at which the pupils arrive at the door, we can see from the outset how language plays a role in marking the boundaries of the lesson. Here they are asked to wait in a line until most of the class has arrived, marking the boundary of a transition from the previous lesson and the other site. The teacher checks on her memory of names as this is a Year 7 class who have been in the school for only six weeks or so and, with a single art lesson a week, she has not had much time to become familiar with the class. Her tone is friendly and interested and at the same time maintains appropriate social distance. This type of discourse is, of course, generic to schooling. Knowledge and utterance of names establish both social contact and a form of control. Rapidly, however, talk turns towards an 'idea' of an art and design lesson. The 'wheels' referred to are not ordinary wheels used for locomotion, they are printing wheels, made of fired clay and used to imprint a strip of design on a soft slab of clay. Instrumentally, this talk serves to remind the teacher how far this class has got with the task. More broadly, in drawing from the collective memory of the assembled pupils, it anticipates the lesson to come, turning and orienting both teacher and pupils to the specialised nature of the task in hand.

'Sit where you usually sit'. The class enter the room where, as one might expect, image and artefact are dominant. Again there are the generic school rituals of placement in the classroom and then the final marker of the start of the lesson proper, the taking of the register of names. In this ten-minute sequence, the framing of the lesson in time and place is established.

In the next sequence, before students are instructed about the practical task that will fill most of the lesson, the teacher sets homework. A main function of setting homework at the beginning of the lesson is to use writing and speech to introduce some major concepts and themes. More broadly, it is to fill out the conceptual stuff of art and design as a subject discipline.

> Teacher hands around sketch books used to do homework and as she does so, pupils are interested in the comments and grades they've been given and read them aloud to each other.

Teacher: A few seconds to read comments on homework, if you can read my writing . . . [*in response to a comment/complaint from a student about the grades she's got*] Yeah, but I asked for colour. It's a beautiful drawing, but I asked for colour . . .

I'll give you a moment to write it down then I'll explain it [*reads*] Due in Friday 30th period 5. An observation drawing of a vessel – use TONE. [*repeats slowly and deliberately*] First of all . . . put your hand up if you know, what's observational drawing?

Pupil: When you look at it.

Teacher: What, your drawing? Or . . . what are you looking at?

Pupil: . . . [*unintelligible*]

Teacher: Excellent. To observe something, looking at, really seeing something and drawing it. What is a vessel? An unusual word . . . what is a vessel? It's always the boys. Let's have a girl.

Pupil: . . . [*unintelligible*]

Teacher: Well done . . . we've had 'a pot'.

Pupil: It could be a boat.

Teacher: Yes, well done. It could be . . . But here a vessel is a container. A jar, a jug, a cup of some sort. Something in the kitchen cupboard . . . Tone . . . what do I mean by tone?

Pupil: Shading.

Teacher: Shading. That's all it is . . . where the shadows fall . . . so tone is another name for shading . . . light and dark. Any other questions?

Even in this early sequence the sense of the lesson begins to emerge in stronger terms, defining conceptual and disciplinary fields of activity. Circling around and working with the meaning of words in writing and speech helps to develop the sense of learning and doing. There is clear emphasis on three key terms: 'observation', 'vessel' and 'tone' and this is enforced on several levels. First, there is what may appear to be the purely mechanical task of reading from the board, or listening to reading aloud, and the copying down of the homework task in homework diaries. We can discern from the concision and precision of this operation that the teacher shows a clear pattern of design and intention that works partly by the repetition of terms and their inscription. In this sequence the meaning of the terms emerges to give the sense of their specific (and technical) usage. Pupils *observe* an object to make it the subject of a drawing. This category of 'artistic' observation is marked off from ordinary 'seeing' with particular emphasis because it is closely articulated with the action of drawing, it is 'really seeing something and drawing it'. Second, the object under observation has to be a *vessel* and this observation and drawing makes the vessel a particular kind of object for art; it has three dimensions, it is hollow, it has volume, and is therefore capable of containing stuff. It could, as the pupil suggested, be a boat; here the teacher's regulation acknowledges the play but firmly states that a vessel in these circumstances has to be a container of some sort. This pupil's contribution is teasing and playful, his humour lies in challenging the sense of *vessel* in the teacher's terms. Third, there is an accent on *tone*. The teacher is quickly satisfied with the response from the student who says that tone is 'shading' because it is apparent that the student has got the sense that tone, 'where the shadows fall' and 'light and dark', is achieved through the technique of shading.

Here subtle connections are being mediated in words referring to the system of the activity of learning about and making art. First, there is seeing with artists' eyes, a way of 'seeing' or observing a vessel that is necessarily different from the way that a design technologist, physicist, chemist or archaeologist might see it. This way of 'seeing' is marked in the written instruction for the homework by the use of the phrase 'an observation drawing' which, in this form, appears to give particular emphasis to a type or category of depiction.

Second, there is the drawing, representation or depiction of the three-dimensionality of the vessel through the use of tone and the technique of shading. Again, this is different from the way one might want to represent the volume of a vessel as an exercise in the mathematics of shape and volume, or might design a vessel in design technology. Possibly the teacher's intention here is for pupils to work on the rendering of volume through observation of the way that light affects the object's surface. The teacher's feedback elaborates and reinforces the answers she elicits. Third, in choosing to set and elaborate a homework task at the outset of the lesson, the teacher establishes a certain kind of conceptual framework. However, at this stage in the sequence of work, the homework task is not explicitly articulated within the remainder of the lesson.

It may well be that this setting of homework is an established ritual for this particular teacher, department or school. It may, furthermore, be less like consciously realised and meticulously planned activity and more like second nature, derived from 'experience' and tacit knowledge. However, she is making sets of choices and framing and sequencing certain patterns of action in specifically marked ways. In this instance, 'framing by homework' not only sets the conceptual boundaries for learning about art through observation, visualisation and making, but also orientates pupils towards the pattern of action that will unfold in the lesson.

In moving away from the board, first making sure that pupils have put away their homework planners, the teacher next turns the attention of the class towards the main activity. Perhaps the putting away of books signifies something of a shift in the role of language in the lesson. From here on, language accompanies or is embedded in action. It is language that accompanies display, gesture and instruction through demonstration.

> The teacher moves to a table of prepared materials and equipment: blocks of terracotta clay pre-sliced into segments; paper cylinders that are models for the vessels; A3 sheets of purplish pink sugar paper, later used to roll out clay and squares of thin white paper marked 'TEMPLATE'.

Teacher: Put your things away quickly and come round . . . We've got to put a pattern on. Before I put out your clay . . . got to roll out some more slabs. Everyone take one. Good practice is to stand up. You shouldn't need an apron . . .

> Meanwhile the teacher is demonstrating how to roll out a slab of clay.

There are several moves being made here, but the main shift is towards the central purpose of the lesson, taking steps towards the making of a vessel. The shift is clearly marked in her move away from the board, where the homework is written, towards the table with its equipment. First, there is the generic regulative discourse of schooling in phrases like 'put your things away' which, incidentally, marks the economy of time imposed by timetable. Next there are some brief checking procedures. Written language impinges less on proceedings, except for the labelling of paper squares as 'TEMPLATES'. This labelling represents a small but significant transformation of a rather generalised category of object (a stack of square pieces of paper of particular dimensions) into a rather specialised and technical object, the template, with which one can (in theory) produce a number of objects with the same dimensions. The template, although a flimsy object, has a rather solid conceptual role in this lesson because its application ensures that the work 'looks nicer' and the aesthetic of 'the look' is a key feature of what makes art. Rolling pins, on the other hand, remain rolling pins but they serve another 'aestheticised' purpose which is to make the tile 'nice and flat', and facilitates the application of pattern by stamp wheel.

From this point, pupils disperse to various tables and begin the task of rolling, cutting and wheeling. The teacher moves around the room watching, instructing, assisting, patrolling. At one stage she stops and draws the attention of the class to what she has to say.

Teacher: If you make it too pancake thin the problem is that the wheel will go through. What Sam's doing is he's used his wheel and he's rushing through it. I want you to slow down. Take your time and think about what you're doing.

> The teacher stands by a table occupied solely by boys. This appears to be a monitoring device to slow their rather frenzied activity. A boy goes to retrieve stamps.

Teacher: I want you to see what a wheel . . . the effects you can practise on . . . it's a very good idea to try and keep your lines tidy otherwise you'll waste space [*teacher is rolling wheels across a slab*] I think you can fit on 5 or 6 wheels.

Pupil: I got 8.

Here, reference to the best use of time is bound up with the need for care and consideration in realising a design. The analogous image of 'pancake' thinness evokes a material that is too flimsy for the task; it is implicitly contrasted with the category of robustness that would allow the controlled application of embossed or imprinted pattern to produce a 'good' aesthetic effect. The boys' tendency towards speedy operations, possibly a competition against time, appears to work counter to producing aesthetic effects. At the end of this sequence, the competitive element is further compounded by the emergence of another competition: how many lines of pattern will fit onto the slab. It is possible that this boy fixes on the teacher's comment about not wasting space as a measure of success for his eight lines of pattern. His final say in this sequence competes with the teacher's edict that it ought to be possible to fit on five or six 'tidy' lines.

Apparent in this dialogue is a small but significant struggle between value systems. On the one hand is the teacher's concern for care, consideration and neatness, and this is towards the purpose of designing aesthetic effects. The boys, on the other hand, valorise the activity of this lesson according to different criteria, those of speed and quantity, faster operations and more lines of pattern are good. It is, of course, an unequal struggle, as in the art classroom, in this lesson, under the hierarchical social order of schooling, the teacher holds most power. In this instance, the pupils' assertion of their own values in action and speech are relegated to a realm of minor dissent.

This is played out in the final sequence of the lesson. Again elements of routinised or ritualised activity can be detected. It is about ten minutes before the end of the lesson when the teacher asks students to finish off their work:

Teacher: We'll have a two-minute 'crit', what went well and what didn't work . . .

The teacher lays out the clay slabs.

Teacher: Right, we're waiting for three people . . . and boys put the clay down. Put your hands on the table. I need to see what you're doing. It's important to position yourself where you can see. This is taking too long and we've got to clear up yet . . . What I need to say is that you really need to see the work. Look at them carefully to see what worked.

Teacher looks carefully at the display of printed slabs laid out on the table

Teacher: Can anyone point out one particular pattern? . . . I've got two favourites. What really, really works?

Pupil: [*pointing*] That one.

Teacher: Yeah . . . positive and negative . . . and it works really well . . . Right, you've got four minutes to tidy up . . . I want to remind you of your homework.

Teacher moves to front of class by board

Teacher: I want you to draw what you see. Not what you imagine but what you really see. I want you to draw a vessel, you're making one, so I want you to draw one.
Pupil: Can we use colour?
Teacher: No, just tone . . . the soft pencils . . . Class is dismissed.

If homework setting appears to have established the opening frame of the lesson in setting the conceptual ground for activity, so in this final section the stretch from the 'crit' to the reinforcement of the homework task appears to fulfil the function of closure. Let us trace this through the above sequence. The 'crit' is centrally involved in 'finishing' the whole lesson.

In this phase there is a chance to reflect on and evaluate the work of the lesson. When the teacher calls it a 'crit', she locates it within the field of art more generally. There is the implicit suggestion that art and design is continuous with the art school tradition. This she reinforces by locating the 'crit' towards the back of the classroom on a working bench, furthest from the door and the board. There is a parallel here with the routine of giving 'crits' for work in progress in art schools, in which students traditionally track around studios looking at people's objects in the places of making. In this classroom the teacher defines the 'crit' as being about 'what went well and what didn't work'. This formulation perhaps signals that the major emphasis in the art classroom is on the making as emergent process, rather than placing too heavy a value on finished products.

The slab tiles are laid out in two parallel lines from a corner of the bench and the teacher's order is to carry them carefully. This is closely followed by the doubly endorsed exhortation to 'really see' and to 'look carefully.' The purpose of this 'real seeing' and 'careful looking' is to look for 'what works'. This appears to be defined according to two main criteria: first, in terms of practicable working of the material, that the tile is thick enough to withstand being rolled into a cylindrical vessel without the pattern being too distorted; second, in terms of aesthetic working of the piece, how the lines of pattern work with each other (for example, the 'positive and the negative'). The theme of 'really seeing' is picked up again right at the end of the lesson when the teacher refers to the homework. There is a further embellishment of what constitutes 'really seeing' in contrasting observation with imagination as the teacher says, 'Not what you imagine but what you really see.' This brings the lesson full circle.

So where have I been, and what have I found about the role of language in relation to the multimodal curriculum? I began with the teacher and pupils as agents and makers of meaning. Work is always given a context in particular historical, social and cultural locations. So, for example, it becomes a problem if meaning-making is reduced to a circumscribed definition of 'literacy'. This kind of reduced plan cuts across and shapes and squeezes into conformity the multimodal capacities shown by young people in their imaginative play. *When focusing on the value of words, words like 'vessel', 'observation' and 'tone' act as a pivot around which the sense of the term revolves and develops in its particular art and design context.* More than this, we have seen how, by using narrative, teachers articulate a long and complicated temporal sequence of activity, that of the making of vessels, into a meaningful and purposeful sequence. Teachers use questions to elicit information, and this for the double purpose of assessing levels of awareness and knowledge and at the same time, ensuring that information circulates among the class. The teacher uses language to direct the attention of learners alongside action to give operational instruction, and together with close observation, to evaluate the work of the class.

It becomes obvious, though, how language works in relation to, alongside and together with other modes. The vessel is a particularly fascinating and culturally loaded example in this context. As well as making an observational drawing, the pupils 'read' a vessel, reinterpret it and make sense of it within a frame of reference of their own experience, a wine glass, a chalice or a *particular* kitchen implement. The pupil who plays with the example of the vessel as boat is in some ways making an imaginative move. After this lesson, pupils go on to make vessels and then assemble them into an installation. All this moves across boundaries, from word to image, the action of rolling and printing, observing and back to word. Young people are fascinated with the possibilities of space, bodies and various materials, and play with these, often accompanied by talk to imagine and help them make sense of their world. This is work that produces multimodal texts in multimodal environments. The art and design classroom offers a space in the school for pushing the possibilities of making and learning beyond words, but words are still present and contribute to the processes of learning and the making of meaning.

Questions for discussion

1   What role do you think that language has in your teaching and your students' learning of art and design?
2   What is the relationship between different uses and functions of language (e.g. instructional, interpersonal, evaluative) and student learning in art and design?
3   How does language, both written and spoken, work together, with, or against, other modes to make meaning in your classroom?

Further reading

Kress, G. and van Leeuwen, T. (2001) *Multimodal Discourse: The Modes and Media of Contemporary Communication*, London: Arnold.
Vygotsky, L. S. (1978) *Mind in Society*, edited by M. Cole, V. John-Steiner, S. Scribner and E. Souberman, Cambridge, MA: Harvard University Press.

8 The role of art and design in citizenship education

Richard Hickman

Introduction

For this chapter, I identify those elements in the teaching of art and design which play an important part in what has come to be known in the UK as 'citizenship education'. To this end I define the term 'citizenship' and explore some of the rationales from art and design education that are associated with citizenship education.

It is axiomatic that any centrally imposed curriculum seeks to regulate behaviour and attitudes; I would suggest that this is particularly the case when such a curriculum includes 'citizenship'. Citizenship in education has many faces and is perceived differently in different countries. For the purposes of this argument I will focus on citizenship as it is understood within the English National Curriculum. In England, citizenship has, in different forms, been on and off the educational agenda for many years. Since the publication of the report of the Advisory Group on Citizenship (1998; see also QCA and DfEE 1999) for Education for Citizenship and the Teaching of Democracy in schools (known as the Crick Report) it has been definitely 'on'. Pollard and Trigg (1997) note that citizenship resurfaced onto the educational agenda after concerns were raised about the UK's 'moral climate'. These concerns were translated into core concepts within the school curriculum that required students 'to be introduced to values which underpin democracy and be able to understand, and make judgements about, social and moral issues' (Pollard and Trigg 1997: 127). The Crick Report suggests three areas that should run through all education for citizenship: social and moral responsibility, community involvement and political literacy. Social and moral responsibility is concerned with building self-confidence and with developing responsible behaviour in students at school. Involvement in the community, according to the report, involves students' service to the community and their participation in the life and concerns of their neighbourhood. Becoming politically literate involves, among other things, pupils' learning about the UK's various institutions and practices.

Most art and design educators would recognise immediately ways in which art and design can feed into or from these three areas. For example, involvement in community murals and focusing on artwork that is concerned with social commentary. However, such connections are rather simplistic and can detract from more basic concerns about the nature and value of art and design in education.

A fundamental issue is whether, as educators, we are dealing primarily with giving school students an education *in* art and design or an education *through* art and design. An education *in* art and design emphasises the learning of practical skills, which entails school students operating as artists and designers. In such a model, the focus of their involvement with non-studio work, i.e. with art history, aesthetics and art criticism, is the use of others' art work to inform their own. The emphasis in education *through* art and design is on education rather than on art and design; the focus being learning about and making art and design as a way of becoming an educated citizen rather than becoming an artist or designer. It seems to me that an education *in* art and design is necessarily subsumed under the general notion of being educated *through* art and design. However, if becoming 'educated' means different things to different people, then becoming a good citizen does too: certainly art and design has a distinctive role to play in educating people about their role in society.

We as teachers and lecturers can no longer take it for granted that traditional art and design activities, such as drawing from observation and making pots, are inherently a good thing. Although they probably are, we need to locate such activities within the broader context of education and educating young people as citizens who can make a meaningful contribution to society. A 'meaningful contribution' can, and perhaps should, include activities which challenge authority and provoke dissent. One potent myth of modernism is the personification of the artist as transgressor and outsider. Therefore many, perhaps even most, western artists are *not* known for their socially responsive behaviour. It could be said, however, that they have made useful contributions to society *because* of their willingness to transgress social mores and engage in the politics of dissent. If we promote creativity through art we are also promoting 'creative behaviour', which, by its very nature, can often be challenging; I suspect that this is not what governments, or at least controlling governments, want.

While the emphasis in western art and design education still appears to be on expression, different educational systems have promoted the idea of art as a vehicle to learn about their own cultural heritage. In this respect, art and design education can be seen to play an important part in those countries where citizenship is identified closely with national identity. Mason (2000) reports that in Japan there is legislation for the transmission of core cultural values, beliefs and practices from one generation to the next. In Japan, therefore, the development of particular artistic skills needs to be viewed within the context of promoting knowledge of cultural heritage. Elsewhere, in Thailand, the US discipline-based approach has been promoted by some art educators as a way of ensuring that Thai students learn about their cultural heritage through art history, art criticism and aesthetics (Ua-Anant 1987). In contrast to what might be seen as a conservative idea of teaching about cultural inheritance, some countries, particularly South American countries, greatly value art as an agent of social change. This is in keeping with what Efland (1990) referred to as the 'reconstructivist stream' in art education. The reconstructivists see art as a means to an end, as a tool for social change, rather than an end in itself.

There seems to be a consensus as to the aims and purpose of art and design education in the west. The following summary draws from a range of texts and publications from the UK and elsewhere. The aims are to:

- Introduce students to their cultural heritage.
- Introduce students to the cultural heritage of others.
- Develop students' understanding of the visual (and perhaps tactile) world – perceptual training.
- Increase students' understanding of their inner-world, of feelings and imagination.
- Develop practical problem-solving through manipulation of materials.
- Enhance creativity through developing lateral thinking skills.
- Promote inventiveness and risk-taking.

Of these, the first four fall most neatly into the more general aims of educating for citizenship. The first two are concerned with culture and therefore (if this is not too tenuous) with democratic society and its values. Intrinsic to knowing and understanding the 'cultural heritage of others' are the notions of acceptance, tolerance, understanding and respect. In developing students' perceptual skills the third aim is concerned with, among other things, defences against propaganda and the ability to be sensitive to others.

The remaining four aims also have a link with aspects of citizenship: increasing students' understanding of their inner-world is directly associated with the ability to know oneself and therefore to empathise with others; as noted previously, it is concerned with developing the imagination which is essential if one is to see others' viewpoint. The aims of developing practical problem-solving and lateral thinking skills, together with promoting inventiveness and risk-taking, are vital components for a dynamic and evolving democratic economy.

'Learning to know, learning to do, learning to live together, learning to be'

The Thirtieth World Congress of the International Society for Education through Art (InSEA) had the theme 'Learning to know, learning to do, learning to live together, learning to be', which can be seen to relate directly to issues associated with citizenship as it is understood in the UK. 'Learning to know' has a particular resonance with those art and design educators who see their subject area as one that promotes a special way of seeing and understanding. Several commentators, such as Reid (1986), have put forward the view that art is, or promotes, a particular way of knowing. The notion that art and design education has in itself a sound epistemological base has been taken up by Eisner (1998b). However, he warns against using the argument that general cognitive development is enhanced through learning in art (the 'transference' argument) as a convincing rationale for art and design education. Eisner notes that there might possibly be *some* truth in the assertion that learning in art facilitates learning in other areas of the curriculum, but suggests that we should be asking what other subjects can do for learning in art. Perkins (1994) asserts that interacting with art can help develop a particular kind of intelligence, specifically reflective intelligence, described as 'a control system for experiential intelligence'. This type of advocacy for art and design education is known as 'Scientific Rationalism' (Efland 1990; Siegesmund 1998).

Much contemporary art is concerned with social commentary which when introduced into schools and colleges has, in some quarters, been perceived as a radicalisation of the curriculum. Cries can now be heard for a return to traditional art skills, a 'swinging back of the pendulum' towards 'learning to do'. Richmond (1998) represents a backlash against art as a branch of sociology and the reconstructivist view of art education. He argues for the importance of *making* to be recognised, saying that:

> The practice of art in education involves students in skill development, use of materials, and creative process . . . fusing feeling, imagination, perception and skill; qualities that, together with knowledge of tradition, form the genesis of style and originality in art bearing universal significance.
>
> (Richmond 1998; 11)

'Universal significance' is probably stretching the point, but in terms of 'learning to do', art and design education has a vital role to play. We must not forget the pleasure, sense of purpose, and joy which is inextricably associated with making; when learners are makers, they become empowered because they are no longer passive recipients, they develop self-esteem and self-confidence. Such outcomes link directly with the first of the Crick Report's recommended areas, that of social and moral responsibility.

A particular value of art and design education is the promotion of intercultural understanding and 'learning to live together'. The NC document for citizenship (QCA and DfEE 1999) has one reference to the role of art and design in citizenship education under its 'links to other subjects'; this link is related to 'knowledge and understanding about becoming informed citizens'. Specifically, it is related to the need for 'pupils to be taught about . . . the diversity of national, regional, religious and ethnic identities in the United Kingdom and the need for mutual respect and understanding' (QCA and DfEE 1999: 14).

Educators adopting a postmodern stance with regard to the art curriculum have stressed the need for a pluralistic approach that, among other things, promotes cross-cultural understanding. Art and design lessons have the potential to perpetuate and challenge racial and cultural stereotyping. Such stereotyping can be, for example, perpetuated in art and design lessons through caricature, in activities such as making a 'Red Indian' doll and strip cartoons of 'African Natives', both of which I have seen in schools. I have noted elsewhere (Hickman 1999) that there can also be a more insidious form of mis-education if students are ill-prepared or ill-informed about the art and artefacts of cultures other than their own. Ballengee-Morris and Stuhr (2001) draw attention to practices such as making 'totem poles out of discarded toilet paper cardboard tubes' as an example of 'inappropriate

cultural re-representation', where objects and images which have a special significance to a particular social group are appropriated and demeaned. It is in this
respect that formalist aesthetics is shown to be not only shallow but also mis-
educational. Understanding and appreciating art from different cultures enables
students to become more aware of, and sensitive to, a wide range of philosophies
and beliefs, but it is not simply a matter of exposure.

Ballengee-Morris and Stuhr (2001) are firmly in the reconstructivist camp,
declaring that, working with other teachers across subject boundaries would
encourage:

> The art and visual culture teacher to direct attention to the ways that artistic
> production by diverse sociocultural groups can contribute to [this] under-
> standing and lead to informed democratic and socially responsible action.
> (Ballengee-Morris and Stuhr 2001: 12)

The final aspect in the InSEA theme was 'learning to be'. Art is said to act as a
conduit to our inner selves and it can also be a pointer towards something greater
than itself. Hall (2000), writing about the spiritual in art, notes that students
studying art and design are also studying themselves, and so we can see art as a route
to self-knowledge. Before people can cooperate effectively with other people they
must understand themselves; the production of art brings about a greater
understanding of the self through exploration of personal ideas and feelings. In
societies where young people are feeling increasingly alienated, the need for these
aspects of art and design education becomes more urgent. One of the principal
benefits of a broad education in art and design is the enhanced capacity for
exercising the imagination. It would not be stretching the point too much to
associate the development of imagination with the development of political vision,
particularly if taught or facilitated within the context of art and design which is
politically challenging.

Art and design education has developed considerably in recent years and its
remit has grown to include visual culture and aesthetic education; in fact 'visual
and aesthetic education' may well be a more appropriate term for the kinds of
activities which are now taking place and the kinds of issues which are being
considered under the banner of art and design education. The title 'visual and
aesthetic education' also implies greater affinity with areas such as media studies
and the performing arts as well as with a wider range of subjects across the
curriculum; this implies greater cross-curricular collaboration and perhaps more
concern with fundamental issues relating to the place of individuals within society.

Although the seven aims outlined earlier might not be solely encompassed
within the domain of art and design, art and design education can play a significant
role in achieving them. I have argued that the label 'art and design education' ought
to be replaced by the label 'visual and aesthetic education' in order to reflect the
broader purview which is intrinsic to these aims. In any case, if art and design
education is to play any significant role in educating for citizenship, we need to be
concerned with promoting an education that is both *in* art and design and *through*

art and design. However, we should not forget the importance of what I might tentatively term 'educating for transgression'. There is a certain tension here which is all for the good – resisting the status quo, challenging orthodoxies and rule-breaking are essential attributes of meaningful art and design activities and, one would hope, of a healthy society.

Questions for discussion

1   Is there a tension between encouraging self-expression and promoting good citizenship?
2   Should art and design teachers be concerned primarily with educating *in* art and design or *through* art and design?
3   Does art and design education have a role in educating for dissent?

Further reading

Efland, A. (1990) *A History of Art Education*, New York: Teachers College Press.
Harland, J., Kinder, K., Lord, P., Stott, A., Schagen, I., Haynes, J. *et al.* (2000) *Arts Education in Secondary Schools: Effects and Effectiveness*, Slough: National Foundation for Educational Research.
QCA and DfEE (1999) *Citizenship: The National Curriculum for England*, London: QCA and DfEE.

9 Thinking out of the box

Developments in specialist art and design teacher education and ICT

Tom Davies and Pete Worrall

Introduction

Information communication technology (ICT) can be approached in a number of ways and a variety of contexts. Principally, in terms of government policy, ICT is a generic transferable set of skills to be acquired by teachers and learners. Crucially, in the context of art and design, it is the technology's potential to support critical thinking (questioning working methods and procedures) that offers greatest potential (new meanings, interpretations and practice) (Davies 2000a). The authors' collaborative research within Birmingham's Institute of Art and Design (BIAD) postgraduate course in initial teacher training has contributed to the view that ICT is the most powerful catalyst yet for challenging predictable practices (orthodoxy) in the art and design curriculum. Advocating a form of critical pedagogy, loosely based on models presented by Grossberg 1994 (see Giroux and McLaren 1994: 16–21) and further contextualized within the subject area by Addison and Burgess (2000: 327–31), continuing research represents an attempt to empower trainee teachers and their pupils/students 'to reconstruct their world in new ways and to rearticulate their future in unimagined and perhaps even unimaginable ways' (Grossberg 1994: 18). More than any other technology ICT is inescapable and unavoidable in contributing to both the administrative design and delivery of the curriculum, and posing fundamental questions as to what we are teaching and why?

The well-established conventions and procedures within the teaching profession (methodology, standardised outcomes and assessment arrangements) are usually subject to gradual change and repositioning. Current educational policy differs little from previous administrations in its desire to raise standards over time. 'Test scores', and a perceptible reduction in the range of learning experiences available, frequently define these measures and achievements for teachers and their pupils. Digital technology has the potential to counter reductionism and empower and stimulate learning. New specialist teachers of art and design have, in the main, responded positively to the opportunities afforded through the use of new media and have welcomed the messages, centrally promulgated by the Department for Education and Skills (DfES), the Teacher Training Agency (TTA) and the Qualifications and Curriculum Authority (QCA) that teachers know best where to appropriately use the new technology (TTA 2000a) The appropriate context for use of emerging digital media within the subject area is therefore profoundly important as the potential use of the media may surface in a number of related areas of exploration, grouped here under five strands. While each is significant in its own right, well-planned and sequenced project work may range across each strand, reinforcing and supporting experimental learning experiences:

- Software programs facilitate the exploration of complex concepts – e.g. time-based visual imaging and three-dimensional virtual environments (web discussion groups).
- Communication systems, collaborative electronic exchanges (internet/mobile phones etc.).
- Virtual exhibitions – schools/community groups, curated and presented through multimedia integrating digital images, sound, video and text.
- Research tools, information access, retrieval and storage (archive development) (Davies and Worrall 2001).
- Control technologies can provide creative scope for those prepared to reappraise the function and purpose of education through art and design.

Emerging ICT orthodoxy, where it exists in school practice, tends to focus on the superficial manipulation of images (Davies and Worrall 2001: analysis of PGCE/ICT schoolwork in 1996) with little evidence of the medium being used to secure new understanding or questioning. Our aim, within the context of this continuing action research programme, was to challenge orthodox approaches to ICT and promote the 'research tool' potential over the technical and vocationally relevant transferability of skills and knowledge. The potential for teachers and learners usually starts with the technical processes and operational systems acting as a trigger for more sustained project work. From the examination of the basic elements to the more productive exploration of personal issues (relationships/self) to moral, social, political and cultural contexts (racism, disability, human rights) the mediation of the art and design educator related the subject to knowledge acquisition in the broadest sense. In so doing this supported communication media as central to the purpose and function of art and design education.

In some respects the government's 'New Opportunities Fund' (NOF: DfEE 1999a) has provided valuable generic training for teachers in ICT (spreadsheets, databases, etc.) but has missed both the challenge of specific subject specialist support and wider dissemination of a future-oriented collective vision detailed in successive government reports (NACCCE 1999). A significant number of young teachers would like to extend their ICT practice beyond the predictable scanning and digitizing practices that are emerging as a new orthodoxy in our schools. The dangers here are self-evident, as the potential of digital technology is not confined to superficial adjustments to cloned or appropriated images. It is a powerful tool for the analysis and understanding of visual phenomena offering a desirable and accessible means of reinforcing learning and encouraging an ownership of the process.

Much of our work related to the evaluation and assessment of ICT in art and design education is based on action research in schools (11–18 age range) and 'curriculum workshop' initiatives in the initial teacher training programme. Earlier reported findings had more general application, in that parallels existed at all levels of teaching and learning (Davies *et al.* 1999). It was conceivable that ICT, appropriately integrated in practice, could challenge the dominance of the conventions of 'school art' that are endemic in UK schools. The (seemingly) irresistible influence of formal assessment practices in secondary schools was identified with particular emphasis on its impact, in terms of type and execution of coursework. A question for subsequent research was how best to assess progression in art and design given that much of the real learning that takes place is ephemeral and process based (Davies *et al.* 1999).

Since the early 1990s a number of educators within the subject have advocated the importance of personal ownership of learning and have tried to reconcile the need for clear, unequivocal criteria and the demand for a reliable grading system (Binch and Robinson 1994). The issue has always been the degree to which the learner understands the criteria (judgements) and whether or not negotiation is seen as part of the assessment process:

> Learners of any age empowered to argue their case, using the same criteria as the teachers, have increased self-direction in their studies and rapidly acquire a critical vocabulary. Electronic learning is largely based on notions of self-direction and personal ownership.
>
> (Davies *et al.* 1999: 17)

The role of teachers is changing as a direct consequence of developments in electronic learning. Self-directed study and the generation of distance learning materials will transform the traditional relationships and teaching methodologies (mediation, intervention, personal ownership and access). ICT in art and design has the potential to support expanding social contexts, offering improved communication systems and new creative outcomes. Learners, struggling to fashion and form traditional media, are manipulating digital media with relative ease, and their degree of familiarity and competence in the use of ICT is often supported by considerable home use (Worrall and Davies 1997). As National Curriculum frameworks for art and design evolve (website-supported learning – e.g. Becta/ National Grid for Learning/Teachers) there will always be scope for identifying appropriate content and a degree of freedom in charting the development of learners. A checklist in some form may help learners to record these experiences but the task for teachers would be to construct an age/phase specific matrix. In principle, this is not a hugely complex undertaking as teachers invariably design schemes of work/projects that have the teaching and learning objectives (criteria) explicitly stated (DfEE 2000). Learners, however, within this particular research all too often inferred the requirements through the exemplification of past 'successful' responses. Art and design education may be conceptualised in a number of ways but generally the planning process takes account of appropriate learning environments, contexts, resources, materials, form and critical engagement with the issues (conceptual development, thinking skills and understanding) (DfEE 1998).

The associated design, implementation and reflective evaluation of the PGCE 'curriculum workshops' was seen as largely subject specific, however there were issues, mainly related to teaching new computer skills, that had to be addressed in more general terms. It was evident at the time (1994–7) that a significant number of the trainees had underdeveloped computer experience (hardware/software) and uneven contextual understanding in terms of relevance and purpose. Auditing skills and experience on entry to the course revealed that there was considerable variability in terms of undergraduate course provision for ICT. New planning considerations, management, teaching and evaluation strategies emerged through using ICT and these tended to confront traditional teaching and learning methods (Davies *et al.* 1999: 38–42).

Practical work and the content of the workshops revolved around a number of related areas:

- Curriculum design (intended learning objectives).
- Ethical considerations/intellectual copyright etc.
- Pedagogy (learning and teaching considerations).
- Hardware/software (technical competency and safety features).
- Research (access, contextual understanding and application).
- Evaluation (assessment, monitoring and recording progress).

Course-specific data, collected between 1997 and 2000, related to skills and knowledge (annual audit analysis) and were supplemented by informally gathered information from other specialist subject ITT providers. Clearly there appeared to be a problem nationally, as few trainees and their respective institutions seemed ready, or for that matter, particularly interested, in adapting to the digital age.

Training needs, critical practice and digital tools

Developments in the implementation of digital technology in educational institutions are highly variable in terms of their form and range, with evidence of a baseline provision deducible from the *National Statistics for Schools within England and Wales*. In her 2001 White Paper Estelle Morris endorsed the fact that 'ICT can play a major role in meeting individual needs and aspirations' (DfES 2001c) and the relevant paragraphs have numbering similar to those in a report concerned with *Teacher Workload* (DfES 2001b: paras 3.24 to 3.27):

> ICT can transform the way that education is delivered and open the way to a new pedagogy. It can make it easier for teachers to plan and to find high quality materials, and it can help pupils to find out more about the subjects they are studying. Critically, new technology can enable teachers to tailor their teaching more closely to the abilities of individual pupils. High quality online materials mean that pupils and teachers have access to good resources across the curriculum.
>
> (DfES 2001c: para. 3.25)

The Schools Minister, Catherine Ashton, has welcomed figures stating that 'virtually all schools are now connected to the internet', and that ICT targets were reached in 2002. These show that 96 per cent of primary schools are now online, with secondary schools almost 100 per cent. Current baseline statistics: primary: 1 computer to 11.8 pupils; secondary: 1 computer to 7.1 pupils (NGfL targets for 2002 are 1:11 and 1:7.) The 'teachers feeling confident' figure is now 73.4 per cent (DfES 2001d).

Despite these most encouraging figures our research in ITT partnership art and design departments indicates that ICT is frequently 'on and off' the agenda. Rarely is the new generation of mobile technology mentioned, yet related industries see this as the most dominant likely use of the technology. The arrival of the third generation (3G) networks in 2004–5 is expected to provide users throughout Europe with a host of applications based on existing technologies such as short text messages (SMS) and wireless application protocol (WAP). In Europe alone, analysts estimate that the value of mobile data will reach over $80 billion by 2009, divided into four main areas: information, communication, lifestyle facilitators and transaction services. The likely spin-offs for educational use and access are yet to be realised, with the costs prohibitive at present. This said, already universities are 'actively seeking developments in teaching and learning methods that employ the benefits of distant communication and electronic access to knowledge and skills acquisition' (Orava 2001).

In art and design it has been our experience that institutions have moved very cautiously, if at all, and many courses in further and higher education lack the investment and the expertise both in terms of technical support and academic application. Schools have also experienced extremely patchy provision with national initiatives frequently mistargeting specialist interest groups such as art and design education. Teachers, according to our research, require particular assistance in locating the content of art education in a digital context. Clearly, there are many repetitive and comparatively low-level procedures that could be facilitated by appropriate electronic tools and environments and these can be further enhanced by online access. Based on our collaborative continuing professional development (CPD) courses, we have found that teachers are rarely hostile to changes related to digital technology, more needing to be convinced as to benefits for them and their pupils. Detailed audits of school equipment and skills have been collated over the years and while improvements are evident in most art and design departments the data confirms that the basic facilities militate against efforts elsewhere in the initial teacher training programme (e.g. college-based ICT workshops and related curriculum planning).

The requirements for teachers, graduating from all courses of initial training, present exacting standards for competence in ICT appropriate to the subject, and the award of qualified teacher status relies on a level of demonstrable classroom practice. These requirements, while essential to ensure a base level understanding, place enormous pressures on trainees to incorporate the skills and commitment to electronic learning in their respective school placements (TTA 1999).

What we have attempted to do, in advancing the use of ICT since 1995, is to raise the level of debate within art and design departments in schools, colleges and museums using our own teacher trainees as a catalyst for change. What we envisaged, at that time, was a form of permeation that would allow teachers to take ownership of a number of basic applications and processes. This would benefit groups and independent learners and generate coursework that could inform and support other classroom/studio practices. Here case study material has been commissioned and used by the Teacher Training Agency, Her Majesty's Inspectors of Schools and commercial publishers (TTA 2000b).

In many respects the work produced since the mid-1990s is untypical of ICT in art and design in that its origin and purpose was simple and unthreatening to teachers. The project's underlining philosophy was the promotion of digital technology in mainstream schools as a dimension of current practices, and not as a substitute or alternative. Unlike the *Manifesto for Art Education*, presented by the National Society for Education in Art and Design (NSEAD), it did not present teachers with a radical rethink of the future, requiring a paradigm shift in what was understood to be the role and function of the subject within the curriculum (Swift and Steers 1999: 7–13). Importantly, it required little in terms of initial expertise but much in terms of interest in exploring ideas, concepts and possibilities within a model of progression and guided understanding (Davies *et al.* 1999).

Change within the curriculum, if it were to happen, necessitates teachers' acceptance of a technological dimension to their role. What we attempted to offer in 1995 remains consistent with our current policy within ITT and related continuing professional development. In the first publication *IT Works in Schools* we were interested in the notion that the use of the technology could result in outcomes and responses that could not easily, or possibly, be arrived at by more conventional media (Worrall and Davies 1997). Digital cameras, scanners and free sampling software supported the proliferation of experimentation with imagery coinciding interestingly with the explosion of interest and ownership of mobile phone technology and text mail. While having, at this present moment, only ill-formed notions of how this particular advancing text technology may be harnessed to serve the interests of the subject, the new services and faster networks are set to overtake voice traffic by 2004, with an estimated 600 million data-enabled mobile devices world-wide. The ease of communication and access to mobile technology could offer a significant potential for related textual exchanges and field study research in the art and design curriculum (Danet 2001: 355–68).

By far the greatest benefits to us have been the established networks of partnerships and colleagues within Europe and beyond. Immediate access to curriculum material and image banks offers considerable potential for course development over the next few years and our links with the School of Art Education, University of Helsinki have already signalled enormous educational benefits for each of our institutions. In addition to our links through the European 'Schoolnet' we were due to contribute to each other's courses from autumn 2001 and host student exchanges from February 2002.

As mobile phones become ubiquitous, they can also be used for a host of other functions, based mainly on the ability of the SIM card in a mobile phone to carry a host of information. The theory is simple and particularly evident in Finland: why carry around documents when the information can be securely stored on the phone? Crucially it will be cost that will determine whether this particular dimension of digital technology has an educational potential, but we shall see (Orava 2001).

While much has been achieved in developing the debate and raising awareness of the application of the technology (internet, mobile phones, peripheral devices, electronic sensors etc.) global access remains an issue:

> The marketplace for ideas is not open, transparent, global and non-discriminatory. Consequently, a *creativity divide* has existed throughout history, subverting mankind's creative capacities . . . [G]lobalisation and the internet offer a platform that can be developed to nurture and celebrate children's creativity and imagination. This would require a re-thinking on part of educators, policy-makers, foundations and corporations.
>
> (Ishaq 2001)

The issue of 'inclusion' and access has been a dimension of our work in the UK and Brazil and as part of a conference presentation we were drawn to the continuing difficulties of availability in partnership schools (Pimentel 2001).

Conclusion

ICT offers new opportunities for new kinds of art work (time-based work, animation, three-dimensional imaging, digital photography, video, performance). It supports presentation formats, desktop publishing, graphic design/typography and independent access to data (internet/website reference – visual resources/data-museums/galleries, artists' sites, designers' sites and school coursework exchanges). Most importantly it extends the debate beyond regional and national agendas to more global concerns as to the nature and purpose of the subject. Increasingly, our 'work in progress' supports the construction of new knowledge and understanding of cultural diversity. Theoretical visionaries go much further in their construction of new realities with such claims as 'Technalysis accepts the ontological fact that we move in a new layer of electronic reality' (Heim 2000: 44). What has been made possible through ICT is the extension and development of an image culture (rapidly accessible high quality databanks) and a shared visual language (exhibition access, selection, editing, transferring meaning/digital exchanges etc.). Gradually the use of digital technology is changing the nature and sequencing of coursework from the traditional, conventional forms to more personal and purposeful expressive exchanges.

ICT significantly enhances the learning opportunities for students in art and design by enabling a dialogue and a critique of visual phenomena to develop. The media can offer new fields of creativity for visual image-makers and provide continuity with the existing curriculum. Media studies education in secondary schools, for example, offers considerable scope for collaboration on current issues (image analysis, style and representation: Buckingham 2000). Language development and the notion of core skills may be more easily tracked with connections made through the acknowledgement of shared or distinctive curriculum contributions (mapping meanings):

> The rapid development of personal computers and communication networks has not only resulted in a revolution in communication but also in knowledge building. Information networks are internet-connected, accelerating the development towards open source solutions. Massachusetts Institute of Technology's (MIT) release of their learning and teaching materials on the internet is a movement towards self-guided lifelong learning without boundaries. The focus in teaching and learning has shifted from producing materials to supporting individual and community learning processes.
>
> (Orava 2001)

It is our contention that ICT, within the art and design curriculum, supports the development of critical thinking skills and experimentation. It represents important learning through, in part, the acknowledgement of failure and less successful solutions (evaluative analysis, debate, critique and speculation). For pupils and their teachers this ability to discriminate, interpret, and select appropriate digital tools has broad application and its future use will certainly transcend the 'box' (computer).

Questions for discussion

1   Is there a tension between the advocacy of ICT as an integrated dimension of the art and design curriculum, rather than a discrete sub-set (multimedia, desktop publishing, time-based media, lens-based processes)?
2   What possibilities really exist for next generation technologies to transform whole school learning environments and pedagogy, and at what cost?
3   Does the promotion of 'risk' and 'experimentation' in ICT (e.g. 'undo' option) translate into high order thinking skills and new forms of art making/creative visualisation?

Further reading

Danet, B. (2001) *Cyberplay: Communicating Online, New Technology/New Cultures*, Oxford: Oxford International Publishers.
Lunenfeld, P (ed.) (2000) *The Digital Dialectic: New Essays on New Media*, Cambridge, MA and London: MIT Press.
National Advisory Committee on Creative and Cultural Education (NACCCE) (1999) *All Our Futures: Creativity, Culture and Education*, London: Department for Education and Employment.

10 Does visual literacy demand a head for heights?

Dave Allen

Since the early 1970s, I have spoken and written many words on the subject of this chapter. For most of that time I was actively involved in visual arts education at various levels and in a number of different roles (teacher, departmental head, researcher, teacher-trainer, external examiner). In that sense my words had an active relationship with my practice, I shared them with many other fellow practitioners, and the words and practice developed reciprocally.

However, in 2000 I became the course leader of a degree course that has some visual elements, but is more concerned with music technology, multimedia, project management and the whole field of computing. As a consequence, writing this chapter has felt like a valedictory point in my involvement with art education so I am trying to explore my subject from a more personal, autobiographical account than might normally be expected.

In part I am doing this because, after extensive struggles and redrafting, this is the way the chapter has emerged and *feels* right. In a more academic sense I can justify it because for some years I have been interested in autobiography as one mode of writing-up the kind of interpretative research that is most effective process of evaluating and developing pedagogy (see e.g. Stake 1985). In that sense, although much of what I am offering, particularly in the first part of this chapter, is personal and retrospective, it is not intended to be nostalgic or sentimental. Rather, I hope it will stimulate thinking about the future of a vital subject that is now in the custody of a new generation.

In particular I want to offer an account of why I began my professional career as a typical secondary art teacher of drawing and painting but changed into someone who argued regularly for the transformation of the school subject into something significantly different. In doing so, I intend to juxtapose the particular circumstances of my professional development with the context in which I worked. How did I become an advocate of particular pedagogical practices and do they have any relevance outside my own practice? I can put the questions and offer the evidence, but others must decide if the answer is worth pursuing.

Towards the end of my school career in the late 1960s, I vacillated between an opportunistic career in popular music and a degree in painting. In the end I did not quite manage either, but I eventually graduated in 1975 and became an art teacher. After a brief and insignificant flirtation with the world of 'pop', I have also maintained a semi-professional life in music for more than thirty years.

There are two key points to this dual life. First, each experience has enabled me to reflect on different working practices, institutions, funding practices, assumptions about creativity and expression and contrasts in skills and professional development in the two areas. Second, working in two disciplines and in close proximity with practising artists *and* musicians has offered a fascinating opportunity to examine assumptions about processes and practices. Some of these experiences will inform my considerations of links between the teaching of art and media education.

Between 1975 and 1985 I was an art teacher in secondary schools in Hampshire. I taught in fairly traditional ways, mainly painting and drawing, but in addition, I became interested in teaching with video and photography and in what is now known as critical studies. I think my approach to teaching art was partly determined by my first degree, a BEd in secondary art and design, a route that has not existed for many years. It was a marvellous four years not least because it forced me to consider my creative practice (mainly painting) in a broader context – one which would have an impact on the experiences of many other people. I had enough friends (and relatives) in art schools at the time to know that this was different from many of the courses on offer to undergraduate artists. As a consequence of that experience, I have always thought of myself very definitely as an art *educator*, about which I wish to make one point. I am entirely persuaded that young people who engage meaningfully with art in schools develop a range of attitudes, understandings and qualities that are personal, social and so on. However, I believe firmly that the main point of teaching art is to learn about art because it is an inherently important human activity in itself.

For the sake of brevity, if at the risk of stereotype, I am content to identify the origins of my passions in the arts in much of the work that emerged in the 1960s. In many cases, the origins of that practice can be traced back in turn to modernist experiments in the first three decades of the twentieth century (especially Cubism, Duchamp and Dadaism, the Bauhaus, revolutionary Russia, and the new media including film). These influences led to a number of general features of 1960s arts practice which have been identified by Marwick (1998: 316–18) and they have always exercised my interest in arts practice and education. Marwick describes:

- The cross-over between 'elite and popular art'.
- The 'blurring of boundaries between individual art forms'.
- Privileging the 'idea or concept over any *direct* representation' [my emphasis].
- 'Chance elements being incorporated into works of art'.
- The participation of 'reader, viewer, listener or audience' as an important element.
- The importance of new technologies.
- The influence of 'radical criticism' and 'art as research'.
- Arts' role as social practice and critique of the 'spectacle' (Situationism).

Such ideas and practices led to new forms and work, which no longer fitted into the old categories. The 1960s was a period when the dominance of easel painting and the classical music canon was constantly challenged by new media, new practices, new artists, new audiences and new tastes. In music, the old high/low dichotomy between the music of the BBC's Third Programme and the popular 'pirate' stations dissolved in much experimental work of the late 1960s and the rediscovery/ reinvention of traditional and vernacular forms. The old categories of popular and classical were, and still are, inadequate.

In many cases the presentation of music also created new visual forms and a new theatricality Light shows, extravagant costumes, audiences as performers, pop films or videos and the proliferation of genres all developed young people's sense of a new world. These images, already surfacing in the fine art of the 1950s, were common a decade later proliferating in graphic design, fashion, television and cinema. By 1970 there was a further shift. In 1972 the Hayward Gallery was showing literary texts, video pieces, live art, photopieces, 'real' objects and philosophical discourse and while painting had not disappeared, it was now no more than one of the many visual arts practices competing for attention.

When the Beatles split up in 1969 people in the UK had only just encountered colour television on the three channels (including the relatively new BBC2). Today it is difficult to avoid an almost constant bombardment of digital sounds and images and they play a central role in our experience of the world. Most people over 50 remember where they were when President Kennedy was shot in November 1963 and they have seen the motorcade image many times *in retrospect*; few people will forget the immediate *visual* horror of the terrorist destruction of New York's World Trade Center in September 2001. Major events are now mainly visual and immediate and oil paint just is not quick enough to compete with digital representations. It has a role, but documenting the present is not it.

I believe there is one *key* point about these changes for our work as educators and it is at the heart of *all* my pedagogical arguments here and elsewhere. The cultural practices that people experience increasingly incorporate combinations of image, sound/music and spoken/displayed verbal texts, often generated and broadcast through new technologies. Despite this, too little of what we do in schools reflects the complexity of these cultural forms, whether we are considering news reporting, Hollywood cinema, MTV, televised sport, or subsidised and less popular forms such as opera or conceptual art. I believe that schools should enable pupils to make sense of the dominant forms of representation and expression in their culture both as producers and as consumers, because in this reciprocal process they become makers of forms, ideas and meaning. Further, there should be a clear relationship between the contemporary cultural and (arts) teaching, an argument I became aware of for the first time in a seminal publication by Dick Field (1970) in the year I arrived at college. Even today, I know that not all arts teachers agree with that view, but I wish they did.

One of the consequences of my interest in these ideas is that I have worked extensively on 'visual literacy' and although I have no particular obsession with the term, I need to say a few words about it. One of its attractions is the sophisticated definition of literacy emanating from Street (1993) which has proved useful in developing analogies with the visual, that is, the capacity to use all modes: speaking, listening, reading and writing.

Second, my interest in visual literacy in the early 1990s was opportunistic. The government, in its wisdom, inserted the phrase in the National Curriculum Order for Art (DfE 1995). I took the phrase and defined it more thoroughly, arguing that it would be more productive to offer teachers ways of operating within their obligations than fighting the might of government (Allen 1994). Recently the government took it out of the revised Order so I'm much less interested in the term in a pragmatic sense; I have certainly never considered 'visual literacy' a phrase meriting ideological (or real) battles.

I have offered some reasons why I came to this view through my own work as a producer and consumer of cultural practices. I now wish to consider how these relate to the development of specific pedagogical practices in my professional life.

I arrived at my first teaching post in 1975, having been immersed in the massive changes in arts and cultural practices of the 1960s. Despite that experience, I discovered a dominant pedagogy in art and design that perpetuated a kind of gentle mid-century tradition, combining an expressive, nature-based pictorialism with aspects of basic design. For the most part pupils drew with pencils, painted with powder colour, damaged themselves with lino-cutters and spent the odd term making things from clay. It wasn't bad teaching and the best work was pretty good, but it didn't seem to me to have much to do with the world I inhabited or the contemporary culture of young people. Neither could I find anywhere else on the curriculum where this was addressed, although oddly, as soon as the school day was over, this community school embraced all those activities excluded by the formal curriculum.

Things changed for me when I was asked to take over a photography CSE in 1980. I quickly realised that no one had a clear view where photography fitted into the secondary curriculum. Sometimes it was a science and sometimes an art, usually determined by the enthusiastic teacher who taught it on the basis of personal interest. As a result there was a lot of technical stuff in the syllabus I inherited and the dominant aesthetic was again mid-century, middle-European, quasi-modernist and pretty dull. So I did something that is now impossible and wrote a Mode 3 course (i.e. my own syllabus) which although approved was perceived as essentially media studies and was therefore examined and moderated by English specialists. At the time I did not know what media studies meant but I quickly became a teacher of art, design and media. It was no more planned than that, but has led to twenty years of arguing for the kinds of ideas that follow.

I am content that there are two subjects in the secondary/tertiary curriculum which are called art and design and media studies and I do not intend to suggest that this distinction is wrong, although my own enthusiasm for interdisciplinarity takes me beyond those limits. So, during the rest of this chapter, I intend to write about the broader area that I call visual arts education, which encompasses many aspects of those two subjects. I acknowledge that even this broader area is inadequate since the privileging of the visual also implies exclusion of the non-visual elements of media studies such as radio or music.

In relation to this interest in interdisciplinarity, I see new technology as a vital opportunity to move beyond the limits of the old subjects or even something called visual arts, to something which engages all the senses (and the intellect). However, I am also uncertain whether there is a real contemporary context for developing that kind of pedagogy. For a number of reasons I am pessimistic about the development of the visual arts curriculum as it interests me, and I wonder whether the subject called art and design has a secure future.

The main reason for my pessimism is that during my thirty years as a professional educator, successive national and local politicians of most ideological persuasions have incessantly manipulated teaching. The context in which I was trusted to develop my own Mode 3 in media studies in 1980 is long gone and I see no prospect of it returning. Further, the establishment of a National Curriculum has reasserted subject demarcation in schools despite its decreasing irrelevance in our multi/inter-everything world. The English education system is in a mess and no one has much time to worry about developing a new interdisciplinary approach to visual studies.

However, occasionally examples of innovation do appear, usually as a consequence of the vision, determination and resourcefulness of individual schools, departments or teachers. As a part of research I carried out for my doctoral thesis I spent two years in the early 1990s on a longitudinal study involving participant-observation of a GCSE course at a secondary school. The course teacher had obtained her DipAD in painting in the 1960s where she had studied film-making as a minor option. Her interest in the moving image had then been fuelled by involvement in a film and video cooperative in the early 1980s and she had been involved in a number of broadly feminist video productions. I had shared some of my curriculum development with her and even within the constraints of the new GCSE and National Curriculum she developed a mixed-media course in which her pupils incorporated video, photography, computer graphics, drawing and critical studies. I saw the first and second groups complete their course with generally good results and I observed the first year of the new option. Sadly they were the third and last group to undertake that examination; the following year the teacher reverted to teaching painting and drawing. There were, briefly, two connected reasons: first, the course needed more resources than painting and drawing and the school could not afford to provide or maintain them; second, the pupils worked in different locations (darkroom, classroom, outside) which caused real difficulties. The management of the course was exhausting in comparison with painting and drawing. So, for organisational and resource reasons, this innovative and successful course ceased.

Many teachers teach visual arts subjects for reasons that are different from mine; they might find my emphasis on cultural education at odds with their approaches. I offer one example.

In 'Directions', a special edition of *Journal of Art and Design Education* (*JADE*), a number of writers considered the possibility of developing a postmodern approach to the art curriculum, partly in response to the failings of the 1995 Art Order but also in the wish to address the divisions between all sectors of art education. In it MacDonald (1999) wrote a considered and imaginative piece about strategies for a postmodern art curriculum that focused extensively on the city as a source of practice. At one point he described Douglas Gordon's *Empire* (1997) as a 'site-

specific' neon sign (the word 'Empire' is shown in reverse) which: 'At first glance
. . . is evocative of the many Art Deco cinema or dance hall signs in the city, some of
which survive – indeed it is in sympathy with the neon pub signs in the street'
(MacDonald 1999: 17). The city in question is Glasgow, where Gordon was born,
and MacDonald, a prominent art educator, is director of the *Lighthouse*, described
as Scotland's Centre for Architecture, Design and the City. Macdonald's identification of the local references is apposite and need not be challenged for its
accuracy, but what about its adequacy?

The sign to which he refers is, in fact, a mirror image of the sign outside the Hotel
Empire in which Kim Novak hides from James Stewart after faking her own 'death'
in Hitchcock's acclaimed film *Vertigo* (1963). Were the film merely one more piece
of Hollywood commercialism this would still be interesting, but it is, in fact, a
central work of cinema and one which continues to reverberate with critics and
audiences after more than forty years. The mirror image might be explained by the
fact that Stewart follows Novak to her room where their first (re)encounter takes
place in front of her dressing-table mirror. Subsequently Stewart persuades Novak
to alter her appearance to resemble that of the 'dead' woman and in another mirror
image urges her to sweep her hair back from her face. In terms of making sense of
these references, it is known that mirrors have many significant cultural resonances
not least in the fields of psychology and psychoanalysis.

Gordon has reworked Hitchcock in the past, notably in his installation piece *24
Hour Pyscho* (1995). In this work Gordon slowed the original film to show exactly
what its title suggested and was included in the British Film Institute's *Spellbound*
exhibition of 'Art and Film' at the Hayward Gallery in 1996. Just weeks after
MacDonald's (1999) article was published, Gordon showed another video
installation *Feature Film* which focused on Herrmann's score for *Vertigo*. As a
consequence, Gordon's sign is almost overloaded with visual cultural meanings yet
MacDonald restricts himself to the local associations and makes no references
to *Vertigo*.

Initially, I imagined that MacDonald was aware of these references but had
decided not to mention them. I wrote a letter about this to the editor of *JADE*, who
forwarded it to MacDonald and he replied to me in April 1999. His letter
illuminates some of the issues I have been wrestling with over these decades as
clearly as anything else I can offer. My sharing of this correspondence is intended to
imply no criticism of MacDonald or me as art educators. What it does is to
exemplify two competing pedagogical positions; MacDonald's is incompatible with
a shift towards the kind of visual arts education that I advocate. The question is,
'Where do you stand in relation to these positions?'

At first MacDonald suggested that some people don't know about Gordon,
Hitchcock and '*Vertigo* in particular'. I am quite sure he is right about Gordon, who
is hardly a household name despite the award of the Turner Prize. But I find it hard
to believe that most people don't know about Hitchcock and I will be so bold as to
suggest that if it is so, then it is a failing of our education system. Hitchcock's body of
work is one of the most important in the visual arts of the twentieth century both
for its visual quality and for the themes and issues explored. It is certainly no less

important than work by other major British artists like Hockney or Moore. If people learn about Hitchcock they will probably learn about *Vertigo*.

The following paragraph from MacDonald's letter raises the key issue for me, so I shall quote it in full:

> However, the point I was making in the paper, moving on from the notion of the *Museum of the Ordinary* was that a site-specific work like *Empire* requires to be approached in the first instance as phenomenology. That is what I would do if I were a teacher or a trainer of teachers. Then there is the social/historical context of the site as discussed in the paper. Then there is the *possible* [my emphasis] allusion to *Vertigo*. *Empire* is capable of a multitude reading but I think it would be Po Mo at its most po-faced to go into all of these in a short paper.

I agree entirely with the final point and have no wish to be 'po-faced' about anything. I was sufficiently taken with MacDonald's example of the *Museum of the Ordinary* in the same article to use it as a pedagogical activity with considerable success. But in reading this one paragraph I finally recognised a problem with that part of my identity labelled 'art teacher'. For decades I have seen art as a curriculum site which creates sufficient space to operate in a variety of ways while, in truth, its orthodoxies and dominant practices are a long way from what 'I would do [as] a teacher or a trainer of teachers'.

There are a number of reasons for this. Significantly, I had considerable contact with the pedagogical implications of phenomenology in my first degree and I have continued to work with colleagues who take such a view. I don't propose to explore these ideas here, but merely to say that I don't see it (literally, I don't *see* it). There are almost no cultural practices that I encounter which ever offer themselves up to a pure phenomenological response, because their baggage and their history are always apparent to me. That may be my problem, but I like the baggage, it absorbs me! As a consequence I can't see a 'possible allusion to *Vertigo*', I see *Vertigo* as a central element of Gordon's piece. *Empire* is not *Vertigo* but, for me, it is diminished without seeing it there.

This illuminated more clearly than anything precisely why, throughout my career, I have felt dragged away from my origins as a painter and secondary school art teacher towards the practices of media education, cultural studies and the like. Given the authority of the Orders for Art, especially the new lot which have done away with visual literacy, it is the moment where I begin to think that I was wrong all along. Despite the similarities between the objects produced and studied in art and media education I now wonder whether it might be better to go our separate ways, seeking to stake out different territories. If they both succeed the kids might be grateful!

The benefits might be a far more complex visual education. For example, I wonder whether a description of *Empire* in a media/film journal would be as likely to ignore the local associations and focus on Hitchcock. If my assumption is plausible, this too would be a partial reading, locating meaning almost wholly within a cultural context and paying insufficient attention to the process of making as well as local references. One of my central arguments for the education of visual literacy is that this pedagogy should reflect the complexity of the visual world, seeking to move beyond the limited agendas of specific visual disciplines, be they formal, expressive, descriptive, cultural or whatever. Perhaps it even needs to be done differently in new slots on the timetable?

Gordon's work, whether *Empire*, *Feature Film* or *24 Hour Psycho*, raises another intriguing question at the heart of this chapter. We know that these works were produced, in some part, as a response to the work of another visual artist, Hitchcock, and that both art and media education have wrestled with the relationship between theory and practice in their respective fields. My question is, to what extent are Gordon's pieces 'creative' and to what extent are they 'critical' responses to the art of another? For example, in writing about Gordon's *Psycho*, Taubin (1996: 71) recounts how university students in the 1970s 'were subjected to countless slow-motion screenings of . . . the shower sequence from *Psycho*' and other films as part of their analytic (critical) practice. Gordon's work differs from this pedagogic practice through context, discourse, spectator expectation and intention, but the artefact is essentially the same – a slowed-down version of *Psycho*. How clear is the division between critical and creative work? What is acceptable as critical discourse?

To take this issue a little further, I want to consider another 'case' and acknowledge my debt to Sefton-Green, who raised the question in a joint presentation we made at a conference entitled 'Creative Media' (Allen and Sefton-Green 1999). He was reflecting on the problem of 'practical' tasks in media studies becoming predictable and stifling creativity. He cited the example of a hypothetical video project in which students would be asked to produce a moving-image sequence of 'Mr Smith leaving his house'. During the following discussion I was asked a question about assessing 'practical' work and I returned to Sefton-Green's example.

I offered three possible responses from students. One group might shoot the sequence in a conventional style, using establishing shots, cut-aways and close-ups, taking care to 'match-on-action', using music and sound to enhance narrative and *mise-en-scène* to enrich meaning. In so doing, this group would demonstrate many probable learning outcomes and would, I imagine, be well rewarded. For whatever reason, the second group would fail to demonstrate this level of understanding and ability. They choreograph the action but simply shoot the sequence in one take, on wide angle and with the minimum of camera movement and only 'natural' sound. For them, a D if they are lucky!

The third group produces a piece that appears almost identical to group two. However, they accompany the piece with a manifesto which draws attention to the purity of primitive cinema, relating their piece directly to the Lumières' film of workers leaving a factory. To this they add a polemic in praise of Bazin and admonishing everyone from Melies through Vertov to contemporary TV advertisements for the tyranny of montage. Their manifesto finishes by proclaiming unity with the recent initiatives of the European 'Dogma' group.

Despite this eloquent presentation their sequence is as poor as the second group's; or is it? How much better than D is such a work? Should the piece be considered aesthetically against the work of Bazin's heroes or are the words sufficient? Imagine that the first group had said nothing about their work and had clearly done no more than reproduce dominant practices – is that A for quality but D for originality? What mark should be given for self-consciously acknowledging cultural references?

Foster (1985), in one of the earliest anthologies on postmodernism, wrote:

> The very nature of art has changed; so too has the object of criticism: as Ulmer notes, a new paraliterary practice has come to fore which dissolves the line between creative and critical forms. In the same way the old opposition of theory and practice is refused.
>
> (Foster 1985: viii)

For me, Gordon equally refuses the old opposition of theory and practice. In doing so his work demands our awareness of *Vertigo*. What I am less clear about today is where such ideas fit in the curriculum.

Finally, the problem for visual literacy is not simply crossing the territories between the history of popular cinema and cutting-edge, mixed-media postmodern art. It is also that during the 1990s visual literacy was an aim of every teacher enforced by government legislation. Now it has been removed from the Order it is back in the rarefied atmosphere of academia (if it is anywhere) and that may as well be nowhere. I always argued for the term visual literacy because it appeared in the Order. I believed that the legislation would enable it to become common currency in schools and that this, in turn, would lead to a broadening of practice. I don't believe that this has happened and now that the term has been omitted from the revised Order I don't believe it has much of a future.

I'm feeling dizzy: I think I'll sit down.

Questions for discussion

1   What do young people need to learn about contemporary visual worlds?
2   How can schools respond to those needs?
3   If they cannot respond well enough, what is the alternative?

Further reading

Allen, D. (1994) 'Teaching Visual Literacy: Some Reflections on the Term', *Journal of Art and Design Education*, 13(2): 133–44.

Field, D. (1970) *Change in Art Education*, London and New York: Routledge and Kegan Paul.

MacDonald, S. (1999) 'The Trouble with Postmodernism', *Journal of Art and Design Education*, 18(1): 15–22.

Doubts and fears

11 Monsters in the playground

Including contemporary art

Lesley Burgess

Introduction

> Something's stirring in the unkempt undergrowth of art. Young artists seem to
> be abandoning the manicured lawns and bridleways, and diving into the bushes
> to partake of dark and lurid activities
>
> (Hutchinson 1998: 144)

In secondary education teachers often shy away from most contemporary art
because they consider it too difficult, an art 'full of monsters, replete with vulgarity
and coarseness . . . [monsters] formed in relation to the inability of knowledgeable,
patient and contemplative practice to express the experiences of the actually
existing subjectivities of young artists' (Hutchinson 1998: 144). Contemporary
art's 'monstrosities' are all too often perceived as problematic, transgressive, even
perverse, certainly outside the 'given' remit of mainstream education. To welcome
them into the classroom runs the risk of rebuke from senior management and
parents alike. But by refusing to engage with potentially problematic practices are
we, as educators, protecting students from unnecessary exposure to 'obscenities', or
are we missing an opportunity to confront important personal, social and cultural
issues? These issues are as relevant to the developing subjectivities of students as
they are to the 'actual, existing subjectivities' of young artists.

In this study, I suggest that deliberate avoidance of 'difficult' subject matter in art
is tantamount to paranoia, a failure to acknowledge that it is all-pervasive in a
society dominated by the mass media and its scopophilic apparatus. Although
absent from the curriculum the monsters lurk behind the back of the teacher in full
view of the students, the unacknowledged 'other' that in every other respect
pervades their lives. Such 'monsters', although forbidden entry to the classroom,
roam freely in the playgrounds where students confront 'real' life experiences. Why
such denial?

Usher and Edwards (1994: 8) suggest that education remains modernist, it is still
very much the dutiful child of the British Enlightenment: an Enlightenment with a
deep mistrust of excess and a promotion of education as an essentially civilising

process designed to transform children from little monsters into useful, cultured members of society (Hume 1874). Within this modernist paradigm, education plays a key role in forming and shaping students' subjectivity and identity, reproducing them as a particular kind of subject: reasonable and thus tamed. In contrast, within a postmodernist paradigm subjectivities are theorised as culturally constructed rather than natural. By refusing the reproduction of tradition, postmodernism presents young people with 'a much more ambivalent and less fixed positioning of subjectivity' (Lash 1990: 198).

How can this denial be overcome? I suggest that teachers consider their role as 'public intellectuals' (Gramsci 1971a) and identify how they can cultivate the discursive environment necessary to facilitate more sophisticated responses to contemporary culture. Edward Said insists that 'it is the responsibility of intellectuals to represent oppositional and otherwise unrepresented positions' (quoted in Williams 1997: 58). Therefore teachers must look critically at pedagogic practices that promote fixity and deny students the opportunity to interrogate their immediate cultural environment. In this way students are encouraged to question the constructed nature of personal and institutional voices, recognising how subjectivities are formed and reformed through experiences; an exposure to the good the bad and the ugly.

Safe, sanitised and static: a distortion of reality?

Despite the rhetoric that insists the content of the curriculum is restricted or restrictive, the National Curriculum Art and design Order (DfEE 1999b), along with other externally imposed national examination syllabi, is open to wide interpretation. It was conceived and developed as a flexible framework for teachers to (re)formulate in the light of regional/local circumstances. Unfortunately, too few secondary teachers have interpreted it as an opportunity to extend their practice, adopting instead a literal (mis)reading which merely validated existing orthodoxies (see Steers, Chapter 2 in this volume). Critical studies was designed to offer what was missing, a more plural, more inclusive range of discourses. However, there is still little evidence that this is taking place in schools. Unlike art and design, newer school subjects such as sociology and media studies have not been held back by the weight of 'heritage' in quite the same way as subjects whose genealogy is rooted in the classical liberal arts. In fact, media studies is invading and populating the arena of contemporary visual culture into which many art teachers fear to tread. Its proponents insist that education should not be seen as a prophylactic designed to protect young people from anything that is deemed 'bad' for them. They insist that, far from being detrimental, these kinds of materials are necessary for full human development (Britzman 1997; Buckingham 1998). Buckingham (2000) is particularly concerned with the way young people become citizens and with the role of the media in this process; Britzman (1997) is concerned with the way education adopts a perfunctory or punitive approach to anything potentially contentious.

Making monsters matter: inviting monsters into the classroom

> Aestheticising childhood creates fantasies of children that has little to do with
> actual children . . . To aestheticise children is to offer a Peter Pan world where
> children never grow up.
>
> (Duncum 2000: 31)

Britzman (1997) explains how, when sex is raised in education it is tied to preven-
tion and protection rather than diversity, curiosity and enjoyment. She claims:
'One can barely separate its objectives and fantasies from the historical bundles of
anxieties, dangers, and predatory discourses that seem to render some sex intel-
ligible as other sex is relegated to the unthinkable and the morally reprehensible'
(Britzman 1997: 90). She identifies three ways education defines sex:

- normative
- critical
- not yet tolerated or 'the polymorphously perverse'.

This final form, the 'not yet tolerated', is how contemporary art is often perceived
largely because the media focus exclusively on transgressive works. For example,
the polymorphous perverse is thrust at the spectator in the Chapman Brothers'
sculptural installations (www.gagosian.com/gg/artists/chapman/chapman.html).
Their work contradicts the idea that childhood is a time of innocence; an idea that
the media seem intent on sustaining despite the challenges of psychoanalytical
thought. The not-knowing, asexual child is a remarkably entrenched mythology,
hence the fuss about childhood sexuality.

Higonnet (1998) looks at the ways images of young children have led to
skirmishes between artists, public and the government over privacy, obscenity and
censorship. She positions the romantic ideals of childhood and loss played out in
every family album against what she tentatively calls the 'knowing child' who, when
invited to take control over how they are presented (given a camera), reveal the
presence of death, mayhem and desire. She provides a welcome antidote to the
current fixation with the child victim – the 'Not Knowing Adult'.

The results of research conducted by Barrett (2000) support this notion of the
'knowing child'. He invited pupils in the sixth grade to respond to Sally Mann's
photographs of young children (www.artcyclopedia.com/artists/mann_sally.html).
It turns out that they did not consider the work controversial or exploitative but
representative of children's lived experiences, interests and concerns. In March
2001 the *News of the World* branded Tierney Gearon's photographs of her children
(www.eyestorm.com/saatchi/gearon.asp) 'grotesque' claiming that they were 'child
pornography' masquerading as art. In response the *Independent* (13 April 2001)
warned against creating a culture in which children's bodies can be seen only as a
crime scene. The editor/columnist writing in the Comments section (p. 3) introduces the debate surrounding the work: 'On one side the terror of censorship
provokes alarm about hysteria and police over-reaction; on the other, the fear of

paedophilia generates an adjectival froth of revulsion'. Gearon's and Mann's photographs oblige the Not Knowing/Knowing adult to do just that.

Duncum (2000) insists that people need to recognise images of childhood as an important resource for discussing with young people how they see themselves positioned within society and the extent to which they accept, negotiate or reject these positions. He insists that images of 'all-knowing children . . . prey on powerful [adult] psychological needs, we must point out their pathology' (Duncum 2000: 33). Young people may well be denied access to 'monstrous' representations of childhood via restriction to media technologies in school but find easy access in their 'playgrounds' (home computers, clubs and internet cafes). However, recent developments in the school curriculum including *Thinking Skills* (DfEE 1999c: 23–4) and *Citizenship* (QCA 1998: 56–61) can be interpreted as positively promoting young people's participation in contested fields of knowledge, empowering them to confront and manage monsters, including representations of themselves. Freedman (1997) warns that without teacher mediations young people will have a 'monological' response to media experiences rather than trying to make sense of them in dialogue with others in order to question values, a plurilogue in which the position of the teacher is posited as just one of many value-laden constructs.

Media(tions)

If educators are avoiding a critical analysis of contemporary art in school then where and how are students' attitudes to recent practice formed and developed? I suggest the mass media play a significant part in (re)producing responses to contemporary art. Contentious contemporary art avoided in schools is pursued paparazzi fashion by the mass media. If the publicity it generates is to be believed, the popularity of contemporary art, replete with its monsters, has reached unprecedented heights with 'more people visit[ing] art galleries each year than attend[ing] football matches' (Walker and Chaplin 1997: 10). However, it could be argued that many of these visitors attend merely to enjoy the spectacle inspired by a prurient curiosity fed by negative media hype. Walker (1999) claims the national and tabloid press can be characterised by:

> utterly predictable knee-jerk reactions and populist attacks on contemporary art and artists employing front page headlines such as 'What a Load of Rubbish'. The results have been trivialisation, misleading and inaccurate accounts of what artists had actually produced, manipulation of the readers' emotions and encouragement of philistine attitudes and aggressive feelings
>
> (Walker 1999: 12)

Rachel Withers (2000) insists that in a similar way TV programmes about contemporary art lack real engagement in critical analysis. Instead, they are riddled with in-jokes, deliberately flip oversimplifications and glancing references to art historical jargon. She suggests that the message to the uninitiated is 'don't even try to understand it, just let contemporary art into your life and you too can hang out with Tracey Emin, go to trendy restaurants etc, etc.' Similarly, TV presents a partial rather than impartial view, framed by the camera, contextualised by music and/or voice-over and carefully edited, it presents what is perceived as a 'common-sense' overview. Information about contemporary art practice gleaned from new electronic media is equally suspect; seduced by its superficial signs of newness it is easy to fail to realise that these new technologies often only reproduce dominant orthodoxies (and even faster!) as Gere (2001) claims:

> To some extent all information communication technologies are concerned with power and control . . . despite the hype . . . much of the work in this area produced so far seems more conventional and canonical than work done for museum displays, and on television, let alone in books and journals.
>
> (Gere 2001: 59)

Schools, in line with government policy, implement a 'gateway system' controlling students' use of the web with 'fire walls', preventing access if 'suspect' words or images are included. As a result intriguing, challenging contemporary art sites are edited out of mainstream education.

Hall (1977: 335) insists that the mass media should be recognised as 'ideological state apparatuses'. He points out that they command a decisive and fundamental leadership in the cultural sphere. He believes that even though social groups and classes live increasingly fragmented lives, the mass media are more and more responsible for providing the basis on which groups and classes construct an 'image' of the lives, meanings, practices and values of other groups and classes.

Young people quickly pick up the media's stereotypical attitudes because they are not offered alternative methods of interpretation. Attempts to introduce or include such works in the curriculum fail because they are not judged on their own terms. Instead they are evaluated within the formalist criteria of an anodyne and conservative formalist modernism. Consequently, the view promoted by the mass media is allowed to go uncontested.

US research

Research carried out in the USA by Freedman and Wood (1999) confirms that there is a high degree of literalism in high school students' verbal responses to fine art. They suggest that this 'literalism' is indicative of a limited conception of art; one that prevents students from realising that art has the potential to influence their understanding of their social world. They suggest that students' understanding involves three important misconceptions:

- Fine art is mainly a form of emotional expression (and decoding the literal image will reveal the emotion of the artist at the moment of creation).
- Images do not have the power to influence.
- The act of understanding is unrelated to social norms.

(Freedman and Wood 1999: 129)

However, this research also identifies that when encouraged to make 'inter-graphical' links between different forms of visual imagery (fine art and popular culture), students reveal a far more sophisticated understanding of images and their power to influence. Interestingly, these 'extended interpretations' were not the result of formal art teaching, rather, it was only in the context of the research project that students felt able to reference popular culture (while this clearly layered their work it did not necessarily result in a critical analysis). The research also reveals that students had difficulty interpreting metaphor in images without substantial cueing: even by those who used metaphor in language/writing (Freedman and Wood 1999: 132). This suggests that art students' understanding of contemporary art/visual culture is restricted by the atheoretical nature of the teaching they receive. As a result they are limited to reading images literally, responding to the surface spectacle rather than engaging in interpretation, looking for deeper meaning.

Giroux (1994) has questioned the type of representations that constitute 'hyper-ventilating realism' (a realism of sensationalism, shock and spectacle) which simply register rather than challenge dominant social relations. He claims that spectacle foregrounds our fascination with the hyper-real and positions the viewer within a visual moment that simply registers horror and shock without critically responding to it. Barthes explains how this 'immediacy of translation' functions as a myth, because:

> It abolishes the complexity of human acts, it gives them the simplicity of essences, it does away with all dialectics, with any going back beyond what is immediately visible, it organises a world which is without contradictions because it is without depth, a world wide open and wallowing in the evident, it establishes a blissful clarity: things appear to mean something by themselves.
>
> (Barthes in Giroux 1994: 198)

Giroux uses the above to explain the impact of the Benetton advertisements on the public. He implies that such advertisements are 'representations of hopelessness'. He explains how they militate against a reading in which the content and the context of the image is historically and culturally situated and how they fail to rupture the dominant ideological codes (i.e. racism, colonialism, sexism) (Giroux 1994: 198). Similarly it could be argued that the Chapmans' sexualised mutants, Hirst's DIY butcher's shop, Sarah Lucas's 'bunny' series, although they might briefly terrorise their audience, never really threaten the polite psychological distance between the artifice of art and the viewer's security in their detached positions. Other potential meaning(s) are rendered obscure or inaccessible. The role of art education in developing an understanding of how this distancing process works and how to move beyond it becomes important.

Aesthetics?

There are conflicting views about where art fits into society, the function it serves. Becker (1994b) claims that art that appears complex, which deals with subjective or psychological concerns, is often considered obscure and inaccessible to those outside the art world. She suggests art educators reconsider the work of Marcuse, particularly his last book *The Aesthetic Dimension* (1979) in order to re-evaluate his mission to make sense of the senseless modern world in the light of postmodernism.

Marcuse suggests a great deal of the radical potential of art lies in its ability to play within, as well as outside, the (Freudian) reality principle (Becker 1994b: 118). Art that deals with complex issues, subjective or psychological concerns is often perceived as obscure and inaccessible to the general public. Becker explains how, for Marcuse:

> Art is a location – a designated imaginative space where freedom is experienced. At times it is a physical entity, a site, a painting on a wall, an installation on the floor, an event chiselled in space and/or time, a place in the mind where one allows for a recombination of experience, a suspension of the rules that govern daily life, a denial of gravity. It 'challenges the monopoly of the established reality' by creating 'fictitious worlds' in which one can see mirrored that range of emotion and experience that does not find an outlet in the present reality . . . . For Marcuse, the strength of art lies in its Otherness, its incapacity for ready assimilation . . . to be effective art must exert its capacity for estrangement.
>
> (Becker 1994b: 119)

Becker explains how Marcuse believes that art must dislocate the viewer by its refusal and inability to become part of the reality principle, in other words it is not the function of art to enable viewers to become assimilated in society; art should challenge its assumptions through 'the demands of intellectual and visual rigour and the heightened recognition of pain and pleasure'. Becker draws out of Marcuse's writing an understanding that art which is too literal (without metaphor) misses the point, to be effective content needs to be embodied in an aesthetically challenging form 'that would further the question, push the viewer or reader to a more complex or revelatory understanding of the problems posed by the work' (Becker 1994b: 121).

Writing in a similar vein, hooks (1995) claims that art is a realm where 'every imposed boundary can be transgressed'. She insists: 'one can be critically aware of visual politics – the way race, gender and class shape art practices (who makes art, how it sells, who values it, who writes about it) – without abandoning a fierce commitment to aesthetics' (hooks 1995: xii). Becker (1996) describes the expectations commonly held by the general public that 'art will be somewhat familiar yet also transcendent that it will be able to catapult its viewers outside their mundane lives' (Becker 1996: 173). These expectations about contemporary art prevent people from engaging with it when it fails to realise their preconceptions. Becker believes that art students who wish to communicate a commitment to social/political issues, who have a 'message', need to avoid the temptation to try too hard to prove their point. They need to realise that:

In its attempt to convince – its sense of its own correctness and also its own isolation – the work often goes overboard, becomes heavy-handed. And that which is designed to persuade, to demonstrate that art can educate, concern itself with the issues of the world, succeeds in pushing its viewers away

(Becker 1996: 178)

She explains how, too often, students producing issue-based work try to tell others what to think; even when they do study theory they are rarely taught strategy. Instead of adopting a didactic approach they need to employ the humour and irony (and/or metaphor) that professional artists use to communicate issues and ideas.

Threatening theory

Theory is more sadistic than politics. It beats you every time. The enforced discipline of theory expels the lazy reader. I read each sentence again and again. Slight distractions flaw me. Trying to get my head round this is like a snake swallowing a pig.

(Cussans 1993: 17)

One of the things I most consistently find is an incapacity of art students to read their own work or the work of others. They are not equipped to think their way into the actuality of the work . . . This underdeveloped discursive culture of art in English art schools culturally disempowers students

(Brighton 1994: 34)

Given the above opinions it is hardly surprising that art and design teachers are notorious for being atheoretical. There are exceptions, but they remain few and far between. Hughes (1998), Steers (2001) and Tallack (2000) have bemoaned the fact that most art graduates remain resolutely resistant to theory. This can, in part, be traced back to their experience at degree level. Research undertaken by Robins and Woollard (2001) suggests that the understanding of art fostered by degree courses continues to influence teachers' attitudes in the classroom. They, like Davies (2001), infer that PGCE courses can do little to change this attitude. Until recently these courses (BA and PGCE) have sidelined any intellectual/theoretical debates in order to concentrate on studio production, thus allowing modernist myths and traditional orthodoxies to be perpetuated. As a result monsters emerge fully formed in their work without them realising why or how they came to be there. Recently there has been a noticeable shift in emphasis; some BA and MA courses in art have been reconceptualised to give greater emphasis to theory, especially within the broader field of cultural studies. This is starting to filter through to teaching but it will need to be championed and developed in initial teacher education and continuing professional development if it is to have a significant impact on mainstream education. This is not to suggest that this is an easy or straightforward task. Suchin (1998) contends that any attempt by art educators to recognise the importance of theory 'hardly ever manages to smash the spell of the artist as the bearer of an alienated but esoteric persona, a subject somehow different from the pack' and theory as 'a necessary evil to be confronted in order to obtain a higher degree' (Suchin 1998: 104).

Stallabrass (1999) suggests that the theoretical readings layered onto the work of artists such as Jake and Dinos Chapman can be seen as superficial and jargonistic. Such readings are little more than a defence against a concern that the Chapmans' kiddie dummies, sprouting sexual organs in unusual places or showing mutilated victims of torture, would be condemned as simply attention-seeking and sensationalist 'a crude gallop over the tender parts of the public and the media' (Stallabrass 1999: 101). Stallabrass insists that theory changes to meet new situations, he points to a 'brand new form of theory combining the disadvantages of elitism with the pleasures of the yob' (1999: 103).

> The Chapmans are triumphantly excremental artists whose art erects an edifice of compulsively anal proportions while depositing the traces of a sepsidic spoor amidst the hallowed halls of culture. Put simply the work is shit.
> (Fogle, quoted in Stallabrass 1999: 103)

It is clear that the relationship between art, theory and the media is complex and at times contradictory. While the Chapmans' work is layered with theory to give it credibility Tracey Emin plays down the conceptual and theoretical sources in her work (particularly its relationship with earlier feminist works) in order to maintain an anti-intellectual, high-media posture. She claimed, and it was well reported, 'Art is not an intellectual mind fuck, I need art like I need God' (Emin 2000: 102).

The 'monstrous-feminine'

> Former misogynist commonplaces are now being seized by women; in rock music, in films, in fiction, even in pornography, women are grappling the she-beast of demonology for themselves. The girl is the heroine of our times, and transgression a staple entertainment.
> (Warner 1994: 10–11)

Warner suggests the adoption of the monstrous is a way for the scorned to gain power.

> Images of blood, vomit, pus, shit etc are central to our culturally/socially-constructed notions of the horrific. A signifier of the split between two orders: the maternal authority and the law of the father.
> (Creed 1986: 51)

In her seminal text *Powers of Horror* Kristeva describes the abject as 'the place where meanings collapse', the liminal, the borderline, that which defines what is human and what is not (Kristeva 1982: 2). It is at the borderline that danger exists; it is dangerous because it is ambiguous. For Kristeva the most significant borderline is the one that separates the inside from the outside of the body, self from other. She argues that the abject holds powers of fascination as well as revulsion and therefore it is subject to a range of cultural and social taboos. Kristeva divides the abject into three main categories: food; corporeal alteration and death; and the female body.

Betterton (1996) suggests that this typology corresponds closely to the pre-occupations of contemporary women artists who 'explore an aesthetic of bodily transgression, often symbolically enacted on the female body' (Betterton 1996: 135). Bordo (1990) argues that the production of the 'normal' body is one of the central disciplinary strategies within society. The late-twentieth-century western ideal of the slender body represents a desire to contain the body's margins; a desire that is encoded morally and socially. In *Purity and Danger* Mary Douglas (1991) identifies the human body as a metaphor for social structures:

> The body is a model which can stand for any bounded system. Its boundaries can represent any boundaries which are threatened or precarious. The body is a complex structure. The functions of its different parts and their relation afford a source of symbols for other complex structures. We cannot possibly interrupt rituals concerning excreta, breast milk, saliva and the rest unless we are prepared to see the body as a symbol of society, and to see the powers and dangers credited to the social structures reproduced in small on the human body.
>
> (Douglas 1991: 115)

The young, fit, slim, female body as a social/medical ideal links critically to the clinical gaze of the medical establishment to produce normative representations (Bordo 1990). Meskimmon (1996a: 7) suggests that 'working in tandem, these institutions define a rigid norm and create "monsters" from all those who do not fit the pattern', an argument that is not only restricted to representations of gender (masculine and feminine), but also applies to race and class (Butler 1993; Mirzoeff 1995).

Barbara Creed (1993) argues that the whole notion of the monster is constructed in and through gender difference and female sexuality. For Creed (1993: 2–3) the 'monstrous feminine' is manifest in two ways:

- Maternity – the pregnant woman as 'shape shifter' defying limits and borders.
- Vagina dentata – the castrating woman.

Representations of the 'monstrous female', rather than merely pathologising that which fails to reach the 'ideal', can be used for the articulation of female subjectivity outside the binary opposition which defines woman solely in relation to man.

Jo Anna Isaak (1996) explains how for Lacan such monstrous femininity is epitomised by the 'femme fatale'. According to Zizek's (1991) reading of Lacan what is so threatening about the femme fatale is that she will go too far, take off all the masks and reveal the 'real'. This 'going too far' is exemplified in the work of artists such as Jenny Saville, Orlan, Hannah Wilke, Jo Spence and Cindy Sherman.

These are women who Zizek would describe as having 'assumed their own fate'. Jo Spence documented her fight with breast cancer confronting the medical orthodoxy and its system of representing her and her disease (see Figure 11.1).

Isaak (1996) insists:

> These works are triumphant, not because the women win the battle; for the most part they don't. They are triumphant in their challenge to society's obsession with masking loss, in their willingness to look steadily at the 'disappearance that everybody denies' (Zizek 1991: 79).
>
> (Isaak 1996: 221)

Meskimmon (1996b) recognises the potential empowerment of the monstrous and the grotesque for women's self representations:

> Thus, the monster becomes an empowering trope for women artists precisely because it cannot be fixed: it is always 'becoming', poised on the borders . . . They exist in a state of becoming rather than a false marker of fixity.
>
> (Meskimmon 1996b: 9–11)

Figure 11.1 Monster (1989), Jo Spence in collaboration with Dr Tim Sherd from Narratives of Dis-ease. Courtesy of Terry Dennett and MAKE, the organisation for women in the arts.

She cites the work of Jenny Saville as an example of 'border crossing' (see www.eyestorm.com/saatchi/biography_saville.asp). Saville's work clearly challenges traditional fine art representations of women, her monstrous self-portraits refuse to be framed, overwhelming the viewer as they overspill the canvas:

> With explicit references to the writings of Irigaray in these works, Saville has placed traditions of mimesis and mirroring into contention. According to Irigaray, traditions of masculine viewing/knowing are the paradigms which have marginalised women, so that techniques of 'jam the machinery' of 'speaking' or 'representing' are necessary.
>
> (Meskimmon 1996b: 9–11)

It is worthy of note that *Make* receives more enquiries about Jenny Saville from school students than any other artist. However, too often her work is seen to fit neatly into a trajectory that focuses on her painterly angst (in the manner of Freud and Auerbach) rather than being recognised as part of a matriarchal lineage. It is a challenge to patriarchal representations. Clearly, an understanding of the construction of the 'monstrous feminine' is necessary if students are to develop a rich understanding of the work of these contemporary women artists.

Conclusion

Meskimmon (1996a) points out that from the same etymological root as 'monster' comes the word 'demonstrate': 'To manifest, show, display to . . . To describe and explain by the help of specimens or by experimentation . . . to show or make evident by reasoning' (Meskimmon 1996a: 7).

As Amelia Jones (1993) explains, subjectivities are historically and culturally constructed; defined within cultural codings that determine which voices can and cannot constitute critical authority in art discourse. She points out that 'within this cultural policing, the possibility of a work of art that is both sensual and conceptual, both eroticized and politically critical is disallowed' (Jones 1993: 383). She quotes Bourdieu, who in *Distinction: A Social Critique of the Judgement of Taste* (1984) claims:

> Only pure pleasure – ascetic, empty pleasure which implies the renunciation of pleasure – is predisposed to become a symbol of moral excellence and the work of art a test of ethical superiority.
>
> (Jones 1993: 383)

The work produced by many contemporary artists challenges such exclusionary value systems and reveals how artists and potentially their critics and audience have agency. In light of this, Pollock's (1988) re-examination of Brechtian 'distanciation' provides a crucial strategy to enable the spectator to become 'an agent in cultural production and activate him or her as an agent in the world' (Pollock 1988: 165). Such agency allows for the deconstruction of the oppositions identified by

Jones (1993: 383) in order also to engage in a consideration and critique of aesthetics, that is critical aesthetics (see Addison and Burgess 2000: 324).

Working in tandem, not unlike an ongoing palimpsest, the theory of the image and the power of the image can inform students' own artistic production and their understanding of art as cultural (re)production. The way contemporary art plays with notions of authenticity and identity through foregrounding the 'monster' should be explored as a signifying system, a fascinating area of study that will enable both teachers and young people to have a voice and to engage in critical debate about important issues in visual and material culture; in the classroom, the gallery and let us hope the playground too.

It is important to point out that it is not my intention to defend the autonomy of the aesthetic or to suggest that art can transcend social reality and achieve autonomy, far from it. Art is unavoidably political and it is without doubt one of the roles of artists today to highlight social, cultural and political issues and concerns. It is the way in which artists do this that is significant and has implications for teaching and learning in secondary schools. Rather than presupposing an opposition between 'difficult' contemporary art and the aims of secondary education, which only leads to a series of intellectual compromises, the art work should be recognised as a meeting place for interpretation, one that cannot be limited to a formal, historical, aesthetic or theoretical methodology but should be fluid and diverse. It is important to acknowledge that in contemporary art value is not set, there are always formalist analyses to be redeployed, social meanings to be resignified, cultural and intellectual capital to be reinvested. Many students in secondary school are engaging in complex theoretical issues and debates in other areas of the curriculum, they can be surprisingly sophisticated readers of visual and material culture. Art educators do young people a dis-service if they confine contemporary art's 'monsters' to the playground. Rather they should coax them into the classroom where young people can confront them and allow them to enrich their developing subjectivities and inform their art production. Young people need a diet rich in explicit fantasy in order to develop confident, complex and discriminating value systems. Hebdige (1996) insists that the multimedia world in which people live, with its array of circulating images, must be 'grazed for meaning since this is where contemporary subjectivity must work itself out' (Hebdige 1996: 139). He claims the power of the image lies in its inherent ability to

> contaminate the pristine, abstract meta level at which theory, left to its own device, seeks to operate . . . I've always liked the fact that the image is both more and less than language, it exceeds or evades whatever we can say. I've always liked what people call the slipperiness of the image.
>
> (Hebdige 1996: 139)

Questions for discussion

1   Should art and design teachers accept responsibility for introducing young people to the issues implicit in 'difficult' contemporary art?

2   How might the 'safe', discursive environment necessary for this to happen be developed?

Further reading

Carson, F. and Pajaczkowska, C. (eds) (2000) *Feminist Visual Culture*, Edinburgh: Edinburgh University Press.

Higonnet, A. (1998) *Pictures of Innocence: The History and Crisis of Ideal Childhood*, London: Thames and Hudson.

Isaak, J. A. (1996) *Feminism and Contemporary Art: The Revolutionary Power of Women's Laughter*, London: Routledge.

Stallabrass, J. (1999) *High Art Lite*, London: Verso.

12 Iconoscepticism

The value of images in education

Nicholas Addison

The entire life of societies in which modern conditions of production reign announces itself as an immense accumulation of spectacles. Everything that was directly lived has moved away into a representation.

(Debord 1977: 1)

The visible is essentially pornographic, which is to say that it has its end in rapt, mindless fascination.

(Jameson 1990:1)

Iconophobia: the fear of images

Western society has become increasingly reliant on images to disseminate its dreams of material well-being, a dependence summed up in the term 'ocularcentric' (Mirzeoff 1999; Rose 2001). In ocularcentric societies the dominant tests of truth, the everyday metaphors by which understanding is commonly acquiesced or questioned, reference the eye – I *see* (what you mean); what is your *view*? (Jay 1993) – an orientation that privileges images in popular discourse but not in education. Thus, despite their omnipresence, or perhaps because of it, there is a real fear of images within educational institutions, of a 'medieval return', a descent into illusion and hyperreality, the 'adman's' dream of the perpetual circulation and consumption of imaginary desires (Baudrillard 1989). This iconophobia is grounded in ancient and persistent beliefs about the nature of the image, or rather, the fear that the image can come to replace the thing to which it refers, a surrogate reality, an untruth. In contrast, words are valorised differently and more positively. For example in the gospel of St John the word is unassailably elevated: 'In the beginning was the Word, and the Word was with God, and the Word was God' (1:1) a revelation in which the word reaches its apogee; neither a substitute for reality nor a confirmation, the word *is* reality; Logos in perpetuam. This pre-material, absolute status is one that the poor mimetic image must never be allowed to attain; for, so the iconophobe claims, if the 'untruths' of appearance come to dominate consciousness the 'higher realities' of metaphysics or critical theory will be as nought. Given this fear, western ocularcentrism is something of a paradox, one that has historically produced an ambivalence towards the image.

The most extreme form of iconophobia, iconoclasm (the destruction of images), was a notable strategy throughout formative periods of European history (Besançon 2000). Today, however, destruction and prohibition are rare, iconophobia is most clearly manifest as scepticism, a doubt as to the value of images. Iconoscepticism in education is therefore the legacy of iconophobic tendencies in western philosophy (the logocentric tradition) so that the image, however much it is used to produce learning throughout the curriculum, is characterised as illustrative, supportive, unthinking, as 'edutainment'. Intellectuals often perceive an ocularcentric basis to the dystopia of contemporary society (Foucault 1977; Baudrillard 1989; Virilio 1997) particularly the regime of surveillance deployed by the modern nation-state and the regime of spectacle characterising the mass media, the mega-visual apparatus of global capitalism. These critics reinforce oppositions between word and image, the logocentric and the affective and, in the popular imagination reinforce the binary principles of western thought.

The dissembling image

Within modern education, particularly within the liberal tradition, some teachers have tried to provide students with the critical means by which 'untruths' can be revealed. Since the Enlightenment the democrat has understood these untruths to be situated in the whole apparatus of the state, the hegemonic structures and discourses of oppression whether maintained coercively and complicitly (Gramsci 1971b) or 'productively' (Foucault 1977: 194). It must be admitted that both the religious and secular state has found in the image a dramatic tool for achieving such hegemony for the image has properties that allow its 'message' to be assimilated with ease, properties such as immediacy and affectivity, a presence and permanence that is persuasive (seeing is believing) and, when replicated, a cumulative effect that can be spectacular, even overwhelming. Given these qualities, the potency of the image has been irresistible to those who would *embody* their 'truths'. But this pretended 'facticity', this simulacrum, this potential to appear true is what has allowed the image to be used to mislead and corrupt, to perpetuate deceptions. Considering this historical and cultural status it is not surprising that the image has become an attractive source for critical analysis and deconstruction by those who would expose the 'emperor's new clothes' in an attempt to empower the people. For these 'empowerers' it is of course the writing that has been used to expose the image's duplicity (see Jay 1993 on Barthes and Derrida). This historical, analytical and rhetorical process has of necessity been word-dependent and has therefore reinforced the anti-sensory, iconophobic tendencies of western religion and philosophy.

Within the progressive tradition, teachers have also tried to educate for a critical student body, one capable not only of participating in democracy but of developing it too, a radical body. This entails the exposure of the hegemonic means of the dominant order, an exposure that might prove uncomfortable in relation to art, for, historically, art has rightly been interpreted as a potent tool of power and is thus the target of analysis and deconstruction (Boime 1990). However, the history of the modernist avant-garde has been co-opted as part of the critical tradition, a means by which the dominant order has been challenged and/or undermined. While this radical potential, art's capacity to produce and transform culture, dominates the theory–practice alliance in art colleges such a proactive role is anathema to the school curriculum which, by and large, serves to reproduce the dominant order. A truly liberatory pedagogy would need to provide an opportunity for students to examine the relationship between their own lives and the dominant order, including an examination of the institution of schooling itself and the place of art within it. This would require students to have a sense of themselves *in* history, a process that would develop analytical and interpretative faculties as well as the potential for agency.

I wish briefly to spend some time examining significant moments in the history of western iconophobia and its relationship to ocularcentrism. Searching so far back into canonic texts for some elusive origin or causal link may seem like a historical indulgence, an unnecessary prelude to the investigation of a contemporary problem in art education. But in order to question the persistence and permutations of such beliefs it is important to demonstrate their embeddedness in western thought. Similarly I wish to question the simple binary opposition, word/image if only to complicate the logocentric/affective opposition that I extrapolate from it and which appears to characterise a bifurcation in the school curriculum.

Ocularcentrism

Already in Greek philosophy sight was privileged above the other senses and Jay (1993) argues that the physical distance afforded by the eye is responsible for a fundamental principle of western thought:

> The externality of sight allows the observer to avoid direct engagement with the object of his [*sic*] gaze. Thus, the very distinction between subject and object and the belief in the neutral apprehension of the latter by the former, a distinction so crucial for much later thought, was abetted by the ocularcentrism of Greek thought.
>
> (Jay 1993: 25)

Observation was the privileged method of investigation and light the dominant metaphor. The resultant subject/object binarism was also the necessary condition for the epistemological bias of western philosophy, an orientation that led inexorably to the bourgeois individual and the solipsisms of subjectivity (Eagleton 1990: chapter 3). Like most in this enterprise Plato too elevated sight above the other senses but it must be remembered that for him only by rejecting forms of material embodiment and sensuous awareness, but particularly all representations, could the citizen achieve a pure apprehension of the Idea (*The Republic*: book 10).

Word/image and Christendom

The Christian tradition of scholastic education was a system dominated by the concept of logos. The place of the image within this system was inconsistent, oscillating between periods of iconoclasm and seeming iconophilia. Bryson (1981) identifies the medieval period as one in which the image was always secondary however splendid the visual effect. In the context of the cathedral the visual and material environment may have functioned as a metaphor for paradise, a theatrical *mise-en-scène* out of which the drama of the liturgy could be re-enacted, but the function of images within this ensemble was even more word-dependent. Because the literate community was limited to a small, educated elite, the Church found it necessary to harness the didactic potential of images in order to educate the population at large; such images were essentially illustrative; as Damisch (1975) confirms, the study of the meaning of medieval images, iconography, *is* the study of texts. Bernstein (2000) also sees language (that is god) in the form of the trivium, as the regulating discourse in medieval Europe; without it the quadrivium, the exploration of the physical world using mathematics, would not be safe. He proposes that this dislocation of languages is transformed into the spatial metaphor inner and outer which in his estimation

> becomes a fundamental problematic of all European philosophy and social science. What we have here, at another level, is the dislocation between inner and outer with respect to the individual, inner and outer with respect to the relationship between the individual and society. This becomes a doxic principle of European consciousness, a principle that we do not find in the Orient [*sic*].
>
> (Bernstein 2000: 8–9)

Inner/outer is an impossible concept within consciousness without some form of mediation, without a bridge; the eye serves that function and, as has been noted, it is its physiological properties that produce the subject/object dualism, a further or perhaps synonymous metaphor. But in medieval Europe the inner world of the majority of the population was limited because they were denied access to the conceptual tools, skills of literacy, through which an 'inner life' could be developed. In this equation the image finds a place because it makes concrete for illiterates the precepts necessary for social cohesion.

When critics refer to a 'medieval return' what they fear is not the image itself so much as the illiterates who depend on it, for them a group identified with the surging masses, the unreasonable and irrepressible mob. However, the texts to which medieval images refer tend to be biblical or hagiographic, a series of canonic narratives illustrating exemplary behaviours and/or moral exhortation. These tales insinuated a system of rewards and sanctions that by and large contained any potential unrest and served the hegemonic agendas of church and monarchy alike. Because of the uses it was put to, the image became tainted by this regulative and illustrative function, what might be termed its dumb didacticism. As painting developed during the Renaissance the revival of classical allegory demanded a different, educated audience. What at first sight appears to be outside the word, the ideal forms of Italian Renaissance art, can in fact be interpreted as a reconstruction based on verbal evidence. But during the sixteenth century a major shift occurred that wrenched art apart from other forms of visual culture. Painting was theorised as something equivalent to poetry, by Lomazzo, for example, as a vehicle by which the grace of god, only faintly reflected in the corporeal world, could be mediated by the angels in the form of 'Ideas' (archetypes) and transferred to the soul of the artist who would then realise the Idea in concrete form (Panofsky 1968). Thus painting joined the liberal arts and was elevated above other types of image. Likewise the artist became a 'creative being' someone who could see beyond appearances and get to the very essence of things; the image in their hands, that is art, could be 'true'.

Idealism: apotheosis and fall

Within the secular tradition it was not until the eighteenth century that the possibility of a world rooted in perception was allocated a parallel if not equivalent place to the abstractions of the logos: 'Aesthetics, Baumgarten wrote, is the sister of logic, a kind of *ratio inferior* or feminine analogue of reason at the lower end of sensational life' (Eagleton 1990: 16), a concrete and thus debased form of logic. For Kant the importance of the aesthetic lay in its potential to provide social cohesion. Eagleton paraphrases:

> The aesthetic is in no way cognitive but it has about it something of the form and structure of the rational; it thus unites us with all the authority of the law, but at a more affective, intuitive level. What brings us together as subjects is not knowledge but an ineffable reciprocity of feeling . . . Paradoxically, it is in the apparently most private, frail and intangible aspects of our lives that we blend most harmoniously with one another.
>
> (Eagleton 1990: 75–6)

Implicit within this equation is the bourgeois ideal of the individual self, who, were 'he' to become fully known to others would be like an object, would lose his subjectivity. However, moments of collective aesthetic feeling could supposedly prevent the fragmentation of society into a collection of unknowable individuals, for in *feeling with*, rather than *knowing of*, others, the individual retains their freedom. Kant suggested that although the work of art is a material object it finds its resonance not as phenomenon but in the realm of noumenon, a bridge between nature, the slavery of cause and effect, and reason, the elusive realm of freedom. In this way art transcends the material and pertains to the ideal. However, Hegel, arguably the philosopher who most profoundly influenced the development of western art history, was intolerant of the split subjectivity of Kant, the cohabitation of logic and intuition. In Hegel's masculinist teleology Kant's dependence on intuition and the imaginary was nothing but a feminisation of philosophy, the patriarchal pedigree of the logos needed to be reasserted and Eagleton suggests that in Hegel:

> The imaginary is elevated from the aesthetic to the theoretical, shifted up a gear from feeling to cognition. Ideology, in the shape of the identity of subject and object, is installed at the level of scientific knowledge; and Hegel can thus afford to assign art a lowly place in his system.
>
> (Eagleton 1990: 123)

Art's moment of apotheosis was short lived. The relationship between word and image comes full circle.

Observation: empiricism

There are however parallel traditions at once less exclusive and more pragmatic. Constable, for example, when reviewing the exhibition at the Royal Academy in 1802 had the temerity to write:

> There is little or nothing in the exhibition worth looking up to – there is room enough for a natural painter . . . *Fashion* always had, & will have its day – but *Truth* (in all things) only will last and can have just claims on posterity.
>
> (quoted in Rosenthal 1987: 35–6)

A cry that can stand for the quest for a strict perceptualism among artists during the nineteenth century. A little later this quest was given moral weight by Ruskin, who advised English artists to imitate the 'handiwork of God':

> Go to nature in all singleness of heart, & walk with her laboriously & trustingly, having no other thought but how best to penetrate her meaning; rejecting nothing, selecting nothing & scorning nothing; believing all things to be right and good, & rejoicing always in the truth.
>
> (Ruskin 2000, vol. 1, section 6, ch. 111, para. 21)

An exhortation that ironically wraps revelation in empiricist clothing and produces a strange alliance between two seemingly antithetical paradigms, a resolution of differences that returns in current secondary art education in the form of perceptualist/expressivist alliances. It is worth mentioning that Constable also stated that 'painting is for me another word for feeling', but it could be argued that the significance of his experiments in opticality belong as much to natural science as to art and, as such, the ocularcentricity of science also deserves mention.

Aristotle found in his natural science a key role for observation and description, although, admittedly, in his poetics, the particularities of science/history are inferior to the universals of poetry; but the visual arts belong to the former: 'Imitation is natural to man from childhood . . . and [he] learns at first by imitation. And it is also natural for all to delight in works of imitation' (quoted in Williams

1965: 20). This faith in appearance enabled the development of philosophical traditions that ran counter to idealist beliefs; empiricism and positivism are its modern legacy. The privileging of experience and sense data within these traditions is associated with *the* scientific method where careful observation, repeated and repeatable, is now institutionalised. Empiricists continuously stress the significance of experience rather than representation and therefore, to them, both words and images are largely necessary as a communicative tool, not as an end in themselves.

Revelation

If for the empiricist words are more suspect than images, St. Paul, brought to the truth through revelatory conversion, was equally wary of 'lofty words' (First Letters to the Corinthians):

> For Jews demand signs and Greeks seek wisdom, but we preach Christ crucified (1:22) . . . When I came to you, brethren . . . (2:1) my speech and my message were not in plausible words of wisdom, but in demonstration of the Spirit and power, that your faith might not rest in the wisdom of men but in the power of God (2:4–5).

When reduced to the cross, Paul's emphasis on the 'demonstration' of Christ cruci-fied suggests a process of condensation, a synecdoche rather than an imitation, a single form out of which the complete narrative of Christ's life and God's love unfolds. With such extreme condensation, the cross becomes a metaphorical meeting of opposites: vertical/horizontal, punishment/forgiveness, death/resurrection, a form that is easily duplicated, whether as word, image or gesture. To the believer this resolution of opposites seems to offer a direct route to the 'true way' ensuring that salvation is available to anyone who possesses the humility to eschew the tempta-tions of doubt and reasoned speculation. The truth of words is essence not enquiry or rational debate; the truth of images is that they can lead one back to the Word.

Legacy

The revelatory and empirical traditions provide an ongoing critique of idealist abstraction, although the significance of the former is much reduced in modern Britain. Historically this has not deterred the idealists from returning the criticism, even Aristotle admitted: 'Nature is what happens always, or almost always' (quoted in Feyerabend 1995: 808). However, for the main monotheistic traditions, Christianity, Islam and Judaism, the word remains sacrosanct and they continue to privilege specifically logocentric literacies. This legacy leaves its traces and effects in current mass education so that, for example, in 1998, for England and Wales, the British government could introduce literacy and numeracy hours for primary school children. This legislation signals that the logocentric curriculum is still perceived as foundational but it also indicates a fear that traditional logocentric teaching is being diluted by child-centred pedagogies. The three traditions I identify – idealist, revelatory and empiricist – continue to develop, some in purist mode others in hybrid form (remember Ruskin). The first two are consistently logocentric, the latter, despite the significance of experiential, experimental data on policy, is often abstracted into number and is therefore accommodated within the logos. Advocates of all three believe they have ownership of the truth and all three find a place in the education system of modern Britain. All three determine the word/number-based practices that tie pupils to the page and screen, reducing the significance of sensory and affective modes of learning and securing the climate of iconoscepticism. Art, dance, drama and music are nonetheless offered a place in the curriculum, but that place is separate, at the margins, a place where 'high' cultural forms can be reproduced (the history of physical education is a different case). Drama and music are however closely allied to the logos through their dependence respectively on text and number, and dance is allied through its dependence on music; art, inevitably ocular in orientation, is left holding the image.

Multimodality

In education the way to counter the prevailing iconosceptic climate is for art teachers to understand more fully, and articulate more cogently, what it is that they are helping students to learn and do. The visual does specific things, makes particular types of meaning possible, but it does not do so in isolation. Theories of multimodality (Kress and van Leeuwen 2001) suggest that meaning is always made across and between modes. A mode is any culturally designated vehicle for the production of meaning; gesture, image, material, sound, speech and writing are the most commonly used. In the way people live their lives these systems of representation and embodiment are never separated, it is only in the context of academic analysis that they are segregated, and only in education that in their isolation they take on a separate and peculiar existence. The perception that the word is a monomodal phenomenon, particularly in its most regulating form, writing, has ensured its hold over the curriculum. In this way the privileging of certain types of writing has ensured an exclusive profile to those students likely to succeed, an exclusivity secured through the examination system. Art and design has of necessity been somewhere outside this stranglehold, however, recent research has confirmed the antipathy felt by teachers and students alike for writing within the art curriculum (ACHiS 2002) and thus a tendency to valorise the visual as an oppositional monomodality. And yet today, the ubiquity of multimodal communications within the mass media has combined with the proto-democratic principles of postindustrial cultures to produce a climate in which people are increasingly multiliterate; able to bypass the false monomodal, logocentricism of traditional academic discourse.

The last stronghold of iconoscepticism

The last stronghold of iconoscepticism is academe, a conglomerate of institutional practices to which primary and secondary education have only a minor sibling relationship. Unlike academe, and despite the wider student body in higher education, maintained schools in Britain accommodate 80 per cent of the population aged between 5 and 16 and therefore have to acknowledge the diversity of social values. However, the form that this acknowledgement takes may often be negative, possibly in the form of criticism or indeed suppression, for schools provide a common social space where the values of the dominant class are paraded and rehearsed. Any transformation at the level of the individual is usually class-based as the dominant values are assimilated by students who then signal their changed consciousness, their recognition of the rules (Bernstein 2000), through conformist or resistant behaviours. In this way schools are self-evidently the key state institutions for reproducing the status quo despite a rhetoric of self-actualisation and empowerment. However, each school is a site where different discourses overlap: academic, ethical, popular, religious, vocational, some allied others conflicting; teachers no less than students participate in these discourses.

Discourses around the image

On the one hand the discussion of images in schools (not their use) is often framed by celebratory popular discourses, on the other, the discussion of the visual arts is often informed by dismissive populist discourses. If the relationship between the image and popular consciousness is therefore characterised by both embrace and denial; embrace of its use, denial of its critical value, what of the relationship between the two disciplines of art history and secondary art and design, the latter of which seeks logocentric credibility from the former. Where are they positioned in relation to the iconosceptic traditions? Within art history Preziosi (1989) recognises both a revelatory (ecumenical) and an empirical tradition, the critical tradition is firmly rooted in the idealist camp. Art, as taught in schools, is equally divided between the claims of the idealists ('creativists' and 'expressivists') and the empiricists ('perceptualists' and 'formalists'). The idealists, however, tend to hold their beliefs as an article of faith, it cannot be said to be an overtly critical tradition although some of its apologists apply a modernist aesthetic terminology (Witkin 1974; Abbs 1994). The critical tradition, in practice, surfaces only in isolated pockets, despite the call to arms since the early 1970s (Field 1970; Eisner 1972; Allison 1981; Thistlewood 1989; Dawtrey *et al.* 1996). Given this mix, it is not surprising that the interactions between those who espouse the different positions and traditions are problematic, producing tensions and conflicts.

Interdisciplinarity

If a recognition of the multimodality of learning is essential to break down the binary opposition that has developed in the whole school curriculum as a result of western logocentricism, how can the tensions in the subject art and design be resolved? The climate of iconoscepticism has led art teachers to take up defensive positions; teaching and learning is often characterised by its fear of words, modernist myths of a mute autonomy are paraded to excuse an acritical, ahistorical insularity. It is true that in many cultures what constitutes art is a differentiated practice, although, unlike its status in contemporary Britain, it is frequently an integral component of social exchange. Nonetheless, even in this context art is often marked off from the mundane, it is making special; Walter Benjamin supposed that before the modern period art was always at the service of ritual, it signalled something sacred (in Frascina and Harris 1992). Even if this is so, art is still only part of a cultural system, it is not all of it; it works alongside other forms, not above or below them. For a more questioning approach to art, educators need to look outside the disciplines of art history and aesthetics to ethnography, psychoanalysis, semiotics and sociology (Geertz 2000; Rose 2001) disciplines and methodologies that refuse to privilege aesthetic categories as truths because they are self-evidently perceived as historical and cultural constructs. Within them art is addressed as one instance of the continuum of human creativity and its contemporary manifestations can be considered unburdened by the baggage of universalising modernist myths.

From an interdisciplinary perspective international, modern art has become a culturally distinct set of practices, largely conventional and institutional in form. It is realised as a range of meaning-making activities that are socially embedded, a part of the way life is lived by a few. However, marked off from the mundane, particularly form the profane world of work, even by those whose work it is to produce it, art signals difference; difference self-consciously made visible for others. But, within modernity, art has to be differentiated yet further because it is simultaneously manifest alongside other images and artefacts that are themselves embedded within larger systems of communication and signification. It might be said that in modernity the radical artist has taken on the role of signalling difference within the homogenising tendency of this larger, global tradition, the mega-visual tradition of corporate capitalism. The way art in schools can regain a radical function is by looking at those artists who in their interdisciplinarity redefine their relationship to consumerist orthodoxy. Such artists signal their difference in the context of modernity by taking on a reflexive role: rather than reflect the worlds of the powerful, or the world of appearances they join philosophy to ask, what is the world? Rather than reproduce tradition in order to reinforce the status quo they engage it in a critical dialogue and thus potentially transform it. The different discourses that surround art are attempts to maintain a separation between it and other forms of visual culture even in the face of artists and theorists who question such boundaries; formal and informal, disciplinary and popular, words, above all else, have been used as the mechanism for separation.

Interpretation

The secondary school is a site where these discourses are either neglected or suppressed. But within the popular imagination, one prescribed by dominant ocularcentric or retinal epistemologies, a key function of art is still that of representation and painting still holds a paramount position. Today painting has two popular representational claims: mimetic objectivity, verisimilitude (assessed in relation to the 'self-evident' criteria likeness to appearance) and expressive subjectivity, feeling (intuited rather than assessed, a condition of empathetic correspondence). But these criteria, products of empirical and idealist modernisms, are often irrelevant in the face of artworks that come from outside western modernism, either historically or culturally, and are particularly inappropriate when faced with contemporary practices where these very criteria may be undergoing critique. It is important therefore that art teachers enable students to understand that systems of representation are culturally and historically conditioned, that the 'naturalness' of art, the self-evidence of the mirror, the notion that art refers and represents transparently is always in doubt. To understand art requires interpretation, or, in more fashionable parlance, a process of decoding (Hall 1997a) a process that is possible only within a discursive environment. Decoding is, however, only a stage in interpretation for it presupposes that the limits of meaning are encased both within the object itself and the contexts of its production, that is that meaning is immanent. What is forgotten here is the constructive work carried out by the viewer who accommodates the meaning-potentiality of the art object to their existing patterns of knowledge, thus for each student the potential meaning is different (Bal and Bryson 1998). Therefore, the word interpretation is capable of accommodating that other vital process, encoding, the means by which meaning is articulated, as thought, or embodied, as speech or as a further work of art. Indeed there may be a false dichotomy between these two codings in that the application of codes or conventions presupposes their understanding (albeit that this understanding may be naturalised rather than cognised or explicated): understanding is manifest both in the interpretation of images and in the image as an interpretation.

The interpretation of art and other images and artefacts in schools is not solely the responsibility of the art teacher and interesting methodological contributions from other areas of the curriculum must be acknowledged. But the special and possibly unique position of art and design as a primarily aesthetic subject (as practised) offers perspectives which English and media studies in particular tend to bypass. But because secondary art educators have, by and large, eschewed the systematic application of methods of interpretation in favour of a more laissez-faire, eclectic, at best, 'organic' approach, the lack of theoretical rigour noted over a number of years (Field 1970; Hughes 1999; Steers, Chapter 2 in this volume), has marked the subject off from those that have begun to look at images more critically, albeit from within an iconosceptic framework.

Recommendations

The simple binary oppositions between word and image, the logocentric and the affective are the means to maintain historical divisions that are no longer tenable. Secondary art educators must break out of their insularity by investigating where their values have come form and what, in reproducing them through their students, they are perpetuating. They should find ways to convince others that art and design is more than recreation, a diversion from the logocentric curriculum. Perhaps they could convince others that learning in the subject does not depend on god-given talents but in the words of one critical theorist that 'the peculiarity of art is to "make us see", "make us perceive", "make us feel" something which *alludes* to reality' (Althusser quoted in Graham 1997: 159–60, original emphasis). If one purpose of education is to draw out from the individual an understanding of both what it is to be *in* reality, and how it is possible to *produce* reality, to have agency, then the visual cannot be sidelined; but neither should it be privileged.

Questions for discussion

1   Art teachers are rarely invited to debate the political implications of their chosen pedagogies because they are encouraged to see them as neutral; should this be so?
2   Talk in the art room is rarely outlawed. Is it possible to direct it towards discursive interpretation without the iconsceptic baggage encountered elsewhere in the curriculum?
3   Is it possible to develop a more critical curriculum in art and design without giving the subject more time?

Further reading

Jay, M. (1993) *Downcast Eyes: The Denigration of Vision in Twentieth Century French Thought*, Berkeley, CA: University of California Press.

Kress, G. and van Leeuwen, T. (2001) *Multimodal Discourse: The Modes and Media of Contemporary Communication*, London: Arnold.

Rose, G. (2001) *Visual Methodologies*, London: Sage.

13 Measuring artistic performance

The assessment debate and art education

David Hulks

Background to the present situation

In the 1980s there was in the UK a broad movement of disenchanted arts educationalists who argued against the idea that artistic performance could or should be accurately assessed. To Ross (1986: 83–93) and his 'radical modernist' sympathisers, the Thatcher government's introduction of successive education reform bills signalled a new oppressive era of public service accountability to which they could not subscribe. The reforms, it was argued, were not about addressing social needs, but rather about the centralisation of power. Assessment, the basis of educational reform, was therefore seen as a dangerous development. The introduction of new assessment regimes into secondary education seemed to signal the end of aesthetic freedoms and so represented an assault on individuality. As a consequence, many an art room in the 1980s developed a fortress mentality. Behind the battlements, the art department became a sanctified space, modelled not so much on the traditional classroom but rather on the artist's studio. Here the right to individual experimentation was more or less enshrined. The essence of post-war modernist art education had been its exhortation to explore the 'formal elements' of art, a conformist prescription. But now it was argued that the purpose of acquiring a basic 'visual vocabulary' was to develop personal freedoms, to be able to depart or conform according to individual will (Clement 1986). In this intensely serious yet also playful oasis of creative free-play, students and teachers were supposed to be unconstrained by society's conventions and were encouraged to develop a discipline so complex and colourful that no attempt to capture it could ever do the subject justice. So Ross's proposal to seal off the studio-based art room must have seemed to many quite a reasonable proposition. Art would continue to enjoy a place at the heart of the curriculum, but students would be protected from the ravages of assessment in an inner sanctum of joyful, artistic production.

As it turned out, the fears about assessment were to some extent justified because the assessment regime had become over-burdensome, this proved off-putting for those caught up in the red tape. It was not only in art and design that deep reservations were expressed. But the politics of resistance were more pronounced, making art departments defensive and uncooperative. Inevitably, the serious weakening of the subject was as much self-imposed as externally inflicted. Ross felt to secure a special place at the heart of the curriculum the arts would need to be hermetically protected. In practice, however, it meant consigning them to the sidelines. Not that the Whitehall bureaucrats nor the curriculum reformers who had in mind an assault upon the arts any more than they were attempting to attack any other subject. The official refrain was that the arts, like the other subjects, would need to conform to assessment imperatives; no one could be allowed to escape accountability, so the argument that the arts should be exempted either was seen as non-viable or was simply not listened to at all. The attempt to resist the introduction of rigorous assessment consequently had a largely counter-productive effect: art and design departments were perceived to be uncooperative, design was split off and moved to technology which had, in contrast, emerged from its former backwardness. On the performance side, dance was removed to physical education, which fragmented the expressive arts curriculum even more. Inevitably, art became even more convinced of its own special but beleaguered position.

At the same time other art educationalists declared themselves opposed to modernist views (Abbs 1996). Many advocated a more critical approach to the teaching of art, and questioned the dominance of practical work (Field 1970; Taylor 1986). The new approach to art teaching tentatively invited more methodical assessment techniques; especially when it came to learning about art and its traditions. This might have led to a complete overhaul of the subject: both dismantling the dominance of intuitive, experimental, practical modes and introducing an academic core. Art and design might have been renamed art and design studies to reflect a greater balance between the practical and theoretical aspects (Allison 1981). Most, however, did not want to diminish the practical mode, which after all was the most enjoyable aspect for students and teachers. It was argued that, in an ever-tightening curriculum, time off from making would mean never getting anything done. Instead, ways had to be found to include a critical studies component without reducing time for practical activities.

The result was a critical studies programme that seemed to represent a significant step in the direction of creating a more rational and therefore more assessable art programme. But it was a programme that lacked any clear will to change; instead of introducing a new taught programme, in practice, critical studies resources were simply used for added visual stimulus (Taylor 1986; a practice subsequently problematised in Thistlewood 1989). Rather than showing how the powerful combination of teaching and assessing might provide a much better understanding of art even if less art would be made, instead art advisers proposed a range of 'practical activities' whereby learning about art and learning how to make art were supposed magically to merge. The idea that art represents an essentially mysterious field of human endeavour, one that cannot be measured, was consequently left unchallenged, as was the idea that 'high art' is too complex for children to understand. Many in art education still believe that their subject somehow defies analysis, that aesthetic knowledge can hardly be taught, let alone assessed.

Falling into line

It is important to acknowledge both the objections and the failures of will. But not all art educators since the 1970s have dragged their heels in the face of the new reforms. When the literature on this issue is surveyed more evenly, constructive contributions to the development of modern notions of assessment and art are evident. Despite expressing their reluctance to grasp the assessment nettle, most art advisers, even in the 1980s, recognised that new modes of art learning were on the horizon and advised teachers not to run to the barricades but rather to cope. Those who encouraged an unofficial policy of resistance appear now rather extremist compared to their more reasonable colleagues. Those who feared the introduction of rigorous assessment based their concerns on the idea that creativity is almost bound to be reduced or confined with the introduction of an assessment mentality. But enough water has now passed under the bridge to demonstrate that by introducing rigorous assessment systems into the art classroom creativity is not inevitably reduced. In practice the effect is negligible. And on some occasions, if handled carefully, assessment can provide a helpful stimulus and produce a richer experience. The determining factors include fairness, relevance and how sensitively systems are introduced. So, the challenge is to find an assessment regime that actually encourages aesthetic sophistication one producing results that are artistically more satisfying.

Among the strongly defensive group of art educationalists that emerged in the 1980s, Allison stood out as someone willing to admit that the intelligent application of assessment mechanisms was perfectly feasible, even in art and design. In his pragmatic contribution to the assessment debate Allison recognised that assessment was not in itself oppressive or even unhelpful, and that effective assessment systems were in fact quite easy to devise (in Ross 1986). A more sanguine and constructive argument was made by John Steers, who spoke on behalf of the National Society for Education in Art and Design. The NSEAD's influence changed the level of debate and created a powerful lobby group; the challenge had now become how to opt in, not how to opt out. The real danger, according to this view, was not that art teachers would be subjected to assessment systems that they could not live with, rather it was that they would fail to contribute to the debate about what should be used and how it should be applied. Allison's more pragmatic approach was not, however, without its false assumptions. He was wrong, for example, to assume that technologies of assessment were readily available, and too eager to work solely on the basis of crude 'performance objectives'. In fact, the science of assessment systems was at the time hopelessly underdeveloped; although many of the teething problems have been ironed out, how to assess the arts is still very much up for grabs. The realists perhaps underestimated the extent to which their colleagues would need to reassess what they were doing in order to make their contributions meaningful. The truth was that although in some areas of educational practice art teachers could be said to have developed advanced teaching strategies (group work, for example), when it came to assessment strategies they had very little purchase on what it was that was required.

This was to become acutely obvious with the arrival in 1993 of general national vocational qualifications (GNVQs). It was the introduction of the vocational curriculum that brought modern systems of assessment to the top of the educational agenda. While traditionalists and philosophers were arguing that the very essence of art would be threatened by the introduction of vocational subjects, a number of art departments showed that they welcomed the new range of courses. Largely this was about gaining position. The new vocational qualifications greatly expanded the range of provision, and students embarked upon courses of art study that finally had enough hours included in them to incorporate 'historical and contextual studies' in line with the critical studies advice. What GNVQ also brought along was a new, rigorous scheme of continuous assessment that had been developed primarily for learning in the workplace. In schools and colleges it proved an awkward and hopelessly idealistic system. It was unrealistic to expect that external assessment could be almost totally done away with, a fact that has now been recognised and the system amended. It was the complexity of the system that caused so many problems. The assumption is often that assessment systems need to be highly detailed in order to capture every nuance on the student's 'learning curve'. But in practice such systems prove unmanageable, especially within school and college settings. So GNVQ was soon seen as over-burdensome both for the staff who tried to administer it and the students who were suddenly asked to track their own progress with little support and little obvious benefit. Because of this, the argument that assessment was anathema to the arts received an unwelcome boost.

However, creativity was not reined in by vocational assessment. Despite the alarmingly high drop-out rates, GNVQ art students *did* progress to university, and were often able to skip the foundation year, unlike their A level colleagues. Exhibitions of GNVQ students' work often demonstrated that far from stifling their imagination, they were still able to express themselves imaginatively within the assessment framework, while at the same time building realistic careers. But perhaps the most useful thing to come out of the GNVQ experiment was the introduction of self-assessment, which invited students to improve their own learning and levels of performance. However, when introduced in the form of self-monitoring tracking sheets, the process proved detrimental since it encouraged a tick-list mentality misrepresenting the more complex mechanisms used to acquire knowledge. Nonetheless, it can be seen as common sense to transfer some of the responsibility for learning onto the student; if done sensibly, self-monitoring can be a spur to active engagement in the process of learning. It is not so much the administration of paperwork that is burdensome, because this can be reduced by a process of streamlining. Rather, the effort arises as the benign effect of self-monitoring itself which, if really taken on board by students, foregrounds their needs in such a way that the teacher has to be increasingly flexible and responsive. If student feedback is taken seriously, teachers will have to become far clearer about what it is they are trying to convey responding to the real needs of students rather than following predetermined or ideological imperatives.

Perhaps a good example of the extra-educational rigour and responsiveness that self-monitoring can stimulate can be found in the area of adult and continuing education (ACE). ACE advisers who, unlike school teachers, have to 'follow the market', have for some years been trying to tighten the fit between 'desirable learning outcomes' (what it is envisaged students will be able to do on completion of the unit) and the 'assessment criteria' used to determine each student's final level of performance (what students actually *can* do at the end of the unit). Self-motivated adults, it is argued, require a 'Plain English' set of 'learning goals' accompanied by a detailed yet straightforward record of attainment that they can use for the purpose of advancing their careers. The Holy Grail for this kind of work is the idea that the myriad of current qualifications might one day coalesce into one qualification that will measure more clearly and accurately the level of ability that has been attained, whatever the subject. Working towards this distant dream, regional providers and local authorities in England have developed credit accumulation transfer systems (CATS) which conceive of completed units of training as conceptual building blocks. There are now parallel organisations throughout the UK; further afield there is a European credit transfer system (ECTS) and similar systems in New Zealand (NZNQF) and South Africa (SAQA). The advantage of assessment following the student is that transferable skills are easier to identify and so do not have to be expensively relearnt. A spin-off bonus of CATS is that educational credit is more easily summarised, so that an individual's educational history can be described graphically as an overall profile reflecting the learning that has been completed and the achievement to date. CATS might suggest a brave new world where educational assessment is closely linked to employment. In such a world, employers would no longer need to ask for an applicant's *curriculum vitae* but instead could look up the individual's profile on a national educational achievement database before they decide to interview. If this is indeed what CATS implies, then it is a glimpse of an even more accountable future than Ross and others could have imagined. CATS, in other words, would be a gift to bureaucratic government and oppressive state control, a fact that has not yet been admitted in the eagerness of the drive towards greater efficiency and better customer focus. One of the reasons why fears about CATS have not been raised before now is that it has proved practically impossible even to coordinate CATS nationwide, let alone link it to employers. At present CATS works only locally, and even then is far from systematically applied.

Sinister though such a development might sound, much of the work that has gone into devising a national format for adult education has had undeniably beneficial effects. Unit design has focused many people's minds on what it is exactly that is being taught and how it might be assessed in each subject area. Teacher-assessors, in collaboration with their peers, have been able to agree assessment regimes sophisticated enough to capture the essence and substance of the subject content, yet expressed with such clarity that their students can at last understand what it is they are being asked to learn and how exactly they should go about learning it. With such systems, students have not only been able to understand what is being asked of them, but also collaborated in assessing their own work, gaining a better understanding of their progress and how to improve their performance. The enormous amount of new research on the impact of students' 'learning experience' in connection with retention is the outcome of this kind of work. It suggests that the focus has shifted from summative assessment, like those produced by examination boards, to ongoing assessment devised by teachers, which in future is bound to be increasingly standardised so as to provide an early warning system for those about to fail.

The introduction of the vocational curriculum at secondary level has produced similar arguments in favour of increasingly standardising the whole school curriculum. The positive aspects of the GNVQ experiment may be more difficult to demonstrate and the negative memories more difficult to erase, but the extra rigour that programmes of continuous assessment have introduced have put such pressure on the academic programme that the traditional academic route has had to be revised so that there is now theoretical parity between the two routes. Hence the GCE A Level has been divided into units of assessment much like the GNVQ, and the GNVQ has been renamed the Vocational A level (AVCE). It has also been given an A–E grading scheme to replace its former system of pass, merit or distinction.

The tick-list mentality is gradually being eroded. More pragmatic assessment systems are being developed that aim to place students in control of their own learning. They are increasingly involved in devising their own learning goals identified at the all-important initial assessment phase and then monitored closely throughout the course of study. Even in the pastoral curriculum, personal tutors, after some initial scepticism, are now finding it quite useful to work with the aid of numerical feedback systems, seeing that such measurement does not do away with one-to-one counselling but rather encourages it. The major discovery has been the simple fact that students (and the parents of school-age students) need to have clear and regular feedback at every stage of their course if they are to do well in their subjects. Verbal feedback will no longer do; hard, numerical data are what is required (Spours and Hodgson 1997, 1999). The teacher's traditional mark record, therefore, has been opened up for scrutiny to become a public document and part and parcel of the process of lesson plan-and-review. If assessments are fair and accurate, the mark record, renamed the monitoring student achievement booklet, will reveal patterns of achievement that are much easier to interpret than marks out of ten accompanied by comments.

Foreseeable futures

What has been introduced so far is clearly only the tip of a very large iceberg. The dream that has arisen is that the extra sophistication produced by the new assessment systems might allow managers of schools and colleges to do their jobs better and so produce more commendable results. Curriculum managers may in future be able to spot non- or low-achievers early enough to help them back on course with their studies before it is too late, and so improve retention and completion. At a more senior level, the data produced by assessment might enable head teachers and principals to gain a better grasp of the real issues that are facing the students in their care, rather than waiting until the end of the year to see the effectiveness of their policies. Further up the chain of command, education authorities and the politicians who direct them insist that they should be able to set performance targets for institutions and then easily assess whether these are being achieved, and take immediate action if they are not. While, at the sharp end, parents, and even the students themselves, may in future be able to understand the progress they are making and so make better decisions about what to do next. Whether or not these dreams are realistic they are being implemented, and art and design will not be allowed to withdraw from what has now become a national effort.

The worry must be that there will be a backlash. There is plenty of material to encourage another wave of resistance from those who claim to speak for the arts and who will argue for art and design teachers to 'take a stand'. The tightening up of the curriculum and unifying effect described above is surely precisely what Ross (1986) warned might occur. Should the arts stand up for the voice of the non-conformist and advocate a sense of rebellion? Isn't this what art is all about? Many will think so. But they should pause to consider the detrimental effects that such an argument is bound to cause. Perpetuating the politics of resistance would be damaging, not only to the position of the remaining subjects within the expressive arts curriculum, but also to the students who would undoubtedly suffer if teachers continue to give them only vague or derisory feedback. By derisory, I mean the use of brief comments or ticks based on unstated and only intuitively understood assessment criteria. Such practices are still widespread, particularly in the marking of sketchbooks. In future students may well become sophisticated enough managers of their own learning and performance to realise exactly what they are entitled to; better assessment inevitably leads to more purposeful tuition and so to better results. It is difficult to counter this argument, since, by and large, greater rigour produces more impressive results. However, in the present audit culture, and notwithstanding advances in continuous assessment, end-of-course results will continue to matter most.

Opting out these days is simply not an option. But for those who still want art and design to symbolise individuality or to elevate 'the right to fail', there may yet emerge some surprising avenues of hope. If assessment is embedded and implemented intelligently, which is by no means guaranteed unless there is an investment in training, there are grounds for believing that creativity might not be squashed in the new assessment-led curriculum. Instead creativity, albeit a different kind of creativity, might become rife. This view would see that diversity, rather than conformity, is likely to be the defining characteristic of the new assessment-led curriculum. More sophisticated assessment, for example, holds out the possibility for fast-track learning whereby students are not confined to a certain level simply because of their age or location. This may well prove a headache to administer, but it may also get people thinking about how to break down the traditional boundaries of the existing curriculum. The new thinking on assessment suggests the possibility of new modes of learning, and particularly encourages the exploitation of information and communication technologies. Within interactive learning environments, new conceptions of what it will mean to be creative and to make art might emerge. Digital communications technologies are unlikely to dampen creative potential but rather are likely to encourage a greater appetite not only for art-making but also for learning *about* art, which was one of the original aims of the critical studies approach but only ever partially achieved. There are still very few opportunities for truly critical discussions within the strongly process-oriented art rooms, and because of this, the end-of-key-stage attainment targets, with respect to these aspects of the Art and design Order, are hardly being met. The extent to which the attainment targets stated in the National Curriculum Orders (DfEE 1999b) require a sophisticated level of critical ability is remarkable. I refer to the expectations for pupils above the age of 7. The minimum expectation is that students can 'comment on differences in others' work, and suggest ways of improving their own'. At the age of 11, however, they should already be able to 'compare and comment on ideas, methods and approaches used in their own and others' work, relating these to the context in which the work was made' (DfEE 1999b: 38–9). It was precisely this that Brandon Taylor, in his sceptical paper 'Art History in the Classroom: A Plea for Caution', objected to. He claimed that children cannot do critical work because they lack maturity, even at secondary-school age (quoted in Thistlewood 1989: 100–12). Whether or not he was right about this, the existence of unrealistic National Curriculum standards undermines the idea that there is currently any systematic assessment of students' critical abilities in schools.

Is there really, then, anything to fear from assessment? Certainly there is. The real danger is that assessment can become burdensome in the extreme. This in itself can cause enormous damage as has been shown time and again in many a pilot and in the bulldozing through of educational reform. The answer, however, is not to bury one's head in one's hands, but rather to insist upon systems that really work; to accept only those systems that clearly benefit students and to jettison others. The best assessment systems are the simple and transparent ones, based on pre-existing, sound educational principles and common-sense practice. On the question of assessment feedback, students generally want to know the bottom line rather than the detail. If the feedback they get rings true they will trust the judgements that are being made and trust the teacher, which can only benefit their ability to engage with the subject. Assessment is, then, in many ways, a false enemy. The introduction of assessment should not indicate the end of traditional values, but rather should allow greater efficiency in disseminating and developing artistic ideas. Students of course will always have the option to accept or reject what it is they are being taught, and assessment transparency should make them better able to do so. Assessment should be considered the starting point for further reflection. In order to self-assess, most students need to be given, as often as possible, a general measure of whether their current work is excellent, good, adequate, less than adequate or unacceptable, in other words a score on something like a one-to-five scale. This is simple enough to do and not half as crude as is often imagined. Simple assessment systems allow students to be told clearly how they are doing and how to improve, none of which is new. What will change is the way lessons will be based far more precisely upon identified needs and in response to much more accurate guidelines. None of this needs to be particularly onerous, yet it should generate plentiful, accurate and rich data suitable for curriculum reporting and, more importantly, for curriculum planning.

Art teachers resist these changes at their peril, but they should not lose their critical view. Instead of arguing against the encroaching shadow of assessment, they should look out for impositions and evaluate them on a case-by-case basis. A cynical attitude is self-defeating. Instead teachers and arts specialists should contribute their expertise to the debates. Specifically, they should be able to advise on how it is possible to work within strict limitations yet produce surprisingly fertile and innovative solutions. The point is not made often enough that the creative response usually thrives on constraint; it is how you work your way out of the box, not the box itself that is important. It should be clear by now that, in the new millennium, holding on to traditional craft-based notions of what it means to make art, or holding on to insular ideas about the nature of art as a place of retreat, will only cause the subject to become even more marginalised and art and design students to become increasingly disenfranchised from mainstream learning. Quentin Blake's crude statement that 'art and design is not just a subject to learn' (DfEE 1999b: 14) should not discourage art teachers from defining and assessing the learning that takes place so as to give it parity with other curriculum subjects; art and design needs to move away from the idea that it is only about play and that it feeds only nebulous ideas into the rest of the curriculum. Too much credence is given to the idea that art education works by some mysterious process of osmosis, which is why art and design is so often perceived merely as an enrichment. Art and design needs to grow up. It needs to look at its own specificities, at exactly what it wants to teach. Working on assessment systems is one way it can do this, and should be its first priority. Teachers should also be able to state more clearly that art and design is a subject to learn. They should not only be engaged in putting on colourful exhibitions of students' work, but also have at their fingertips the data to show students' achievement, exactly what has been learnt. The extent to which art and design specialists are able and willing to do this will determine whether the subject survives.

Questions for discussion

1   To what extent did the 'Against Assessment' view in the 1980s have real influence in schools?
2   How has Curriculum 2000 refocused the assessment debate?
3   How will ICT alter the way we think about the assessment of learning and the creative responses?

Further reading

Ross, M. (ed.) (1986) *Assessment in Arts Education: A Necessary Discipline or a Loss of Happiness?* Oxford: Pergamon.
Spours, K. and Hodgson, A. (1999) *New Labour's New Educational Agenda Issues and Policies for Education and Training from 14+*, London: Kogan Page.
Thistlewood, D. (ed.) (1989) *Critical Studies in Art and Design Education*, London: Longman.

The principle of collaboration

14 Temporary residencies

Student interventions in the gallery

Kate Schofield

The increasing trend towards collaboration between practising artists and museum curators has in some cases involved the rehanging of existing collections or redesigning gallery spaces. In this way the probing instinct of the creative mind counterbalances the sense of permanence and order associated with the museum in a constructive dialogue involving elements of the past, present and future.

(Putnam 2001: book jacket)

Background

When James Putnam curated an 'intervention' with the work of Sophie Calle at the Freud Museum, London in 1999, the idea of a student intervention project was crystallised. I had previously seen 'The Time Machine' (1994–5) at the British Museum, another of Putnam's inspired exhibitions and I knew of the ground-breaking interventions made by Fred Wilson. Normally these artists' interventions are set up through liaison with a particular museum, an artist or artists and a curator, but as far as I knew no one had arranged such a museum installation or intervention involving art and design PGCE students. Although the fifteen students in my tutor group were all regular gallery and museum goers, few had knowledge of 'interventions'.

Manipulating the museum: interventions by artists

An intervention by an artist is a way of creating and placing work in a gallery or museum that responds to both the collection and the location. In making such site-specific work the audience is necessarily implicated; responses can be hostile, pleasurable, or the intervention may induce a sense of discomfort (see p. 147). Such self-conscious installations set up an immediate dialogue between the artefacts already *in situ*. Host spaces are disrupted by the visitor and can give radically new meanings to the collection. A good example is the work done in the USA by Fred Wilson. Wilson shook the museum world when he reinstalled items from the Maryland Historical Society's collection in such a way that the public had to reconsider the collection's significance. The intervention was entitled 'Mining the

Museum' (1992) and brilliantly brought out how African Americans had been treated, mistreated and ignored:

> People expected to see the society's rich holdings of silver on display, but it was startling to see silver made for 19th-century Maryland households next to iron slave shackles. The juxtaposition forced you to confront the fact that many of the wealthy white Marylanders who owned the silver also owned the African-American slaves who polished it.
>
> (Guilliano 2001: 1)

Like many other artists who make interventional work Wilson poses the question:

> Is our reliance on seeing making us blind to other ways of understanding ourselves, our cultures and those of others? Could the way we see and the studied act of looking be only a partial view; a beautiful, tantalising, satisfying view, perhaps, but very narrowly defined?
>
> (quoted in McShine 1999: 158)

Sometimes artists, such as Wilson and Sophie Calle, work as curators, bringing already existing artefacts to an established exhibition, whilst others such as Andy Goldsworthy, Daniel Buren and Gillian Wearing, create work for a specific site. The PGCE students had to respond to and make work for the Soane Museum following these ideas. What follows is the rationale for this project, a new way of working for PGCE students.

The Sir John Soane Museum, London

> The charm of the Soane Museum is that the spirit of Sir John Soane still hovers over it . . . It is a personal collection. You feel you are calling on someone who will be down directly . . . As you step out into the well mannered calm of Lincoln's Inn Fields, you feel inclined to say to the retainer: 'Thank you very much. Please tell Sir John I am sorry he was out'.
>
> (Betjeman 1934: 29)

Considered by many to be one of the lesser known and 'secret' museums of London, this house/museum is a unique one-man collection. Soane (1753–1837) is famous for being the greatest architect of his day, designing among others the Bank of England and Dulwich Picture Gallery. He bought two houses, Nos 12 and 13 Lincoln's Inn Fields, using them not only as a home but also as a setting for his antiquities and works of art. After his wife's death in 1815 he lived alone, constantly adding to and rearranging his collections. In 1823 he purchased and rebuilt No. 14, not only as a letting proposition but also to extend the physical space of his museum. The facades of these three houses form a symmetrical composition facing Lincoln's Inn Fields and ostensibly seem domestic in appearance.

However, what confronts the visitor on entering the house/museum is a most eclectic collection of artefacts, all of which were acquired or bought by Soane. The museum is a veritable time warp; since Soane's death in 1837 nothing has been altered. In fact in 1833 he established the house as a museum open to the public by means of an Act of Parliament, ensuring that it be left 'as nearly as possible in the state in which he shall leave it'. Soane was a great teacher of architecture at the Royal Academy and mindful of what could be learned from collections as resources. Students were welcome in his house where they made visual aids for his lectures. Soane himself called his collection an 'Academy of Architecture' and as such saw it as a place for teaching and learning which made the idea for this project particularly meaningful for beginning teachers of art and design.

The Soane Project

The project was arranged for October 1999 to coincide with the major retrospective of Soane at the Royal Academy of Arts. Fifteen PGCE students were asked to make practical art work in response to the Sir John Soane Museum as an 'intervention' to his 'frozen' collection of art and artefacts. On completion, their work was to be placed in and among the collections in locations the students would select. The Soane Museum gave them *carte blanche* with free access to all rooms, spaces and artefacts with the proviso that no object could be altered or moved. I was mindful of Bloom's comment: 'Quite distinct from the motives of the public museum are those psychological imperatives that drive the private collector's almost fetishistic desire to assemble, organise, touch and cohabit with objects' (Bloom 1999: 81); indeed Soane's idiosyncratic collection did prove a rich source for mining.

Here is a museum that was and remains a one-man idea, crammed full of artefacts, painting and sculpture including casts, vases, tombs, glass, marble fragments, clocks, cork models, mirrors all placed *touche-touche*, ostensibly with no narrative and which presents a non-didactic approach to display. Within the museum the accumulation of artefacts is compelling although there seems to be no hierarchy, no immediately obvious order or taxonomy, no sequence of approach for the visitor and the labelling is almost non-existent. It might be said to speak with the authority of a past survivor. Two opposing critiques needed to be highlighted. On the one hand Heumann Gurian states:

> Old fundamentals of museums-collections, preservation, contemplation and excellence and the methods represented by these values, should not be discarded in our enthusiasm for the new and the next.
>
> (Heumann Gurian 1999: 35)

On the other hand, revisionist thinking within a postmodernist arena suggests that spectators revisit such modes of display and the ethics of collecting, questioning the deracination of artefacts from their 'proper' contexts. Certainly, today one can question the imperialistic approach of Soane's Grand Tour, his requisitioning and purchasing of classical antiquities, paintings and relics. But the Soane is a museum that, because of its remit, had not taken on the burden of trying to reinterpret its display to reflect a modern re-examination of its histories, this intervention was one such re-examination, which in my opinion makes it rather special and quite refreshing. Students for their part were asked to examine critically how the artefacts were displayed and what messages this communicated.

The aims of the project were to:

- Study the Soane Museum, the collection of artefacts and their contexts.
- Consider an issue or idea raised by the museum.
- Respond by installing an 'intervention'.

The Curator of Education encouraged students to question whose history was being told, and how visual and textual devices revealed Soane's unconscious agenda and the supposed neutrality of visitors to the museum. They were reminded of Vergo's statement that:

> Every juxtaposition or arrangement of an object . . . means placing a certain construction upon history, be it the history of distant or recent past. There is a subtext comprising innumerable diverse, often contradictory strands.
>
> (Vergo 1989: 2–3)

Back in their studios students discussed what they had seen and began to formalise ideas and consider what issue or aspect of the collection they wished to investigate. They had ten days to design, make and install the work in the museum.

Taking up residency

Students quickly established a focus for their work. Because of the urgency of the task, there was little time to procrastinate. After group discussion, some revisited the museum whilst others felt they needed to read about Soane and his ideas; Richardson's and Stevens' (1999) catalogue proved a valuable academic text. Others sought books on gallery and museum education where methods of collecting and display are discussed. As students were completing their pieces ready for exhibition they were invited to talk to a video recorder about their ideas and feelings:

> I found my visit [to the Museum] to be somewhat unsettling. The chaotic way in which the vast collection of objects is displayed throughout made my viewing seem intrusive and uncomfortable . . . there was little that interested me. However, in the breakfast room I noticed an empty glass cabinet. I discovered that originally it contained Napoleon's pistol but it was stolen in the 1960s. This pistol is the only item to have left the Museum since its opening and because of its disappearance has become of great interest to me. Using only collected objects of my own, I am attempting to make a replacement.
>
> (Student interview 2001)

One student's newly constructed 'pistol' was placed in the empty glass vitrine and had an intriguing resonance, being roughly the same shape and size as the original. Only modern scrap materials such as off-cuts of wood and copper piping were used to make a replica of what was an expensive armament acquired by Soane from a sale room some time after Napoleon's exile on Elba.

Three students found the Soane a very masculine domain and wanted to explore ideas about gender. Soane was married, but there is little evidence of his wife in the house.

> Mrs Eliza Soane seems to be conspicuous by her absence. Whilst her husband has sought to immortalise himself and his work in stone, Eliza's interests, dreams and fears remain opaque to us. I looked at her sketchy portrait and imagined the interior life contained within it; the story of her estranged sons, her patience and her silence.
>
> (Student interview 2001)

And:

> My thought came from the realisation that the whole style and feel of the house was inherently masculine, fashioned for a man, by a man. Where was Mrs Soane?
>
> (Student interview 2001)

Today's students are operating and teaching in a post-feminist arena but were very keen to engage with the feminist view that the subordinate position of women is neither natural nor inevitable, but socially constructed. These students' own art practice refers to their continuing struggle to reclaim their bodies whilst making comments on motherhood, censorship and exploitation. Their perception of the masculine Soane household became their vehicle to continue their exploration of ongoing ideas. One student made a memorial to Mrs Soane, an ethereal, text-based installation that hung over a tombstone in the crypt.

The breakfast room was the site chosen by another student, who celebrated traditional women's crafts by crocheting a rug which, with its bright, chemically dyed coloured yarns, looked strangely out of kilter when placed on the floor (Figure 14.1).

> I decided to make something Mrs Soane might have made since there is so much creative energy in the house but no evidence of anything that she might have done . . . The game is Twister, a modern game about spatial orientation . . . it is also a clumsy and boisterous game which is a reaction to my feeling that one needs to tread very carefully when you're there. It's a game that she could have made for the boys [her sons] to play.
>
> (Student interview 2001)

The unique spatial and atmospheric quality of the museum was another issue with fascinated many in the group.

Figure 14.1 Mrs Soane plays Twister with her sons, Sir John Soane Museum Interventions
         Project, PGCE student (Institute of Education, University of London).

There is an aura of unreality encapsulated in this house and it evokes a sense of
uneasiness . . . evidence of domesticity is everywhere . . . would Soane's house
be featured in *Hello* magazine today? I have always found those who seek public
exposure rather puzzling.

(Student interview 2001)

Notably others commented on and made work about nostalgic feelings evoked by
the Italian souvenirs that Soane brought back from his Grand Tour. They probably
evoked for him personal or collective memories and emotions. These associations
may have been projected onto the objects, but equally the objects themselves
possess a history.

The snowstorm subverts Soane's impeccable taste whilst referencing the
classical. My piece represents the Temple at Tivoli, purchased from a street
vendor and kept in the Museum ever since.

(Student interview 2001)

This student created a trashy, contemporary souvenir that was supposed to subvert the idea of Soane's rather more beautiful pieces, which no doubt strongly reminded him of Italy.

All students related to the project in an engaged and highly focused way. All produced work of a high technical standard and in many cases their ideas were pushed to new levels. The word 'learning' comes with a great deal of baggage but if it is to be believed that the consolidation of knowledge, and the layering of meaning through making new connections are important, then this project proved effective. Students learn in settings that are both physical and psychological constructs and this museum was in my view a stimulating context. As Falk and Dierking (1992: 100) insist, 'The light, the ambience, the 'feel' and even the smell of an environment [museum] influence learning'. Students attempted to remove artificial barriers by intervening within the collection creating fictional narratives and instigating a dialogue between old and new. In the act of doing this they actively considered how the museum space might be transformed into an arena for ongoing debate.

In conclusion this résumé does no more than to lay out a model for future work. I believe that this idea could be deployed by PGCE students in other contexts, in different museums and with any age group. The immediacy and power generated by doing this work was palpable. The museum too was affected by their interventions, which I have coined 'the temporary residents'. These interventions had an effect on the static artefacts that curators had for years taken for granted. At the end of the project Christopher Woodward, Curator of Education at the museum remarked:

> It was one of the most rewarding educational projects we have done here and completely refreshed my own enthusiasm for the Museum . . . [the responses] made me see objects I had never noticed before.

Questions for discussion

1   What might be the key questions to ask when contemplating making work as an intervention for a museum collection?
2   What types of learning might be taking place during an interventional project such as the one described in the chapter and what method/s would you employ for evaluation?

Further reading

Corrin, L. (1994) 'Artists Look at Museums', in F. Wilson (ed.) *Mining the Museum: An Installation*, Baltimore, MD: Contemporary and New York: New Press.
Hein, G. (1998) *Learning in the Museum*, London: Routledge.

15 Creative partnerships or more of the same?

Moving beyond 'it reminds me of . . .'

Neil Hall and Pam Meecham

The current impulse by government and its quangos to engineer creative partnerships across formal education and the museum sector should give us pause for thought. Galleries and museums do seem to hold out the prospect of a complementary location for teaching interdisciplinary studies and may offer the art teacher much needed contact with gallery professionals and original art works. Many subjects, so the theory goes, could benefit from integration with the visual arts. The integration of other subjects into the gallery or museums, however, is fraught with contradictions and paradoxes, not least the conflicts aroused by government enthusiasm for measurable accountability, access and inclusion. The initial impetus for many cross-curricular partnerships stems from government concerns about educational standards rather than an enthusiasm for an inter-disciplinary approach to education. All too often, it is not the breaking down of subject chauvinism that is on the agenda but the prospect of improved numeracy and literacy scores.

At present it is the burden of galleries and museums to be coerced into the utopian promise of enlightenment through Arts for Everyone initiatives, although in reality *everyone* seems to be those designated 'disadvantaged'. Museums as agents with responsibility for social inclusion, beyond the paternalism of an earlier age, is a relatively new idea. What this means in practice has been highlighted in literature that explores these ideas at some length (DCMS 2001; Group for Large Local Authority Museums (GLLAM) 2000; Newman and McLean 2000; Scottish Museums Council 2000; Allen 2002). Galleries and museums are required to answer new questions in return for public funding. Lottery monies and government support require both the rejection of entry fees and the recognition of the need for accountability in order to secure public usage, broad social inclusion and education initiatives. These institutions can no longer maintain existing barriers to public access, those exclusive barriers that reinforce their positions as the custodians of high culture, as centres largely for the middle classes, as collectors' playgrounds, for connoisseurship, or as cultural capital for the moneyed, well-intentioned but uncritical classes. However, the rhetoric behind creative partnership initiatives must be called into question.

While galleries and museums are involved with questions related to their func-tion and direction, educators also need to engage in this debate. Some members of the museum and galleries community are likely to wish that many of the initiatives would go away. However, others still insist that they have little to contribute to broader social roles and that their education services exist to dispense knowledge about their special holdings to an unknowing, uncritical and compliant audience. Nonetheless, in the early 1990s some institutions bypassed this position, exemplary practices issuing from Tate Liverpool and the Whitechapel in London. A return to a less accountable age remains little more than wishful thinking: funding expectations dictate that there will not be a return to an age where education departments were the province of the well-meaning amateur. If government policy and financial largesse indicate that galleries and museums are to become more inclusive, in consequence, they need partners from the traditional educational community, and especially from schools. As the gallery and museum sector court partnerships with schools, it is timely to ask what schools can expect from these institutions. Indeed, crucially for this chapter, we want to question the government drive to deliver the core subjects in the art gallery and museum.

There is nothing new in an educational remit for galleries and museums. Monolithic museums such as Henry Cole's Victoria and Albert had education at its core and the Geffrye Museum in London's East End was set up explicitly to improve the knowledge and skills of local furniture manufacturers. However, co-option of the art gallery into partnerships under the guise of 'social inclusion' is burdened by a overly patronising certainty that everyone wants to be included in one community and crucially that the arts can successfully accommodate all ventures. A brief incursion into the report world uncovers awesome aspirations for the arts. Although the social benefits of the arts have been central to public funding, debates since the inception of the Arts Council of England in 1945 and the current rash of official reports bearing the words *gallery* or *museum*, bear testament to an increasing awareness of the possibility of using them as a panacea to sort out the social and educational ills that conventional institutions and mainstream agencies have been unable to resolve. The continuous stream of reports since *A Common Wealth* (Anderson 1997) bear witness to an enthusiasm to harness galleries and museums for the national good. *All Our Futures* (NACCCE 1999), *Empowering the Learning Community* (Library and Information Commission 2000), *Libraries, Galleries, Museums and Archives for All* (DCMS 2001a) and *Culture and Creativity: The Next Ten Years* (DCMS 2001b) are all government initiatives to conscript the arts into a utopian project of social and educational reformation. Moreover, the outcome of PAT 10 of the Policy Action Teams set up by government in 1998 to look at so-called problem communities, identified art's potential as a panacea to:

- Creatively engage young people at risk from exclusion.
- Encourage creative activity in order to raise standards of literacy and numeracy.
- Prevent crime and support rehabilitation.
- Augment preventative medicine and combat declining standards in mental and physical health through health action zones.

Furthermore, Chris Smith (1998), while Minister for Culture, Media and Sport, saw the role of the arts as '"principal trainers of imagination" . . . as the greatest resource possessed by a nation . . . enabling higher levels of invention, economic advantage, scientific discovery, better administration, and more security' (Smith 1998: 133).

What government agencies have in their sights is important. According to Re:source (2001), the government quango with responsibility for museums, libraries and archives, in its consultation document *A Learning and Access Standard for Museums, Libraries and Archives,* its ambition for galleries and museums is to support lifelong learning, improve overall quality of life, increase the learning capacity and skills within communities, as well as combat social inclusion, stimulate economic regeneration and 'improve attainment levels in the formal sector' (Re:source 2001: 2; see also www.resource.gov.uk/reports/learnacc.html). The imperative to coax literacy, numeracy and science into the space of the art gallery raises many issues. Projects situated in the art gallery can be difficult to evaluate in relation to the distinct features of the disciplines that actively invite partnerships (or whose funding depends on it). Art collections are both distinct from, and complementary to, formal education but even in a period that sanctions multi-modalities, hasty fraternities are not without casualties: art has its own language.

What galleries, museums, their financial backers and their clients mean by inclusion and partnership is anything but certain; the terminology is fluid. However, it is undeniable that some actions are inclusive, for example, encouraging non-attending groups to participate in institutional activities. Similarly, a non-controversial example of partnership is the museum working with a local regeneration group in the community's plans for redevelopment and educational initiatives: Dodd and Sandell (2001) cite many such initiatives. However, the readiness of gallery educators and schools to participate in literacy and numeracy projects, for example, of the national collection at Tate Britain was highlighted in a three-year initiative (1999–2001) *Visual Paths to Literacy.* The project involved artists, writers, teachers and children from ten inner-city London primary schools and a Year 7 group from a comprehensive school. This is only one of many literacy and numeracy projects that cross the primary and secondary sector. What is at stake in these initiatives is the extent to which meaningful teaching can take place with art collections when practitioners often expert in their own fields of puppetry, story-telling and mathematics are working with collections that have their own histories and procedures and environments.

It would be easy to see this chapter as yet another voice raised in complaint against the diminishing role of art and design in the school curriculum and an attempt to maintain the distinct nature of the discipline and its objects of study. However, we are not making a plea for gatekeeping the fabled autonomy of the art museum: it starts from the premise that galleries are custodians of national collections without a mandate to dictate how the public might use them. It is our contention that attention to the *stuff* of art and an understanding of the rituals of western culture's embrace of reified artworks would enable more meaningful speculations *across an interdisciplinary* field to take place. The research conducted by the Institute of Education during the *Visual Paths to Literacy* project uncovered contradictions and ambiguities that are relevant to those who would take young people to the gallery for an 'educational experience'.

The research revealed that even those familiar with painting and sculpture often struggle to find a language with which to articulate their sense of an art work. It also revealed the importance of the viewer's prior knowledge in making meaning. For instance, pupils working on the National Numeracy Hour were quick to incorporate the language acquired from their most recent lessons onto the abstractions of a Fernand Léger painting. Although this approach was often accompanied by 'it reminds me of', it gave very young pupils a way into the art work from their own experience. Sensitive teaching in the gallery encouraged further exploration of the use of mathematical concepts frequently utilised by modern artists in the search for a formal vocabulary. It is here that some tensions exist. The pupils quickly incorporated what they knew into what they saw thus abandoning any notion of the reified art work, a process that is still considered heretical in some quarters (Institute of Ideas). We want to pursue this further.

Collaborations based on other forms of language, whether mathematical or literary, offer a challenge to the formalist orthodoxy of silent contemplation in the presence of the art object. Literacy projects such as *Visual Paths to Literacy* are heavily dependent on two principal strategies when working with original art works: the search for a 'poetic equivalent' of the image, a largely outmoded nineteenth-century practice, or the imposition of narrative readings onto art works which pay scant attention to artists' intentionality and modes of production. The relationship of narrative to modern art has a complex history. In brief practitioners of modern art rejected the narrative form, familiar in nineteenth-century genre painting and the epic novel, in favour of an emphasis on formalism; a concentration on the intrinsic properties of the medium that renders storytelling obsolete. In 'The Storyteller' (1936) Walter Benjamin (1970) objected to modernism's 'will to silence' and to the primacy of the visual over the literary. He argued that the 'eclipse of storytelling was the final destabilization of the social identity which existed in Europe for hundreds of years' (quoted in Wallis 1995: xii). For Benjamin, the story, especially in its epic form, was a mode of resistance to the formalist aspects of modernism. The story's power came through 'experience', artisan activity and craftsmanship in opposition to 'industrial technology' (Benjamin 1970: 91). We are not suggesting that *Visual Paths to Literacy* or related projects are an extension of a Benjaminian philosophy, but there is something to be gleaned from his observations. The young people working with art works as varied as Henry Moore's *Family Group* (1949) and Michael Craig-Martin's *Knowing* (1996) were encouraged to delve into their own experience and make stories from their imaginations; a practice that runs counter to both art historical and modernist procedures.

The embrace of postmodern theories into the critical practices of art history has enabled educators to admit other ways of knowing beyond the rational and ocular focused intellect: art works are now read within a climate of contingency with all meanings subject to inevitable revision. That is not to say that all meanings are equally valid or sustainable: it is possible to be very wrong about what a work might mean. The issue at stake here is the extent to which a non-art specialist is willing, knowingly or not, to adopt a position of 'productive fiction' in order to advance their particular subject needs. It is always worth reversing the question to ask what would be at stake if mathematics and English were to wilfully introduce art into their subjects in order to advance the art and design curriculum. As a part of a demythologising agenda, the new art historians initially adopted draconian procedures to readings invested in uncovering art's conditions of production, representing it within a socio-political structure. They did this because they were anxious to distance themselves from connoisseurial art appreciation which was usually typified as reactionary and representative of bourgeois values. They often undermined the reification of art works and the secularised quasi-religious ritual of the gallery visit. Through this rigorous methodology the sacred 'aura' of art works was declared bogus and the status accorded to the artist as genius was demystified. However, while not wishing to reinstate aura as a principal means of accessing work, a qualified use of aura can help create a distance that might give rise to speculation, exploration and, crucially, interpretation.

Contemporary theory has placed the viewer as a participant in the meaning making process (Bal and Bryson 1998). Having wrested that exclusive responsibility from the artist's vision, many possibilities are opened up as alternative frameworks for interpretation are sought. However, while applauding the possibility of interpretation it is here that the issue of partnership founders. Here art works become the subject of speculations that bare no relationship to their specific histories and rituals: we insist that such a collapse into relativism cannot be countenanced. The *Visual Paths to Literacy* research also revealed that those teachers who were the most effective in the gallery, were those who understood the historical and social production of art works, including the techniques and materials and conceptual strategies utilised by artists and curators. For instance, writers who were also illustrators were able to relate symbolism and metaphor to imagery in order to encourage deeper layers of reading art works and writing stories. The research also demonstrated that the *power of the image*, reinforced through close reading of the work at the level of form and content and the relationship between the two, was effective in supporting young people's writing.

We want to return to a point left hanging earlier: ritual. The project raised another issue that cuts across the grain of orthodoxy. Many of the research interviews conducted with participants – teachers, children and gallery educators – were punctuated with a quasi-mystical vocabulary from adult and child alike: 'something magical and spooky happens'. It would be easy to dismiss this with a nod in the direction of false consciousness, but the encounter with original art works accompanied by a popular writer (familiar to the children through books absorbed in the classroom) encouraged pupils and staff to see the experience as very special and to work accordingly. The ritual visit to the art gallery reproduces both a mythology of awe and wonder and the notion that the origin of art is magical and religious. This may be a productive fiction but the project demonstrated how young people's confidence in an alien and awesome space, such as both the London Tate galleries, could increase beyond induction into middle-class rites. The way children draw on knowledge gained from across the curriculum to make meaning in the gallery is therefore one way of opening up possibilities for learning. If this is coupled with a belief in the art work as 'a real thing' and 'a thing in itself', possessing a powerful presence both physical and metaphysical, then perhaps there are reasons to locate teaching within the gallery space.

Although the gallery offers the possibility of a complementary location for teaching across the curriculum it is important to recognise that it is not a neutral space and that a reliance on the mystical aspects of the visit needs to be tempered by another aspect of the research. It became clear that the most effective teaching and learning practices took place where the aims and objectives were made transparent to the learner and where links were carefully established between the gallery, art work and the classroom (reproductions for use became crucial in this respect). Art has its own language, a language that reveals other possibilities for being in the world, possibilities beyond the utilitarian, imaginative possibilities. Art works can also be used to develop a critical vocabulary, both visual and verbal, beyond the pragmatics of the literacy hour.

If we are to move beyond 'it reminds me of . . .' we reject the notion that one way of ensuring art experiences in a government controlled, closely inspected and crowded curriculum is to teach art and design through other subjects. Importantly, perhaps even sacrilegiously, we do not support the uncritical acceptance of mathematics and English as subjects to be valued above all others as somehow practical, essential, in some way capturing the very essence of western develop-ment; we challenge the preeminent position of numeracy and literacy. We do not accept this position as given, justified and unassailable. However, we do seek to justify art and design, in partnership with gallery education as a field of knowledge and practice in its own right, with a justified place in the curriculum. We argue here, that given the present political interference in schooling with its attendant curriculum, regulatory and inspection constraints, an effective way of presenting some aspects of art is through those concepts that art, mathematics and literature genuinely have in common. All too often cross-curricular projects set up with galleries to explore numeracy and literacy are unequal partnerships. While intent on maintaining the importance of their disciplines, projects motivated by a numeracy or literacy agenda pay scant attention to the historical materialism of art works in pursuit of justifying a trip to the gallery through improved standard assessment task scores. While this may be laudable, it is our contention that if little account is taken of what is special and often unique about an art work and its location in a gallery then an expensive educational opportunity is only of a secondary value. Meaningful relationships with other subjects, particularly where those subjects have never had their position at the apex of an educational hierarchy questioned, makes equal partnerships unstable. Collaborations require a level of research into the language, procedures and histories of art. Only then will the full potential of partnership be achieved in developing critical verbal, written and visual skills that will enhance learning across the curriculum. With a commitment to learning from the host discipline (in this case art) core subjects can abandon their traditional subject chauvinism and collaborate in a symbiotic relationship. A parasitic relationship will ensue if those charged with the delivery of core subjects in the gallery and museum sector assume working in the gallery is a one-way street.

There is one further consideration. Teachers have many skills that are undervalued, skills that are appropriate to learning in the gallery context. Many gallery education departments assume that artists as 'experts' are the most appropriate interpreters of artworks, and for some reason do not need training in teaching methods. However, it has been recognised that artists' training is just as important as that of teachers (Burgess 1995). It is evident that a symbiotic relationship will not develop until there is an end to the notion of teacher 'deficit', a notion still promoted by many art schools and galleries. Partnership also means questioning the assumptions behind the historical understanding of educational roles in schools, galleries and museums.

Acknowledgements

The authors would like to acknowledge the work of Dr Eileen Carnell and Kate Rabey as research officers working respectively on the Visual Paths and Young Cultural Creators Projects.

Questions for discussion

1   Consider the benefits to be gained from building 'creative partnerships' across interdisciplinary fields.
2   If we consider that community-based literacy learning can and should be delivered in the art gallery, what possibilities does this open up for the art teacher engaged in a critical practice?
3   Some well-known artists knowingly use mathematical concepts in the design and construction of their art works. By studying work by Rothko, Mondrian and Schwitters try to identify the mathematical principles they applied. Does this approach to understanding artwork open up the possibilities for interpretation?

Further reading

Dodd, J. and Sandell, R. (2001) *Including Museums: Perspectives on Museums, Galleries and Social Inclusion*, Leicester: Research Centre for Museum and Galleries, University of Leicester.

Milner, J. (1992) *Mondrian*, London: Phaidon Press. (This book provides a detailed account of the ways in which Mondrian used mathematics as the very foundation for his paintings.)

16 Challenging orthodoxies through partnership

PGCE students as agents of change

Nicholas Addison and Lesley Burgess

The most popular route to becoming a secondary school teacher in the UK is the postgraduate certificate in education, a model that relies on a partnership between schools and universities. Although this model is recognised as efficient and effective it brings together institutions in collaboration whose aims do not always converge. Often one side is accused of pragmatism while the other is denounced for its unrealism. Neither institution seems fully to appreciate the other and so simple oppositions may be set up and perpetuated through misunderstandings. When this arises student teachers are positioned uncomfortably in the middle and in order to survive they have to negotiate a pedagogical identity that acknowledges potential differences.

In art and design these differences are frequently most pronounced around the issue of a critical curriculum. University lecturers and art educators have criticised school practice for its insularity, disparagingly referring to it as 'school art' (Efland 1976; Taylor 1986). The difficulty they have with this phenomenon is its conservatism and populism so that, despite a rhetoric of creativity, it remains a hermetically sealed field of knowledge in which 'making' is privileged in a persistently self-referential way. This is in contrast to the programmes of study outlined in the National Curriculum and examination syllabuses which all include a historical and critical dimension (although they do not necessarily suggest the integrated model of critical study that we promote elsewhere: see Addison and Burgess 2000). Unlike most school art, students engaging in critical study have to recognise art as a differentiated instance of a wider phenomenon, that of visual and material culture. Here they will have to question both the hierarchisation of practice implicit in the fine art emphasis of the curriculum, and interrogate the modernist myths (however diluted) upon which school art is dependent. What critical study suggests is a reflexive process in which making and understanding, production and reception are held in a symbiotic relationship, a relationship that makes the construction of meaning possible. Such study enables teachers and pupils to make connections between activities in the classroom and the broader field of social and cultural practice; it allows them to make sense of what they do and why they are doing it; it allows for the possibility of critique.

The difficulties are exacerbated by a false dichotomy set up between the notion of a creative as opposed to a critical curriculum. Advocates of the former assume that subject knowledge in art and design is predicated exclusively on practical activity, what is usually called 'making'. In this instance emphasis is placed on the formal elements of art, in particular its visuality, not only is the discursive neglected but also the other senses are marginalised. This promotes a technical, skill-based programme at KS3 during which it is hoped pupils will attain some competence in the 'basics': line, tone, texture, colour, space, shape etc., before moving onto more exploratory activities at GCSE. This largely two-dimensional programme privileges the paradigm of the picture, which in alliance with formalist procedures produces what we term the 'perceptualist orthodoxy' (Burgess and Addison 2000). This paradigm is predicated on what Hughes (1998) describes as:

> Processes and practices which reach back to the nineteenth century – processes and practices which cling to a comfortable and uncontentious view of art and its purposes . . . a Hybrid, divorced from contemporary ideas in the spheres of art practice, critical theory, art history or museology.
>
> (Hughes 1998: 41)

On the art and design PGCE course at the Institute of Education (IoE), University of London student teachers are immediately asked to consider the meaning and purpose of the subject within the school curriculum. At this stage their responses invariably include the notion of 'self-expression', art as a peculiarly 'creative' phenomenon, something quite alien to the remainder of the school curriculum. These views rehearse modernist myths about the function of art in society, myths that perpetuate the notion of art as something autonomous even transcendental, something apart from and above the prosaic and mundane (Abbs 1989). These myths are not to be dismissed, like all myths they are fictions but fictions that may be productive nonetheless (Meecham and Sheldon 2000): art undoubtedly provides an alternative to the logocentric curriculum.

Student teachers are also asked to identify how their own experience of art in school relates to their subsequent experience in college, the studio and industry. Invariably they perceive a wide discrepancy between the two. In particular they remember the fixity of school art, the rehearsal of long-tried 'experiments' and stultifying exercises, the former exploring teenage identity and angst the latter based on reflections in bottles and negative spaces between upended stools. Such practice is given credibility by reference to the work of exemplary artists (rarely designers or craftspeople the exceptions being Morris and Gaudi): for example the ubiquitous experiments in 'alienation' in the form of pastiches of Munch, Kahlo and African masks, explorations of 'beauty' in the form of transcriptions of ideal portraits and exercises based on artists whose perceptual development is seen to depend on studying everyday objects: apples, Cézanne; flowers, O'Keefe; water, Monet. In contrast, student teachers' experience of art in society is one of response to perpetual change: the needs of differing audiences, the impact of new technologies, the spectre of commerce. Of course, there are differences between those students/artists who have followed degrees and/or careers in craft, design and fine art; there are differences in terms of the relationship between theory and practice and the relationship between internal and external needs. But they begin the PGCE course fired up by the desire to reconceptualise the art curriculum so that it engages with contemporary culture, subject knowledge in the expanded field. This is where differences may produce tensions. In schools, especially at KS3, they often find a restricted curriculum, one squeezed of resources, with management demanding 'pretty pictures' for the walls and a site where even the 'unacademic' pupil is expected to achieve a degree of success. It is not difficult to see how this militates against the introduction of a critical curriculum, pupils' and parents' expectations are sustained ensuring significant numbers for GCSE courses which, in turn, ensure good results in the league tables. This way the status quo is assured, art becomes merely a means of cultural reproduction. Only with the introduction of a critical curriculum is transformation possible.

But, just as with fictions, tensions can be productive. In many schools, student teachers find resistance to reconceptualisation, their desire is frustrated. The simple binary oppositions: creative/critical, perceptualist/expressive, fine art/design, traditional/contemporary, on which these tensions are fuelled, are the basis of investigation during workshops at the IoE. Over the year they culminate in a curriculum assignment which involves two core components, one, a written rationale, the other a visual display. Student teachers are asked to identify an aspect of subject knowledge in art and design education that, as a result of their experience in schools, merits investigation. Often the tensions resurface. 'How can I assess pupils in relation to normative standards whilst at the same time extolling the virtues of self-expression?' 'Why do I show canonic exemplars of historical western art when my pupils are immersed in the global culture of the mass media?'

We intend to suggest the productivity arising from these tensions by examining two examples of these displays which in this instance are installations. We argue that rather than reinforcing the binary oppositions by which the school curriculum regulates and controls normative standards, these tensions enable a dialectical process in which such oppositions collapse under the weight of scrutiny.

Modernist myths and pedagogic orthodoxies

Universality

In schools reproductions of the work of abstract artists may be introduced to offer an alternative to the mimetic or expressive exemplars that typify the proto-modernist profile of much school art. However, the supposed 'universal' forms of such artists as Kandinsky, Mondrian and Rothko merely become another resource for transcription and pastiche. Their historical and cultural specificity is ignored in favour of some 'spiritual essence' or a capacity to evoke 'mood'. Even here the potential of these works to suggest anything beyond a 'harmonious' arrangement of formal elements maybe neglected and they are often subject to the orthodoxy whereby all phenomena are reduced to their 'look', to surface. Such decontextualisation reinforces in pupils the notion that art is all about 'style' and technique, as if it were legitimate to appropriate any image however contested its history and subsequent place in critical discourses. Although most pupils go through the motions, many find the process alienating, something difficult to relate to their lived experience and developing tastes.

In the installation *The Destroyer* (Figure 16.1) a PGCE student simulates a teenage girl's bedroom, the place in her home where she has the opportunity to forge some sense of personal identity, where she is able to 'express herself', albeit dependent on the resources of the mass media and mass-produced consumer goods. In other words the bedroom is a multimodal site where, using available material resources, she makes meaning. The penetrating 'Destroyer' signifies the 'pure' forms of high modernism (typical of this student teacher's own work). Here it becomes a crushing monolith that annihilates the diversity and messiness of the pupil's youthful tastes, reducing her collecting and display of artefacts to the kitsch and sentimental (Greenberg 1992). The 'destroyer' (a metaphor for the effects of modernist teaching) is reductive and exclusive, totally at odds with the plurality of the subject positions of pupils in a postindustrial, postcolonial classroom.

Originality

Exemplars of artists from the western canon also reinforce the notion of originality and genius, here exemplified by a transcription after Raphael, academic art personified. Modernists, developing the Renaissance concept of authorship believed that the authenticity of the artist's personal 'signature' guaranteed the work of art its integrity, its uniqueness. However, in the age of mechanical, that is

Figure 16.1 The Destroyer. PGCE student (Institute of Education, University of London).

digital reproduction, signs of originality proliferate so that although the original artefact retains its aura to the point of fetish, the reproduced image undergoes a process of perpetual semiosis.

In this floor piece '*I can't draw either*' (Figure 16.2) a PGCE student mechanically transcribes the drawing by delineating the face from a projected reproduction. His transcription may appear spontaneous, immediate, but such signs are contrived. The piece is a parody, no more indicative of a 'passionate sensibility' than the random scribblings of the battery operated toy cars which encircle and slowly obliterate the 'master' drawing. This is a guerrilla tactic, a subversive gesture that ridicules the decorum and deference usually afforded the canon. Here traditional classroom notions of skill are turned on their head, nothing is what it seems.

Figure 16.2 '*I can't draw either*'. PGCE student (Institute of Education, University of London).

Conclusion

The pressure on art teachers to reproduce school orthodoxies is immense and it could be argued that despite notable exceptions these pressures deny teachers the opportunity to reflect on their pedagogic practice. It is therefore within initial teacher education that school art needs to undergo critique. This may not be comfortable for any of the partners. PGCE students form the bridge between classroom pragmatism and the 'not yet possible'. Their need to ensure that their work is both applicable and accessible makes them realistic critics of any tendency by universities to divorce subject knowledge from application, theory from practice. Their position 'in between' enables them to construct a space for reflection, to engage partners in dialogue. In this way the possibility of all teachers, from whatever sector, becoming agents of change is acknowledged. Dialectical processes no doubt produce tensions, but they prevent stagnation in the form of rigid orthodoxies.

Questions

1   This chapter identifies two of the modernist myths that continue to pervade art and design education: universality and originality. Identify other myths and consider ways that they can be used productively.
2   How might teachers' potential as agents of change be further developed?

Further reading

Addison, N. and Burgess, L. (2000) *Learning to Teach Art and Design in the Secondary School*, London: Routledge.
Meecham, P. and Sheldon, J. (2000) *Modern Art: A Critical Introduction*, London: Routledge.

Part 3
Towards an ethical pedagogy

17 Do hope and critical pedagogy matter under the reign of neoliberalism?

Henry A. Giroux

The conception of politics that we defend is far from the idea that 'everything is possible'. In fact, it's an immense task to try to propose a few possibles, in the plural – a few possibilities other than what we are told is possible. It is a matter of showing how the space of the possible is larger than the one we are assigned – that something else is possible, but not that everything is possible.

(Badiou 2001: 115)

Reclaiming education as a democratic public sphere

There is a growing sense in the popular imagination that citizen involvement, social planning, and civic engagement are becoming irrelevant in a society where the welfare state is being aggressively dismantled (Bauman 1998). Those traditional, if not imagined, public spheres in which people could exchange ideas, debate, and shape the conditions that structured their everyday lives increasingly appear to have little relevance or political significance, particularly as important social and economic issues are trivialized in mainstream media. Emptied of any substantial content, democracy appears imperilled as individuals are unable to translate their privately suffered misery into public concerns and collective action. The prevailing modes of domination have been reversed. As Bauman (2001a) points out, the public no longer dominates the private: 'The opposite is the case: it is the private that colonizes the public space, squeezing out and chasing away everything which cannot be fully, without residue, translated into the vocabulary of private interests and pursuits' (Bauman 2001a: 107). As the idea of the public is dissolved into constituencies and the concept of public interest disintegrates into talk about privatization and personal scandals of public figures, the language of commonality, shared values, a just society, and public goods are severed from the imperatives of a critical and substantive democracy (Wolin 2000: 10). Civic engagement and political agency now appear impotent, and public values are rendered invisible in light of the growing power of multinational corporations to privatize public space and disconnect power from issues of equity, social justice, and civic responsibility (McChesney 1999). As democratic public spheres are either eliminated or commercialized, agency is no longer linked to challenging and producing a crisis in established power. As the vast majority of citizens become detached from public forums that nourish social critique, agency not only becomes a mockery of itself, but also is replaced by market-based choices in which private satisfactions replace social responsibilities and biographic solutions become a substitute for systemic change (Beck 1992: 137). As the global space of criticism is undercut by the absence of public spheres that encourage the exchange of information, opinion, and criticism, the horizons of a substantive democracy disappear against the growing isolation and depoliticization that marks the loss of a politically guaranteed public realm in which autonomy, political participation, and engaged citizenship make their appearance (Brenkman 2000: 124–5). As Kohn (2001) points out, '[p]ublic sidewalks and streets are practically the only remaining available sites for unscripted political activity' (Kohn 2001: 71). Few sites now exist 'that allow people to talk back, to ask a question, to tell a story, to question a premise' (Kohn 2001: 71). Rapidly disappearing are those public spaces in which people meet face-to-face, removed from the ravages of a market logic that undermines the ability to communicate through a language capable of defending vital institutions as a public good. One consequence is that political exhaustion and impoverished intellectual visions are fed by the increasingly popular assumption that there are no alternatives to the present state of affairs (Jacoby 1999; Boggs 2000; Bauman 2001a). Within the increasing corporatization of everyday life, market values replace social values and people appear more and more willing to retreat into the safe, privatized enclaves of the family, religion, and consumption. At the same time, power is removed from politics to the degree that it has become global and exterritorial; power now flows, escaping from and defying the reach of traditional centers of politics that are nation-based and local. The space of power now appears beyond the reach of governments and as a result nations and citizens are increasingly removed as political agents with regard to the impact that multinational corporations have on their daily lives (Bauman 2001a: 203). Once again, the result is not only silence and indifference, but also the elimination of those public spaces that reveal the rough edges of social order, disrupt consensus, and point to the need for modes of education that link learning to the conditions necessary for developing democratic forms of political agency and civic struggle (Giroux 2001).

As these critical public spaces disappear under the juggernaut of neoliberal policies, it becomes crucial for critical educators to raise fundamental questions about what it means to revitalize an *ethical politics*, one that takes seriously 'such values as citizen participation, the public good, political obligation, social governance, and community' (Boggs 2000: ix). A renewed and vibrant politics would take on the challenge of creating the necessary discourses for investing in public life and for keeping open democracy as a site of permanent struggle and ongoing possibility 'where the fullest human experiences – social, intellectual, political – could best be realized' (Boggs 2000: 95). The call for a revitalized politics and civic consciousness grounded in a thriving democratic society substantively challenges the utopian promises and dystopian practices of neoliberalism – with its all-consuming emphasis on market relations, commercialization, privatization, and the creation of a world-wide economy of part-time workers. Such an intervention confronts critical educators with the challenge of developing those atrophied public spheres (the media, higher education, electronic communities, and other cultural sites) that provide the conditions for creating citizens who are capable of exercising their freedoms, including their ability to question the assumptions that govern political life and their participation in shaping the social, political and economic orders that govern daily existence. Neither homogeneous nor nostalgic, the public sphere points to a plurality of institutions, sites and spaces (Fraser 1990); a sphere in which people not only talk, debate, and reassess the political, moral, and cultural dimensions of publicness but also develop processes of learning and persuasion as a way of enacting new social identities and altering 'the very structure of participation and the very horizon of discussion and debate' (Brenkman 1995: 7).

As the promise of radical democracy and social, economic and racial justice recedes from public memory, unfettered brutal self-interests combine with retrograde social polices to make security a top domestic priority. One consequence is that all levels of government are being hollowed out as their policing functions increasingly overpower and mediate their diminishing social functions. The police, courts, and other disciplinary agencies increasingly become the main forces used to address social problems and implement public policies (Giroux 2001). Labelled by neoliberals and right wing politicians as the enemy of freedom (except when it aids big business), government is discounted as a guardian of the public interests (Ferge 2000). The forces of hyper-capitalism have disparaged the USA government when it has provided essential services such as crucial safety nets for the less fortunate, and as a result government bears no obligation for either the poor and dispossessed or for the collective future of young people. The disappearance of spaces for reactivating our political sensibilities as critical citizens, engaged public intellectuals, and social agents is happening at a time when public goods are disparaged in the name of privatization, and critical public forums cease to resonate as sites of utopian possibility. The growing lack of justice and equity in American society rises proportionately to the lack of political imagination and collective hope (Unger 1998; Unger and West 1998). We live at a time when the forces and advocates of hyper-capitalism and the marketplace undermine all attempts to revive the culture of politics as an ethical response to the demise of democratic public life. Understood as both a set of economic policies and an impoverished notion of citizenship, hyper-capitalism represents not just a series of market-driven programmes but also a coherent set of cultural, political, and educational practices.

Politics devoid of a radical vision often degenerates into either cynicism or appropriates a view of power that appears to be equated only with domination. It is therefore crucial that critical educators respond with renewed efforts to merge politics and ethics with a revitalized sense of the importance of providing the conditions for forms of critical citizenship and civic education rather than believe the fraudulent, self-serving hegemonic assumption that democracy and capitalism are the same, or indeed that politics as a site of contestation, critical exchange and engagement is in a state of terminal arrest. Such efforts would supply the knowledge, skills, and experiences necessary to produce democratic political agents. In part, this would demand engaging with the alleged argument for the death of politics as not only symptomatic of the crisis of democracy, but also as part of the more specific crisis of vision, education, agency and meaning that disconnects public values and ethics from the very sphere of politics. Some social theorists such as Bennett (1998b), Hunter (1994), and Gitlin (1997) make the plunge into forms of political cynicism easier by suggesting that any attempt to change society through a cultural politics that links the pedagogical and the political will simply augment the power of the dominant social order. Lost from such accounts is the recognition that democracy has to be struggled over, even in the face of a most appalling crisis of political agency. Within this discourse, little attention is paid to the fact that the struggle over politics, power, and democracy is inextricably linked to creating public spheres where individuals can be educated as political agents equipped with the skills, capacities, and knowledge they need not only to actually perform as autonomous political agents, but also to believe that such struggles *are worth taking up*. The struggle over politics, in this instance, is linked to pedagogical interventions aimed at subverting dominant forms of meaning in order to generate both a renewed sense of agency and a critical subversion of power itself. Agency now becomes the site through which, as Judith Butler has pointed out in another context, power is not transcended but reworked, replayed, and restaged in productive ways (in Olson and Worsham 2000: 741). Central to my argument is the assumption that politics is not simply about power, but also, as Castoriadis (1996) points out, 'to do with political judgements and value choices' (Castoriadis 1996: 8), indicating that questions of civic education and critical pedagogy (learning how to become a skilled citizen) are central to the struggle over political agency and democracy. Civic education and critical pedagogy emphasize critical thinking, bridging the gap between learning and everyday life, understanding the connection between power and knowledge, and extending democratic rights and identities by using the resources of history. However, among many critical educators and social theorists, there is a widespread refusal to recognize not only that this form of education is the foundation for expanding and enabling political agency, but also that it takes place across a wide variety of public spheres mediated through the very force of culture itself.

Democracy has now been reduced to a metaphor for the alleged 'free' market. It is not that a genuine democratic public space once existed in some ideal form and has now been corrupted by the values of the market, but that these democratic public spheres, even in limited forms, seem no longer to be animating concepts for making visible the contradiction and tension between the reality of existing democracy and the promise of a more fully realized, substantive democracy (Unger 1998). While liberal democracy offers an important discourse around issues of 'rights, freedoms, participation, self-rule, and citizenship', it has been mediated historically through the 'damaged and burdened tradition' of racial and gender exclusions, economic injustice and a formalistic, ritualized democracy which substituted the swindle for the promise of democratic participation (Brenkman 2000: 123). Part of the challenge of creating a radical democracy is in constructing new locations of struggle, vocabularies, and subject positions that allow people in a wide variety of public spheres to become more than they are now, to question what it is they have become within existing institutional and social formations and, as

Chantal Mouffe points out, 'to give some thought to their experiences so that they can transform their relations of subordination and oppression' (Olson and Worsham 1999: 178). In part, this implies resisting the attack on existing public spheres such as schools while simultaneously creating new spaces in clubs, neighbourhoods, bookstores, cyberspace, and other locations where dialogue and critical exchanges become possible. This way the pedagogical and political conditions for individual resistance and active social movements can be created.

In spite of the urgency of the current historical moment, critical educators must avoid crude antitheoretical calls to action. More than ever, they need to appropriate scholarly and popular sources and use theory as a critical resource to name particular problems and make connections between the political and the cultural, to break what Homi Bhabha has called 'the continuity and the consensus of common sense' (in Olson and Worsham 1998: 11). As a resource, theory becomes important as a way of critically engaging and mapping the crucial relations among language, texts, everyday life, and structures of power as part of a broader effort to understand the conditions, contexts, and strategies of struggle that will lead to social transformation. I am suggesting that the tools of theory emerge out of the intersection of the past and present, and respond to and are shaped by the conditions at hand. Theory, in this instance, addresses the challenge of connecting the world of the symbolic, discursive, and representational to the social gravity and force of everyday issues rooted in material relations of power. If theory is to escape from its most retrograde academic uses, critical educators and other progressives must avoid any form of theoreticism, an indulgence in which the production of theoretical discourse becomes an end in itself, an expression of language removed from the possibility of challenging strategies of domination. Rather than treating theory as a closed circuit, academics and others must mine it critically in order to perform the bridging work between intellectual debates and public issues; at best, theory should provide the knowledge and tools to connect concrete academic issues with broader public debates, opening up possibilities for new approaches and ways to address both social problems and social reforms.

The overriding political project at issue here suggests that critical educators produce new theoretical tools (a new vocabulary and set of conceptual resources) for linking theory, critique, education, and the discourse of possibility to the demands of a more fully realized democracy. In part, such a project points to constructing a new vocabulary for connecting what we read to how we engage in global movements for social change, while recognizing that simply invoking the relationship between theory and practice, critique and social action is not enough. Any attempt to give new life to a substantive democratic politics must also address how people learn to be political agents; that is, what kind of educational work is necessary within what types of public spaces to enable people to use their full intellectual resources and capacities to both provide a profound critique of existing institutions and struggle to create, as Stuart Hall puts it, 'what would be a good life or a better kind of life for the majority of people' (in Terry 1997: 55). Bauman (2001b) adds to the gravity of such a political project by calling for progressives to fully address the 'hard currency of human suffering', to undertake an ethical activism whose task is 'to cry at the wolves, not to run with them . . . to count human costs, alert others to them, arouse consciences to resist them, to think of alternatives, less costly, other ways of living together' (Bauman 2001b: 343). One challenge currently facing critical educators is that they need to understand more fully why the tools used in the past often feel awkward in the present; more often than not they fail to respond to problems facing the USA and other parts of the globe. More specifically, critical educators need to understand the inability of existing critical discourses to bridge the gap between how the society represents itself, and how and why individuals fail to understand and critically engage with such representations in order to intervene in the oppressive social relationships they often legitimize. Such forms of intervention are complicated by the pressing requirement to construct a politics that runs counter to the 'natural order of things' but on a scale in which individual empowerment is viewed as inseparable from broader social and political transformations. Intervention in this sense is also complicated by a dialectical understanding of the relationship between local change and global structures, as well as the imperative to view public engagement within a global notion of social transformation (Dirlik 2000).

If emancipatory politics is to be equal to the challenge of capitalism, critical educators need to theorize politics not as a science or set of objective conditions, but as a point of departure in specific and concrete situations (Badiou 2001: 104). They need to problematize the very meaning of the political so that it can no longer be used to provide complete answers. Instead they should ask why and how particular social formations have a particular shape, come into being, and what it might mean to rethink such formations in terms of opening up new sites of struggles and movements. In the absence of such languages and the social formations and public spheres that make them operative, politics becomes narcissistic and reductionist and caters to the mood of widespread pessimism and the cathartic allure of spectacle. In addition, public service and government intervention is sneered upon as either bureaucratic or a constraint upon individual freedom. The age of manufactured politics and neoliberal values no longer translates private problems into public issues or collective solutions. Emptied of its political content, public space increasingly becomes a site of self-display: on the one hand a sphere dominated by a notion of freedom that is located exclusively in an inner-world marked by the spectacle of the media confessional, and, on the other, the social Darwinism of reality-based television with its endless instinct for the weaknesses of others and its masochistic affirmation of ruthlessness and steroidal power. Escape, avoidance and narcissism are now coupled with the public display, if not celebration, of those individuals who define agency in terms of their survival skills rather than their commitment to dialogue, critical reflection, solidarity and relations that open up the promise of public engagement with important social issues.

Educated hope

We should be, without hesitation or embarrassment, utopians. At the end of the twentieth century it is the only acceptable political option, morally speaking . . . irrespective of what may have seemed apt hitherto either inside or outside the Marxist tradition, nothing but a utopian goal will now suffice. The realities of our time are morally intolerable . . . The facts of widespread human privation and those of political oppression and atrocity are available to all who want them. They are unavoidable unless you wilfully shut them out. To those who would suggest that things might be yet worse, one answer is that of course they might be. But another answer is that for too many people they are already quite bad enough; and the sponsors of this type of suggestion are for their part almost always pretty comfortable.

(Geras 1999: 42)

Against an increasingly oppressive corporate-based globalism, critical educators need to resurrect a language of resistance and possibility, one that embraces a militant utopianism. Simultaneously they must be attentive to those forces that seek to turn such hope into new slogans or to punish and dismiss anyone who dares to look beyond the horizon of the given. Hope, in this instance, is a precondition for individual and social struggle, the ongoing practice of critical education in a wide variety of sites and the mark of courage on the part of intellectuals in and out of the academy who use the resources of theory to address pressing social problems. But hope is also referent for civic courage and its ability to mediate the *memory* of loss and the *experience* of injustice as part of a broader attempt to open up new locations of struggle, contest the workings of oppressive power and undermine various forms of domination. At its best, civic courage as a political practice begins when one's life can no longer be taken for granted. In doing so, it makes concrete the possibility for transforming hope and politics into an ethical space and public act that confronts the flow of everyday experience and the weight of social suffering with the force of individual and collective resistance and the unending project of democratic social transformation.

The profound anti-utopianism that is spurred on both by visions of the market and some post-structuralist and postmodern visions of displacement, either commodifies the subject or eliminates the possibility of theorizing a notion of agency based on the fashionable discourse of pluralized subjectivity. Educated hope combines the pedagogical and the political in ways that stress the contextual nature of learning, emphasizing that different contexts give rise to diverse questions, problems, and possibilities. In doing so, such hope brings to the fore the call for progressives and other critical intellectuals to be attentive to the ways in which institutional and symbolic power are tangled up with everyday experience. Any politics of hope must tap into individual experiences while at the same time linking individual responsibility with a progressive sense of social destiny. Politics and pedagogy alike spring 'from real situations and from what we can say and do in these situations' (Badiou 2001: 96). Emphasizing politics as a pedagogical practice and performative act, educated hope accentuates that notion that politics not only is played out on the terrain of imagination and desire, but also is grounded in relations of power mediated through the outcome of situated struggles dedicated to creating the conditions and capacities for people to become critically engaged political agents. As a form of utopianism, educated hope engages politics through the interconnected modalities of desire, intervention, and struggle. As Baker (1994) argues in a different context:

> No longer mere fantasy (opium for the masses whose real work is elsewhere), no longer simple escape (from a world defined principally by more concrete purposes and structures), no longer the elite pastime (thus not relevant to the lives of ordinary people) and no longer mere contemplation (irrelevant for new forms of desire and subjectivity), the imagination has become an organized field of social practices, a form of work . . . and a form of negotiation between sites of agency ('individuals') and globally defined fields of possibility.
>
> (Baker 1994: 12)

Educated hope both engages the imagination as social practice and takes seriously the importance of civic education. As a form of utopian thinking, educated hope provides the foundational connection that must be made among three discourses that often remain separated: democracy, political agency, and pedagogy.

The concept of educated hope rests on an expansive notion of pedagogy by pointing to broader considerations. First, an understanding of the role that education now plays in a variety of cultural sites, and second, an understanding of how these sites have become integral to producing models of human nature through the pedagogical force of a 'capitalist imaginary', one based almost 'exclusively on economic exchange' (Castoriadis 1997: 347). Given the omnipresence of this 'imaginary' it will require more than simply the language of critique if critical educators are to develop an oppositional cultural politics. As important as immanent critique might be, it always runs the risk of representing power in the absolute service of domination, thus failing to capture the always open and ongoing dynamic of resistance at work in alternative modes of representations, oppositional public spheres, and modes of affective investment that refuse the ideological push and institutional drive of dominant social orders (Castoriadis 1991).

Combining the discourse of critique and hope is crucial to affirm that critical activity offers the possibility for social change. An oppositional cultural politics can take many forms, but given the current assault on democratic public spheres, it seems imperative that progressives revitalize the struggles over social citizenship, particularly those struggles aimed at expanding liberal freedoms and civic rights. Simultaneously they must develop collective movements that can challenge the subordination of social needs to the dictates of commercialism and capital. Central to such a politics would be a critical public pedagogy that attempts to make visible alternative models of radical democratic culture in a wide variety of sites. These models will raise fundamental questions: what is the relationship between social justice and the distribution of public resources and goods? What are the conditions, knowledge and skills that are a prerequisite for political agency and social change? At the very least, such a project involves understanding and critically engaging with dominant public transcripts and values within a broader set of historical and institutional contexts. Making the political more pedagogical in this instance suggests producing modes of knowledge and social practices that not only affirm oppositional cultural work but offer opportunities to mobilize instances of collective outrage, if not collective action. Such mobilization opposes glaring material inequities and the growing cynical belief that today's culture of investment and finance makes it *impossible* to address many of the major social problems facing both the USA and the larger world. Most importantly, such work points to the link between civic education, critical pedagogy, and modes of oppositional political agency that are pivotal to elucidating a politics that promotes autonomy and social change. Unfortunately, many progressives have failed to take seriously Gramsci's insight that '[e]very relationship of "hegemony" is necessarily an educational relationship' (Gramsci 1971a: 350). This implies that education as a cultural pedagogical practice takes place across multiple sites as it signals how, within diverse contexts, education makes us both subjects of and subject to relations of power. In order to address the current attack by corporate culture on democratic public life I want to invoke the spirit of pedagogical and political resistance by building on Gramsci's insight.

Ethical pedagogy

A radical, ethical pedagogy as a form of resistance should be premised, in part, on the assumption that educators vigorously resist any attempt by liberals and conservatives to reduce them to either the role of technicians or multinational operatives. Struggles over pedagogy must be accompanied by sustained attempts on the part of critical educators to collectively organize and oppose current efforts to disempower teachers through the proliferation of standardized testing schemes, management by *fixed* objectives, and bureaucratic forms of accountability. This requires that critical educators and other progressives organize against the corporate take-over of schools, fight to protect the power of unions, expand the rights and benefits of staff personnel, and put more power into the hands of faculty and students.

Accordingly, progressive educators and social activists should reject forms of schooling that marginalize students who are poor, black, and least advantaged. This points to the necessity for developing school practices that recognize how issues related to gender, class, race, and sexual orientation can be used as a resource for learning rather than being contained in schools through a systemic pattern of exclusion, punishment and failure. Similarly, if curricular justice suggests that school knowledge be organized around the needs of the least advantaged, then school and classroom authority should rest in the hands of teachers and communities and not be under the control of 'experts', imported from the business community or the world of 'for-profit schools'. In addition, assessments in schools should draw upon multiple sources, be attentive to the cultural resources of the communities in which students live their daily lives, and recognize that any viable approach to assessment is as much about the discourse of equitable and fair distribution of resources as it is about issues of testing and accountability. In this perspective, the conditions for teaching and learning cannot be separated from how and what students learn. Schools don't need standardized curricular and testing. On the contrary, they need curricular justice; forms of teaching that are inclusive, caring, respectful and economically equitable. This aim, in part, is to undermine those repressive modes of education that produce social hierarchies and legitimate inequality, while simultaneously providing them with the knowledge and skills needed to produce well-rounded critical actors and social agents.

What educators teach is inseparable from what it means for them to invest in public life and locate themselves in a public discourse. The responsibility of educators cannot be separated from the consequences of the knowledge they produce, the social relations they legitimize, and the ideologies they disseminate to students. At best, educational work represents a response to questions and issues posed by the tensions and contradictions of public life, and only when work is critical can educators hope to understand and intervene in specific problems that emanate from the material contexts of everyday existence. Teaching in this sense highlights considerations of power, politics and ethics fundamental to any form of teacher–student interaction.

The fundamental challenge facing critical educators within the current age of neoliberalism is to provide the conditions for students to address how knowledge is related to the power of both self-definition and social agency. Central to such a challenge is providing students with the skills, knowledge, and authority they need to inquire and act upon what it means to live in a radical, multicultural democracy, to recognize anti-democratic forms of power and to fight deeply rooted injustices in a society and world founded on systemic economic, racial, and gendered inequalities. Such educators should address the practical consequences of their work in the broader society while simultaneously making connections to those too often ignored institutional forms, social practices and cultural spheres that powerfully influence young people outside of schools. This is especially important within the ongoing and constantly changing landscape of popular culture with its shift away from a culture of print to an electronic, digitally constructed culture of images and high-speed hyper-texts.

At the beginning of the new millennium, educators, parents and others should re-evaluate what it means for adults and young people to grow up in a world that has been radically altered by a hyper-capitalism that monopolizes the educational force of culture as it ruthlessly eliminates those public spheres *not* governed by the logic of the market. Galeano (quoted in Espada 2000) has stated that:

> [B]y saying no to the devastating empire of greed, whose center lies in North America, we are saying yes to another possible America . . . In saying no to a peace without dignity, we are saying yes to the sacred right of rebellion against injustice.
>
> (Galeano quoted in Espada 2000: 9)

Galeano speaks clearly to the urgent task of elevating the politics and possibility of resistance to address all those issues, spaces, and public spheres in which the intersection of language and bodies plays a strategic role in the process of forming and disrupting power relations. Intellectuals cut off from the wider society often fall prey to forms of professional legitimation that not only deny the political nature of their own labour and theoretical work, but also reinforce a deep-rooted cynicism about the ability of ordinary people to take risks, fight for what they believe in and become a force for social change.

The issue is not whether public or higher education has become contaminated with politics, it is more importantly about recognizing that education is already a space of politics, power, and authority. The crucial matter at stake is how to appropriate, invent, direct and control the multiple layers of power and politics that constitute both the institutional formation of education and the pedagogies that are often an outcome of deliberate struggles to put into place particular notions of knowledge, values, and identity. As committed educators, we cannot eliminate politics, but we can work against a politics of certainty, a pedagogy of terrorism and an institutional formation that closes down rather than opens up democratic relations. This requires that we work diligently to construct a politics without guarantees, one that perpetually questions itself as well as all those forms of knowledge, values, and practices that appear beyond the process of interrogation, debate, and deliberation. Against a pedagogy and politics of certainty, it is crucial for educators to develop pedagogical practices that problematize considerations of institutional location, mechanisms of transmission, and effects. They should also make room for ongoing student critiques of how teacher authority functions by analysing the ideological baggage and subjective investments that teachers bring with them to the classroom experience.

Neither democracy nor schooling should become synonymous with the language of capital, oppression, control, surveillance, and privatization. Interrogating how power works through dominant discourses and social relations, particularly as they affect young people who are marginalized economically, racially, and politically, provides opportunities for progressives to challenge dominant ideologies and regressive social policies that undermine the possibilities for connecting the struggles over education to the broader crisis of radical democracy and social and economic justice.

Now that the fate of an entire generation of young people, if not democracy itself, is at stake, the time for radical democratic change in the USA has never been so urgent. This challenge gives new meaning, if not impetus, to the importance of resistance, the relevance of critical pedagogy and the significance of political agency. It is hoped that the challenge will not be lost on educators and others who are interested in social change and the problems to be confronted in creating those crucial democratic public spheres, cultural institutions and social relations that give substance to what Derrida calls 'the promise of democracy' (Derrida 2000: 9). The promise of democracy is present at best in a project of resistance and possibility, one that is propelled by both a dream and a collective practice that makes justice, equality, and freedom operational for all members of a democratic social order.

18 Loaded canons

Tom Gretton

This chapter presents an argument, grounded in a critical pragmatism, for continuing to teach the canon. Critical pragmatism is compromised and compromising. My argument may tend to associate me with advocacies which present themselves as principled, and of which I am highly critical. I share many of the critical positions that seek a disengagement from the canon as a focus for art historical studies; I am aware of the possibility that my strange bedfellows may find my arguments more useful (if not more palatable) than may my 'natural' allies.

What is a canon? At the Synod of Laodicea, AD 340–81, Christian leaders agreed to name almost the same New Testament books as the Church does now. The Synod was the highest council of the Christian church, and its decisions were termed *canonical*, given the status of rules or yardsticks. Since Christianity was by that time the official religion of the Roman Empire, it was vital that not only priests and their flocks, but also pedagogues and police knew clearly which texts defined the faith. The decision meant that a few works became 'the [new] word of God'; other texts became not-the-word-of-God. The processes of authority and validation at work between the canon and the Church were circular: the Synod gave authority to a particular group of texts, and then took its authority from those texts, since the Priesthood was the interpreter of the word of God. This benign circle functions perfectly only if the body of work so hallowed is both fixed and understood to be different in kind from non-canonical works. This assertion of difference in kind is crucial: the claim 'these works are different because we choose them to be different' recycles no authority onto the choosers. The canon depends on and authenticates the authority; the authority depends on, defends and perpetuates the canon. Teachers have historically been no more immune to that sweetheart deal than have priests; it turns out that I am not immune to it either.

Art has taken on some of the functions that religion used to discharge; this essay explores implications of the canonical sweetheart deal, both for teachers and for students of Art's history. Of course no secular work of art is canonical in the way that *the Gospel According to Saint Luke* is canonical; this is a metaphor. Talk of 'great artists', 'masterpieces' and 'works of genius' reinforces the metaphor; in talking thus the claim that there are a few works in which the word of God (or its functionally equivalent) is clearly and fully present, and a host of other works whose worth is conditional and contextual is reproduced. Harold Bloom (1994) speaks of the canon as unique and unitary, just as the Fathers of the Church did. This strong original concept of the canon requires the existence of an unique, authoritative, unified and unifying set of works: thus its extension to the place of old art in contemporary culture can only be metaphorical at best, and the metaphor can be used in a stronger or a weaker sense. Teachers may argue strongly that there is or should be a small group of works whose excellence is understood as being different in kind, and not merely in degree, from 'ordinary' art, works of fundamental importance, both because they make manifest the values of art, and because they are the ideal types of tendencies, movements and aspirations in the history of art. Works in this canon are thus sources both of value and of history; protected by concepts of genius and by claims to both historical and transcendental importance, this is, if you like, the armoured canon. To speak of a western canon is to imply the existence of parallel lists, drawn up by other criteria, or, perhaps even worse for the fundamentalists, of a different list drawn up by the same criteria. In this weak usage, one may emphasise the existence of a more inclusive and flexible but still restricted group of works which are given special, exemplary status in narratives about art and its history. Works may move into or out of this group, but the relationship of mutual support between pedagogic and wider cultural power remains constitutive. This may be called the loose canon, which is the version I address in this chapter.

In the vital and unavoidable process of the reproduction of cultural values through education, the role of 'high culture' has been to provide a justification and a template. However, since the rise and triumph of cultural relativism and its practical application in multicultural curricula, both these uses of high culture have become highly problematic. Cultural relativists understand high culture as the 'core curriculum' of a pedagogy of oppression, an indispensable tool of cultural dominance, reproducing not inspiring ideals and transcendent values, but ethnocentricity, patriarchy, and the norms of bourgeois individualism. From this point of view, one man's canon is another woman's water-cannon. Any discussion of the possible usefulness of the canon immediately confronts the problem of cultural relativism, of finding a legitimate position from which to make, communicate or critique judgements of cultural value. But if I, or any other cultural authority, can solve the problem of cultural relativism, then there is no problem of cultural relativism.

The evolution of art history since the early 1970s has left teachers with a pragmatic problem. Despite the demonstration that the canon is the product of ethnocentrism, sexism and the operation of class interests, the loose canon continues to be reproduced. There are various ways of demonstrating the conservatism of actual research and publishing practices in contrast to the progressive radicalism of discursive practice. In these circumstances we as teachers can either join the party of those who denounce and reject the canon; or we can accept that its definition and reproduction meet some powerful cultural needs, accept that it is there, and that we, and our students, need to come to terms with it. In this case, we need to find acceptable ways of dealing with it in our teaching, ways which neither worship the sorts of cultural power the canon represents nor stare down cultural relativism with cultural authority.

But first, a question of fact. Given the thrashing which the canon has in theory taken in recent years, is it still being reproduced? To give a crude empirical answer to this question, I checked the CD-ROM of the Getty Institute's annual *Bibliography of the History of Art* (BHA), which took over the work of the two pre-existing art bibliographies *Répertoire internationale des livres sur l'Art* (RILA) and *Repertoiré d'art et d'archaeologie* (RAA) in 1991, and surveys books, exhibitions and articles in scholarly journals. I asked it two sorts of questions using the indexes from 1975 to 1999: how many times certain keywords characteristic of 'old' and 'new' art histories occurred, and how many times the names of a selection of artists occurred, concentrating on mid-nineteenth-century France (data lists, and a methodological discussion, can be found on my pages of the UCL History of Art website; words in this chapter followed by three dots indicate that the search used the wild-card facility).

The 'keyword' data present a complicated picture. Whereas in RILA there are more than 127,000 occurrences of the word 'art' out of 139,000 entries, in BHA the proportion has crashed to 70,000 out of about 170,000 entries. This suggests that 'art' is on the run. However, closer study indicates a subject in which old ways of thinking and old preoccupations remain dominant, but one where there has been an infusion into the 'classical' discourses of art history of the vocabulary and problematics associated with some aspects of 'the new art history' and its postmodern inheritors. The sensational increase in the use of words such as 'representation' (950 to 5,556) and 'gender' (21 to 621) suggests that literary theory and gender studies have been taken up into mainstream art history with considerable success, as have concerns with ethnicity and colonialism ('ethnic...' 43 to 166, 'colonial...' 432 to 833), whereas the preoccupations associated with a class vocabulary ('class' 338 to 436, 'proletar...' 50 to 26), have been relatively less attractive to recent art historians. It is unclear whether this selective incorporation of 'progressive' agendas represents the fact that the old art history, focused on the reproduction of the canon and its values, is changing in fundamental ways, or whether it is just demonstrating its resilience. The continued occurrence in thousands of entries of those 'old' preoccupations 'iconography' (24,535 to 14,199), 'influence' (10,663 to 7,119), and 'patron...' (6,269 to 5,528) suggests resilience, and prompts two further observations.

The first is that people tend to be more aware of change than of continuity in the institutions (in this case 'history of art') with which they are familiar, so that they are more impressed when 'gender' increases its score from 21 citations to 621 than when 'influence' continues, despite a 30 per cent decline, to be used in article titles almost 12 times as often as 'gender'. The second depends on another argument. One common claim concerning the difference between high-quality works of art and 'ordinary' ones is that the really good ones can sustain and repay a wide range of sorts of scrutiny. Whether this is or is not actually the case, it is certainly true that an evolution in discourse does not of itself entail an evolution in the work studied: but then the concept of the canon addresses the set of texts, not the discourse that surrounds them. Consideration of the occurrence of named artists in the two data-sets may illuminate these questions. Certain artists have been cited more often recently (Renoir 55 to 106), some major women artists among them (Morisot 31 to 62), and certain artists (Degas or Delaroche) are indexed markedly less frequently. However, the relative proportional stability of citation rates for major artists (and the relative infrequent instances of artists dropping far down the ladder or rising swiftly up it between the two databases) suggests that there is a relatively stable hierarchy of artists preferentially selected for study, and confirms the impression of conservative topical and discursive conservatism given by the massive continued weight of keywords like 'patron...' and 'school'. In the world of scholarly art history, the canon is still being energetically reproduced; it is evolving, though considerably less quickly than do the discourses which support and validate it. These themselves are evolving less quickly than people may care to believe: multiculturalism has had a strictly limited impact on the artist-focus of the art history which gets published.

The impression of continued stability is confirmed by another search I did, this time on the Unesco annual bibliography, *Repertoiré d'art et d'archaeologie*, which has a long continuous run, from before 1939 (under different auspices) till 1989. I searched the paper version of this resource from 1952 to 1989, and then from 1990 to 1999 using the electronic BHA. I counted the number of separate references in the artist index to five 'canonical' figures – Raphael, Michelangelo, Rembrandt, Manet and Cézanne – expressing the total as a percentage of the number of entries in each year's bibliography.

The results show that, apart from one canonical surge in 1956, and a set of low readings from the late 1960s through the 1970s, the percentage has generally remained between about 0.9 per cent and about 1.8 per cent. Ratios go up and down, but if anything proportions are higher now than they were a generation ago. The moment when the reproduction of the canon came under serious threat is in the revolutionary upsurge of the late 1960s, rather than under the onslaught of feminist and other critical theories since 1990. This critique has resulted in a renewal of old art history, rather than in its eclipse. While new discursive vocabularies have emerged to take a minor place alongside still-healthy old ones, the works and the artists to which attention is still paid are by and large, the usual suspects.

This reliance of research and publishing activity on the canon and on the ways of thinking that it has in the past richly supported means that we, the teachers, are going to go on finding it easy to lay our hands on material about the canonical figures, and quite hard to lay our hands on stuff about even the minor 'great artists', let alone the foot soldiers of cultural production: one can expect that most of us, most of the time, will find ourselves on paths of least resistance. Continuity of reproductive practice in research and publishing damps change in teaching; its effects will be most deadening and conservative when unexamined and unacknowledged. Uncritical recourse to canonical works and figures will reproduce the canon as something natural and inevitable, not as an institution in which social structures, relations of cultural power, are reproduced and legitimized. Canonical ways of thinking about and of doing history of art and design imply not merely a high culture but a dominant culture. It seems a logical move to argue that they imply the endorsement of such a culture and its dominance. Such a premise is of course anathema to a defender of the canon such as Harold Bloom, who wrote:

> Nothing is so essential to the Western canon as its principles of selectivity, which are elitist only to the extent that they are founded on severely artistic criteria.
>
> (Bloom 1994: 22)

This is an excellent example of staring down cultural relativism with cultural authority, and helps us to formulate the task more clearly. How may one find a way of defending a reproductive engagement with the canon which does not on the one hand deny the contribution of cultural authority to social power, or on the other hand oppressively assert that acquiescence to cultural authority is itself a good thing for the acquiescer?

Bloom's book, with its trenchant message that 'the Academy' has a quasi-sacred duty to teach primarily from a tightly defined and exalted canon, had a considerable success in the USA in the mid-1990s, because it so clearly communicated the beleaguered sense of righteousness of an interest group which believes that their disinterested desire to educate students by unveiling the greatest works of humankind is under threat of submersion by the tide of post-structuralist and multiculturalist dissent and criticism. Critiques of canon-based teaching come from a variety of positions. There are those who refuse the model of pedagogy (and of authority) which is implied in Bloom's 'great books for open minds' fantasy of enlightenment, with its transfer of power and authority away from the reader, notionally to the text, but actually to the author as creator, and to the teacher as interpreter. There are those who, on the basis of the canon's particular gender and ethnic biases, deny the validity of the particular group of 'greatest works of humankind' which is being offered. And there are those who would reject any canon, however purified, corrected, enlarged or reorientated, believing that all such privileging is anti-democratic and elitist, that it fetishises specific cultural artefacts while demonising whole classes of others, that it misrecognises the productive work which readers and viewers do when they make a work into something of value to them, mistakenly sees this as a labour not of making, but of discovery of what is already there.

Bloom has made me more uneasy about my position than I was before I read his essay, not because his arguments convince me, but because of his incandescent certainty that everyone is out of step except himself and a bunch of writers considerably more successful than me, including Homer, Plato, Dante, Shakespeare, Goethe and Proust. I am impressed by authority of the sort that these figures have in our culture, and Bloom's passionate assertion not only of their authority, but also of their foundational importance and current relevance makes me uneasy about my own relative cultural relativism. But Bloom is a fundamentalist; he believes that a small group of works by a small group of writers has transcendental authority, and that any work on literature (and, by extension, on art) which does not acknowledge this fundamental fact is an institutionalised conspiracy against the truth.

One of the intellectual traditions in which I work is a bourgeois British Marxism, attentive to the workings of contradiction in historical process. E. P. Thompson argued in *Whigs and Hunters* about the struggle over the eighteenth-century Game

Acts that the law could not protect property if it did not deliver justice (Thompson 1975: 263). Thompson's argument characterises a contradiction in capitalist society, shows the contradictory presences of oppression and resistance to oppression within a fundamental social institution. The shape of his argument seems relevant here. Faced on the one hand with those who see little but oppression in the canon, and on the other by invocations of the canon's transcendental power, I feel the need to echo him. My attitude to the canon goes something like this: '[the bourgeois idea of] art could not protect property if it did not deliver a critique of the materialism which underpins bourgeois conceptions of property'; or maybe 'the notion that there are canonical works could not protect cultural authority if it did not deliver to those who make themselves familiar with the canon the cultural-self confidence and range of reference which empowers them to critique that authority'. The idea of art protects property, by making the treasured (and owned) object, and thus the socio-economically restricted *ability* to accumulate treasure, seem like a blessing to us all (which perhaps it is). The ability to operate with confidence when it comes to the canon has very powerful effects on the individual's feelings of worth, including the feeling of an ability to stand away from the pressures of the everyday, to resist the mundane and the material in the name of the transcendental. These are contradictory effects.

I want now to argue first that the production and reproduction of cultural hierarchies, such as that which the canon defines, is unavoidable, second that in the face of this inevitability it makes sense to collaborate in the reproduction of a canonical set whose values and resources for teaching can be understood and endorsed, and third, that if it is done properly (both by the teacher and by the student), a reproductive engagement with a loose canon can produce relevant knowledge, transferable understanding and cultural empowerment.

The production in experience, and reproduction in sociability, of some sort of cultural hierarchy is unavoidable. This is worth pointing out because implicit in the critique of the canon is an egalitarian vision of cultural production and reproduction, where no tastes are authoritative, no forms, genres or individual artefacts within a culture have higher status than others. But both on the level of 'culture' as that which the individual has and on the level of the culture of groups, this vision of a flat and undifferentiated cultural field is a mirage. People are forever bound to discriminate among the cultural artefacts which the past has left and the present makes available to us, and to do so through a set of processes which are both individual and social. Making sense of our experiences in culture is bound to involve both absolute distinctions between the significant and the insignificant, and a hierarchisation of the things people find significant: if people did not operate such criteria, they could neither remember nor forget anything.

What would people do with all the art that is produced if they had no brutal, effective and sanctioned ways of ignoring the vast majority of it? Things are getting worse, not better: the number of practising artist-painters in the USA today is twice as great as the whole population of Florence in 1500. They, and their colleagues the world over, produce a flood, an ocean, of candidates for our attention and veneration. People desperately need to be convinced that, out of this sea of stuff, one object, or a string of objects linked by a maker, deserves the name of art. They cope with the anxiety about having missed something or chosen wrong by a massive disinvestment in the unsuccessful candidates, and a massive investment in the chosen ones. But such practices are not just about reducing anxiety and managing excess. Sharing the work of classification and hierarchisation is also a powerful and gratifying form of sociability, a way of defining and maintaining group identities.

It may be argued that while judging, and the sharing of the criteria for and the results of judging, may be necessary, such judging does not have to take the binary form implied by the canon with its short list of redemptive works and its long list of damnable ones. Granted; but people like and often need to work in binary mode; it may be much less fun, much less functional, to nuance, relativise and contextualise every judgement they make or share. I make culturally constructed dismissive binary judgements in vast ranges of the rest of my life; so does everyone; that is how people are. One of the things they do and have to do is make, share and maintain lists of who and what is in or out. These lists, and the behaviours which go along with them, position people in culture, and no one can escape the culture in which they are positioned (though they may escape the culture in which they used to be).

This is not to say that all consumer-cultural selectivity should be obliged to reproduce the values or the visions of social structure embedded in the canon; it can be argued that different social groups should be encouraged to produce their own classifications and hierarchies since they are going to produce them anyway. But as those processes produce a canonoid list, then that list will produce and be reproduced by its own pedagogic institution, its own mini-cultural authority system. The twin experiences of multiculturalism at home and balkanisation in the Balkans suggest strongly that the politics of cultural identity tends to be highly fissiparous, and that cultural authorities in fissiparous culture areas are likely to be more, rather than less intolerant of difference. One alternative to righteous intolerance is a multiculturalism in which the pedagogical authority grants permission to abstain from being inculcated with the values and defining knowledges of the dominant culture. But is this particular alternative to righteous intolerance actually righteous tolerance or something less pleasant; does this toleration tend to be repressive?

I want briefly to explore the issue of the social and political power implicated in cultural competence using the work of a French sociologist, Pierre Bourdieu (1977). From his study of France in the 1960s and 1970s, Bourdieu identifies education's role in validating and perpetuating social hierarchies: he finds a close correlation between access to post-16 education, and to the various grades of higher education, and the uneven distribution of wealth. The richer people are, the more education their children are likely to have; the more education you have, the richer you are likely to be. Education validates wealth as social status. Of course, the match is not usually perfect; but for a huge block of men and women at the bottom (and thus, the odds are, for their children too), relative poverty and relative ignorance go hand in hand. Bourdieu imagines a world of social competition in which the dominant class is internally divided into two: one segment, well-educated and wealthy, which he calls the dominant fraction of the dominant class, and another fraction, highly educated and less wealthy, the dominated fraction of the dominant class. The dominant fraction tends to emphasise that when it comes to culture, the highest is the best: opera, the classics, great art. Their power supports and is supported by the hierarchy of genres; they tend to endorse and promote a highly elevated canon: almost, one might say, a mortar. The dominated fraction tends to see its best hope for wealth and fame in increasing the anxiety of the dominant about their own culture, in making them doubt that the values of high culture are *really* transcendental, piercing their cultural armour by showing that it is more important to talk a good painting than it is to own one.

Below the dominant class, says Bourdieu, is a group which he calls petty-bourgeois; men and women who have access to some wealth, but who do not have the education to validate it or to ensure its reproduction in the next generation. Their attitude to the values of high culture tends to be submissive and uncritical: they see that education (and the cultural values it transmits) is worth getting for what it brings, and if they have to submit to cultural authority in their search for social equality, then so be it. So the dominant fraction of the dominant class have a clear potential ally when it comes to emphasising the importance of the canon.

Below these, says Bourdieu in a bleak analysis, is a mass of people who are relatively poor, and whom schooling has not equipped to rise. Such people are fenced off from wealth, and, by their lack of education, from the personal satisfactions which the consumption of high-cultural goods can bring. This mass of people tends to experience their exclusion from the table at which material and cultural goods are consumed as their own choice; they find ways to deride the goods which the rich and educated consume, and to value those goods with which they have to make do. Bourdieu calls this 'le choix du necessaire' – the illusion that one chooses that with which one is compelled to make do.

A pessimist, a Machiavellian, might argue that much of multiculturalism is driven on by an alliance between this imperative to find ways of loving one's own exclusion, and the need felt by the dominated fraction of the dominant class to destabilise the cultural confidence of the elite, and drive a wedge between them and their potential petty-bourgeois allies. Multiculturalism does not simply say, 'so-called great art is mostly by and for the rich, the men, and the western Europeans, so why should we, the poor, the women and the people from the third world, give a damn?'; rather it claims a righteousness in rejecting that from which the rejecters are *de facto* excluded. This possibility, that multiculturalism is at least potentially a form of the 'choix du necessaire' suggests to me that multiculturalism has disempowering as well as empowering possibilities.

At least for the purposes of analysis, let me distinguish between social skills and cognitive skills. Bourdieu is discussing social skills, and argues that familiarity with 'the master narrative' of the dominant culture is a *sine qua non* of feeling entitled (and being entitled) to a share in the flow of goods, power and satisfactions which capitalism and the nation-state control. The implied obverse of this position is that those who exclude themselves (or are excluded by their schooling) from familiarity with this 'master narrative' will have reduced access to this flow of cultural, political and material goods; thus one may suspect that multiculturalism may not serve the dispossessed very well, however well it serves their spokespeople.

But as well as skills for the social struggle, teachers teach, and students learn, cognitive skills; one might even argue that this is the central purpose of education. What cognitive skills may be developed when a student learns to operate with the canon? Note that the key cognitive skills I list below could doubtless be got using another list of cultural artefacts. A productive (and thus to some extent reproductive) engagement with a canon involves:

- *Judging*: understanding and replicating the process of discriminating between cultural texts/artefacts on the basis of articulated criteria.
- *Worth-finding*: imagining/learning how groups of viewers in other cultural positions [the past] found worth in texts/artefacts.
- *Meaning-finding and testing*: comparison and assessment of validity of different (e.g. historical and contemporary) meanings (*not* values).
- *Developing awareness of cultural relativism*: coming to terms with the under-standing that both meaning and value are historically determined and changing.
- *Understanding of historical process*: in this case, the intellectual, educational and institutional reproduction of the tradition of production and consumption called 'western art'.
- *Imaginative reconstruction of a historical structure*: the canon as relationships and sets (imitation, influence, innovation; school, period-style, persistence of genres).
- *Mastery of a body of data*: such command circularly requires and develops engagement and learning strategies; if successful it enhances self-esteem.

At this point, cognitive skills shade into the development of a positive self-image, the area in which critics of the canon seem to have their clearest targets and easiest shots: how can working-class black women gain anything other than a sense of irrelevance and exclusion, an experience of humiliation, from exposure to a canon made for the pleasure of ruling-class white men? But even here, I am not sure that the arguments go all one way: here too is a world of contradiction, a world in which pedagogic initiatives and resistances are both good and bad. That group of white men are in the ruling class at least in part because they have been taught to be at ease with the canon whose dominant status is being reproduced every day by the art-history industry. Wishing the canon would go away has not been a notably successful strategy to date; giving it a make-over has had some success, but it still walks and talks and weighs the same. It makes more sense, perhaps, to acknowledge the fact that it survives because it meets needs, and inevitably responds to demands for change, to well-supported demands for inclusion and reinterpretation.

Instead of wishing the canon to oblivion teachers should identify for and with our students the sources of its power and the logic of cultural reproduction and distinction of which it gives such clear evidence, and then use the loose canon because it is an adequate resource for the cognitive training, because it is an indispensable resource for cultural entryism, and because it can form the focus of a critical debate with and among students on the realities of cultural power.

Teaching from the canon rather than from another purged list (a *rifled* canon, one might call it) or a value-free (that is, random) assemblage offers the possibility that as the students begin to feel some sort of cognitive and cultural power over the objects they study, they will develop a sense that the canon and its values belong to them, are theirs to play with as they see fit. This is not the only possible outcome: Bloom, for example, clearly feels that he (and all people) belongs to the canon, not the other way around: 'Shakespeare, as we like to forget, largely invented us; if you add the rest of the canon, then Shakespeare and the canon wholly invented us' (Bloom 1994: 41). This hints, I suppose, at the fundamental objection to teaching from the canon. If it is understood and projected by the teacher as embodying overpowering transcendental merit, then it will be hard for any student to develop a position other than prostrate and dependent. Hard enough for those students whose social background and life-chances already make them candidate members of the world defined and legitimized by the canon; harder still for the outsiders who look to education to change their lives, to give, rather than to confirm, cultural power. For students, as for teachers, the canon remains a two-edged weapon, which is not the same as a double-barrelled one. To understand canons as loaded only with the ammunition of oppression is to miss the point. The connection between familiarity with the canon and cultural power is a circular and contradictory one, as I said right at the start of this chapter. If we as teachers seek to protect our students from the canon because of its racist, sexist and classist dimensions, then we implicitly accept the idea that the canon belongs to the powerful, and that the best we can do is hide ourselves and our students from power. We can do better than that.

Questions for discussion

1   Why do democratic governments in nation-states pay large amounts to keep art galleries open in national capitals?
2   Is being able to discuss a work of art a sort of way of owning it?
3   Is 'the canon' a useful metaphor for understanding the relationship between works of art, the status of teachers, and key cultural values in contemporary western societies?

Further reading

Bloom, H. (1994) *The Western Canon: The Books and School of the Ages*, New York: Harcourt Brace. (A 'know your enemy' recommendation.)

Bourdieu, P. (1984) *Distinction: A Social Critique of the Judgement of Taste*, trans. R. Nice, London: Routledge & Kegan Paul. (From *La Distinction*, Paris: Editions de Minuit, 1979.)

19 Forming teacher identities in initial teacher education

Dennis Atkinson

Introduction

The aim of this chapter is to consider some of the issues confronting PGCE (secondary) students as they begin to form their identities as teachers, specifically issues relating to initiating and assessing work produced in the classroom. For many student teachers their PGCE year and their initial years of teaching are the most challenging as they begin to establish themselves as effective teachers. Although in England the *Standards for the Award of Qualified Teacher Status* (Teacher Training Agency 2000a, 2000b, 2001) provide a list of requirements that all intending teachers must satisfy, it is also evident to most people with a knowledge and experience of teaching, that teaching involves much more than this. Some years ago when profiles of teacher competences were being developed, a colleague made the point that when all the statements were taken together they still didn't capture the reality of teaching.

Although the current Standards inventory ensures that student teachers plan their lessons, establish clear learning intentions, develop effective classroom management skills and assess pupils' work, as an approach it produces a reductive and mechanistic discourse about teacher education. This discourse tends to ignore locally contingent, idiosyncratic and psychic processes as they interact with social and contextual factors in schools. These processes consist of a series of conscious actions, unconscious processes, interactions and conversations, impulses and responses, planned activities, disruptions and unexpected events and situations; in other words, as a series of conceptualisations of teaching, the Standards lie at some distance from the phenomenology of action experiences and discourses of beginning to teach, all of which evade simple description. A common tendency I have noticed is that when faced with the Standards inventory, many student teachers pathologise themselves as teachers; they believe something is lacking in themselves.

This chapter describes some of the difficulties student teachers experience as they begin to learn how to teach art and design; it offers an analysis, through the writings of Jacques Lacan, of social and psychic processes that form teacher identities. My intention is to use Lacan to provide a theoretical framework more commensurate with the degrees of complexity involved in becoming a teacher. The result will be an alternative discourse to the Standards, a discourse in which the articulation between the psychic and the social can be explored in relation to the life-world experiences of student teachers.

Discipline, the (Big) Other, '*objet petit a*' and the Real

One of the most difficult aspects of teaching for any beginner is the ability to supervise pupils effectively. Comments such as, 'They were awful today. They just wouldn't listen to me', are quite common. For some student teachers classroom discipline is a major problem; whatever tactics they employ, their pupils simply refuse to settle down and do what is asked of them. Such experiences are extremely stressful. Many will be able to overcome such difficulties by seeking advice and gradually develop effective management strategies. For a few student teachers there seems to be no solution no matter how hard they try, no matter how much they refer to the Standards discourse on classroom management or try to implement course guidelines. In such cases students may blame their pupils, their course tutors or suggest the course is not showing them how to cope with difficult pupils. There is a clear suggestion that if only they were given the correct advice or actually *shown* how to achieve effective supervision then they would be successful. Often they pathologise themselves and begin to feel that they will never become successful teachers. In many of these pathologising discourses student teachers become involved in a process of fetishising both themselves and others. The students blame everything that is going wrong on something *in* themselves or on something *in* the pupils, or something *in* course tutors or something *in* the course. Alternatively these students perceive good teaching, remembered from their school days or observed on teaching practice, as some quality the teacher *possesses*, something they lack and feel they will never obtain. It is possible to view such students as victims of the discourse of the *charismatic subject* (see Moore and Atkinson 1998), a discourse in which teaching is reduced to aspects of personality.

The Standards offer little hope in helping students overcome such anxieties. In fact they may impede progress because they function at a level of ideality at some distance from the phenomenology of students' experiences; they only pathologise students as they struggle to cope in difficult circumstances. In order to overcome this process there is a need to establish a different kind of discourse, one in which students interrogate themselves as historically constructed within particular discourses and practices. This different discourse would help students realise that interactions with the 'other' (pupils, training programmes, course tutors) can also be *read* as specific discourses that offer a way out of pathology into a more constructive discursive position. In this way students may *read themselves* not as lacking or possessing particular qualities but as constructed through experiences, discourses and relationships. This enables them to comprehend how such histories affect and inform their current relations with others when learning how to teach. Such an examination considers socio-economic power relations involving issues of class, gender, race and sexuality. It involves reflection on classroom practice and power relations as well as the ideologies of knowledge that underpin the school curriculum. By occupying such discursive positions students may then be able to take a different perspective on the task of learning how to teach and avoid blaming themselves and others for the difficulties they are experiencing.

In my work as a teacher educator I have found the work of Lacan useful for developing strategies to help student teachers in their struggles. His writing is deeply concerned with the formation of the subject within symbolic systems such as language. One of his key ideas is that we can never know the subject-in-herself/himself, rather, the subject we know is a subject-of-language and any attempt to understand ourselves and others, is always a self or other of language. Lacan's term for the symbolic order is the (Big) Other. For Lacan, signifiers do not refer directly to specific signifieds, that is to say words do not refer directly to things or people-in-themselves. Language is a material medium, it constructs objects and subjects that it signifies and meaning is accomplished through chains of signification in which 'a signifier represents the subject for another signifier' (Lacan 1991: 207).

The signifier, producing itself in the field of the Other, makes manifest the subject of its signification. But it functions as a signifier only to reduce the subject in question to being no more than a signifier, to petrify the subject in the same movement in which it calls the subject to function, to speak, as a subject (Lacan 1991: 207).

Zizek provides a good illustration of this process. He focuses on the medical chart, which usually hangs at the bottom of a hospital patient's bed. This chart, as a signifier, does not represent the patient-in-him- or herself directly for other subjects such as doctors and nurses, 'but primarily for other signifiers, for the symbolic network of medical knowledge' (Zizek 1998: 74). Similarly a pupil's school report does not represent the pupil-in-her- or himself directly for teachers and parents but for the signifying chains of different institutionalised subject-knowledge discourses.

The idea that people are *constructed* through experiences and discourses allows student teachers to get away from essentialist stances towards themselves and others so that when they experience difficulties in teaching they don't blame themselves or others but try to evaluate the symbolic systems (curriculum structures, management strategies, planning, social and political context) in which both they and their pupils are positioned.

Lacan also uses the term '*objet petit a*' (Lacan 1991: 270) to describe objects of desire that do not exist but which we strive to attain, fantasy objects that have no existence in reality but which structure our desire. Attempts to reveal the essence of society, tradition, intelligence and ability in order to expose their hidden kernel of meaning ultimately always fail because such terms are constituted on an essential lack which is masked by the very term itself. A good example of how this theoretical term can be helpful in teacher education contexts concerns the obsessive attempts of some students to achieve *discipline* before they attempt to teach a lesson. Their focus on *achieving discipline* can prevent them from realising that what this term refers to is in fact a by-product of other more specific teaching strategies which they can in fact develop. These strategies include: effective planning, stimulating and relevant teaching projects, better use of voice, and class management. This is more constructive than allowing students to blame themselves for something they believe they do not possess and persisting in reading their teaching within a discourse of personality. Students may begin to acknowledge that the *actions they are taking are unproductive* rather than thinking that *something in themselves* is lacking. Thus the signifier 'discipline' is not a point of density of meaning, although this appears to be the case, rather it can be viewed as a signifier without a signified (*objet petit a*) in that the apparent reference to a specific object (discipline) is created through a fantasy object of desire (the need to attain discipline).

Student teachers may also begin to recognise that the task of achieving successful classroom management involves levels of actions and responses that cannot be symbolised within discourses such as the Standards for QTS. The latter constructs an essentialised picture of teaching whereas what student teachers need to 'know-in-action' cannot be conveyed in such discourses because the action-space is too complex to be represented in language. Lacan's term the 'Real' (1988: 66) is helpful here because it hints at a 'hard impenetrable kernel that resists symbolisation' (Zizek 1989: 169). Bowie writes:

> The network of signifiers in which we have our being is not all that there is, and the rest of what is may chance to break in upon us at any moment.
>
> (Bowie 1991: 103)

It is the 'rest of what is' which could be said to constitute the Lacanian Real and which people experience purely as contingent encounters that disrupt symbolic networks. On encountering the Real, Bowie (1991: 105) argues: 'the mind makes contact with the limits of its power, with that which its structure cannot structure'. The essential point is that the eruption of the Real within the symbolic order (Big Other) creates a destabilisation of frameworks of understanding. However, although the Real invokes a disturbance of the symbolic order it is important not to forget that the symbolic order introduces a cut in the Real (see Evans 1996: 159); although the Real is always primary it is largely overwhelmed by ideas of reality which are products of symbolisation. So, as well as denoting that which lies beyond symbolisation, the Real, by implication, refers to that which is lacking in the symbolic order, that which is foreclosed by the symbolic and which can never be grasped. In the attempt to define good teaching the Lacanian relation between the symbolic and the Real suggests that there will always be something lacking. What is lacking could be described as 'the Real of teaching' in contradistinction to the symbolic order of teaching.

Points de capiton

Translated into English as 'quilting point' or 'anchoring point' this term refers literally to an upholstery button, a device which pins down the stuffing in upholstery work. Lacan (1977: 303) uses the term to discuss how particular signifiers retroactively stitch the subject into the signifying chain. Zizek (1989) develops the notion of quilting with reference to the Althusserian idea of interpellation and shows how key signifiers interpellate or 'hail' individuals into subject positions. He describes how meaning is structured through key nodal points or signifiers which articulate the truth of a particular ideological discourse. For example, if a discourse concerned with freedom is quilted through communism, the result will be a particular structure of meaning relating to class struggle. On the other hand, if this discourse is quilted through an idea of liberal democracy a different structure of meaning develops. Zizek (1989: 88) argues that ideological struggles hinge on choosing the most effective *points de capiton*, that is to say those key signifiers that capture and thereby totalise the field of meaning. For example, ideological struggles involved in art education depend upon key signifiers around which and upon whose sense a particular discourse is structured. Art practice quilted through the signifier 'self-expression' will produce a different structure of meaning to art practice quilted through the signifier 'critical studies' or the signifier 'basic design'. Currently the English National Curriculum for Art and design has emerged with a new hegemony, a totalising discourse whose key signifiers: technique, knowledge, performance and attainment, produce a particular structure of meaning.

The *point de capiton* therefore is the signifier that unifies a given field and constitutes its identity (Zizek 1989: 95–6). The importance of this term for the constitution of subjectivity and identity is crucial:

> The *point de capiton* is the point through which the subject is sewn to the signifier, and at the same time the point which interpellates individual into subject by addressing it with the call of a master signifier ... – in a word, it is the point of the subjectivation of the signifier's chain
>
> (Zizek 1989: 101)

The National Curriculum for Art and design in England (DfEE 1999b) constitutes the official subject pedagogy according to which student teachers must plan and organise their teaching and assess pupils' art work. This curriculum can be viewed as a discourse underpinned by key signifiers, *knowledge*, *skills*, *understanding* and *attainment* (*points de capiton*) in which both pupils' and teachers' pedagogised identities are formed. Through this discourse they are interpellated as specific pedagogised subjects. In Foucauldian terms the NC discourse functions as a form of institutionalised power-knowledge which regulates and normalises a particular approach to pedagogy and practice. Earlier forms of pedagogy advocating self-expression (Witkin 1974; Ross 1983; Abbs 1987) are underplayed in NC programmes of study which tend to foreground subject knowledge and its application. There are those who believe that the current concern with adopting a technicist approach to art education with its emphasis upon teaching specific skills and knowledge is at the expense of creativity, learning and pluralism (Ross 1995; Hughes 1998; Swift and Steers 1999). In the Order for Art and design the idea of self-expression is not abandoned but it does not figure prominently as it once did. The need to teach specific skills and forms of knowledge within subject boundaries lies in stark contrast, for example, to the report *Opening Minds: Education for the 21st Century* (Royal Society of Arts (RSA) 1999), which emphasises learning and suggests that rigid subject boundaries are inappropriate for the twenty-first century. What educators need to consider in relation to the formation of such teacher identifications are the kinds of *restrictions in production* (Butler 1997: 84) that pedagogical discourses such as the Standards for QTS and the NC subject orders invoke.

I will unfold these more general comments on the formation of pedagogised identities within the ideology of curriculum discourses into more local functioning contexts of learning how to teach art and design in secondary schools. The following vignettes raise several issues relating to the forming of teacher and pupil identities in initial teacher education and to the socio-psychic processes in which such identifications are formed and change.

Angela's story

Angela is beginning her teaching practice in a difficult secondary school in the East End of London, the students are lively and for many teachers the task of gaining their attention to begin a lesson provides a challenge. In an initial interview after teaching a class of Year 9 students Angela said:

> You have to be careful not to give these kinds of pupils any choices otherwise they get confused and just sit there staring at you or each other wondering what to do. This happened in a lesson where we were doing collage and I gave them a choice of how to proceed to make their collages. After I finished speaking they just looked confused. I knew I shouldn't have given them a choice . . . I should have just told them what to do because that's what they expect. After the lesson I felt awful and I know that in future I won't make the same mistake, I won't give them a choice because I've learned that's what they can't handle.

The interesting point for me about this statement is to read it as a discourse in which Angela is already forming herself as a particular kind of teacher and her pupils as particular kinds of learners through the interpretation she makes of her actions and her pupils' responses which are quilted by the term 'choice'. She creates an imaginary identification, an imaginary image of her pupils by conceiving them as unable to cope with choice and who therefore require explicit instructions. In this pathologising discourse she imagines that these pupils are unable to explore and experiment in their learning and, by implication, require a didactic form of teaching. In these very early experiences of teaching therefore, Angela is already beginning to develop specific pedagogic relations and to conceive specific pedagogised identities of herself and her students as she reads them through a discourse in which 'choice' functions as a key term totalising her framework of meaning.

Two or three points emerge here: is Angela's pathologising interpretation of her pupils' attitude and approach to learning a true reflection of their capabilities, or is her discourse a form of defence in which she is able to provide reasons for an unsuccessful lesson? In offering choice is she able to cope with the consequences of her actions and provide detailed support for individual responses? Or, as someone learning how to teach, is it the case that she has not yet acquired the support skills and strategies to allow her to respond to the different ways pupils respond to her actions? In other words her intention to allow pupils a degree of choice in their learning is a laudable strategy but putting this into practice is another matter entirely.

At this moment in her teaching Angela believes that she must adopt a specific teaching strategy with these pupils because of her pathologised image of both herself and them as learners. She proceeds to position herself and pupils within a particular pedagogic discourse where certain power relations are manifest in the form of a didactic and instructional pedagogy. All this seems to be the outcome of a lesson that did not go according to plan. Angela blames herself, that is to say she blames her planning and organisation of the lesson, which she interprets as flawed and unsuccessful and she pathologises her pupils in terms of their inability to embrace choice. For her, giving this class choice is perceived as a mistake. She does not acknowledge at this stage of learning to teach that putting pedagogies into practice is something that requires perfecting, that will involve quite complex management and supporting strategies.

Rather than persisting with a sound pedagogical idea, encouraging difference and variety in pupils' art practices, and rather than consider alternative strategies to teaching in support of choice, Angela wants to reduce the possibility of failure by imposing a tighter form of pedagogic control. This response is not untypical of someone beginning to teach, who, having planned carefully, is not yet able to cope with the responses of pupils due to lack of experience. Yet the difficulty for both the teacher educator and the student teacher is that those processes which constitute the 'experience-which-needs-to-be-acquired' in order to implement effective pedagogy evade symbolisation: they cannot be signified in language.

At this stage in her teaching Angela is unable to enter a double hermeneutic in which she might function reflexively not only upon her pupils' responses but also upon herself (her emotions, feelings, thoughts) by asking herself why she feels this way about what happened. By depersonalising issues she can begin to consider how she is constructing both herself as a teacher and her pupils as learners, through a 'blaming' and 'pathologising' discourse.

Andy's story

Andy's initial observations of art lessons in his teaching practice school are that they seemed uninspiring. He remembers learning art in school as an enjoyable experience, but admits it may not have been such a positive experience for his school friends. However, these initial observations make him feel depressed because they are focused upon technical training in specific skills and not enough upon developing ideas in visual form.

> My main worry is planning schemes of work according to school briefs. I need to fight my corner in terms of the outlook of the department. I'm aware that I'm training and I might not do things confidently and I need support . . . but at the

same time what's it all for . . . I have a stake in all this, I need to pursue that otherwise I won't be able to go for jobs in the places that will support that way of working.

Andy is highly motivated by 'issues-based' art education, a form of pedagogy and practice in which pupils explore social, cultural and personal issues through art practice. Workshops and lectures on the university-based part of the course introduce him to this way of working. He perceives a big problem in not being able to develop work that interests him. He experiences a feeling of being instructed what to teach so that ownership of his teaching, of himself as a teacher, diminishes; he hints at a kind of cloning process, a kind of ventriloquism.

I'm not being told exactly how to do things but they say things like, if you give kids a project on war all you'll get are clichés, hackneyed responses.

However, Andy is also experiencing great difficulty in trying to formulate quite simple project and lesson plans; he struggles to plan a sequential structure to his projects. Andy's desire to 'find himself' as a teacher is strong at this stage, and he perceives the system as militating against this desire, which is driven by his infatuation with a specific pedagogy (issues-based art education) i.e. the desire for a particular pedagogy and practice and the desire to take on a particular identification as a teacher. It is as though Andy is occupying conflictual positions in different discourses, one concerned with a pedagogy he desires to practise, and another concerned with a pedagogy towards which he feels antipathy. Such conflictual discourses involve conflictual pedagogised identifications. Although Andy has this burning desire to employ a particular pedagogy, he struggles to cope with what might be termed the 'basics of planning lessons and teaching projects'. His desire to facilitate a particular kind of learning through art is hampered by a struggle to understand how to plan, structure and sequence projects. His school tutors feel that he needs to grapple with these issues but he reads their guidance as too invasive and as instructing him how to teach.

Angela's and Andy's stories can also be interpreted as consequences of the constraining effects of a one-year teacher education course in relation to developing critical reflection and subsequent effective action. Angela feels a strong desire to slip quickly into forming specific pedagogical approaches; the system does not provide adequate time or space for detailed exploration and evaluation of different pedagogy–practice relations. The front loading of prescribed approaches to planning that takes place on PGCE courses to meet NC and TTA requirements prevents meaningful consideration of alternative approaches. Andy feels that he has to subscribe to a form of teaching and learning promoted by his teaching practice department. He is keen to experiment but believes he is denied the opportunity to do so. His course tutors feel a strong desire to encourage him to grapple with the 'basics' of planning. The conflict of interests here hinges upon *preferred identities* and their related forms of practice and understanding.

Assessment and fetishism

Assessing pupils' art work is one of the most difficult aspects of teaching. As a teacher educator I have real difficulty in providing advice which does not conform, subscribe or pander to discourses which are ultimately suspect. Many students know from their own understanding and experience of making art that the very idea of assessing art work is contentious. It seems to them anathema to the purpose and function of art practice. I can best describe my dilemma and their concerns about assessment by reference to Zizek's writing on fetishism.

Zizek (1997) describes the process of fetishised social relations by the way people treat their king or queen, as if being a monarch is a natural property rather than a political construct. He extends the idea of 'fetishist misrecognition' to institutions:

> The notion of a certain fetishism which is independent of the opposition between 'people' and 'objects': it designates the state in which the effect of a 'structure', of a network, is (mis)perceived as the direct property of an individual entity.
>
> (Zizek 1997: 100)

For example, someone might say: 'the school is responsible for my child's problems', placing the blame on teachers' relationships with their child and failing to acknowledge that such personal interactions are determined by the 'invisible' symbolic order of the institution.

In the process of assessing art work, pupils are fetishised in terms of the *abilities* they appear to possess and their work is fetishised in terms of possessing particular *qualities*. However, notions of ability *in* the pupil or qualities *in* the artwork are 'materialisations of the symbolic institution' and not specific properties of people or things. Yet teachers and pupils proceed to function in this institutionalised process as though they are concerned with identifying natural properties.

> When we are victims of the 'fetishist' illusion, we (mis)perceive as the immediate/'natural' property of the fetish-object that which is conferred upon this object by virtue of its place within the structure
>
> (Zizek 1997: 105)

The important point here is that when functioning within institutions such as schools, everyone is taken over by the symbolic order of the institution. Some student teachers find it difficult to come to terms with this. As in Andy's experience, many student teachers experience conflictual discursive positionings as they enter the symbolic order of the school art department. Discussing 'the primordial substitution' (Zizek 1997: 109–11) Zizek describes social and psychic processes in which *the Other does things for me*, as, for example, canned laughter on television. In relation to institutional performative speech acts (see Austin 1966), such as assessment statements or evaluation comments, where words bring into being that about which they speak, Zizek makes the point:

In the very gesture of accomplishing an act by uttering words, I am deprived of authorship; the 'big Other' (symbolic institution) speaks through me. It is no wonder, then, that that there is something puppet-like about people whose professional function is essentially performative [aspects of teachers' work, Ofsted] they are reduced to the living embodiment of the symbolic institution.

(Zizek 1997: 110)

Here the institution-as-signifier directs action and understanding to the extent that, in assessment, the work of pupils and the pupils-as-learners are given their place in the symbolic order of the institution. Both teachers and pupils as pedagogised subjects are represented and constructed by signifiers of the symbolic order of the institutional discourse of assessment. Zizek's notion of primordial substitution has direct significance for current Ofsted inspections of teaching and teacher education in England; the Ofsted inspector's sole duty is to confer the institutional seal of approval on the work of teachers and teacher-educators and this is achieved through the discourse of Standards.

An illustration of the institutional symbolic order 'at work' can be viewed in discourses of assessment in which pupils' abilities and consequently their pedagogic identities are constructed. I have written previously (Atkinson 1998, 2001) about the use of the term *accuracy* in assessment of observational drawings. The use of this term suggests that the representational purpose of such drawing is to achieve optical truth, that is to say a direct correspondence with viewed reality. Accuracy functions as a Lacanian *point de capiton* in that it provides a semantic pivot around which meaning in the assessment discourse is structured. What fails to be recognised is that the signifier *accuracy* does not refer to a pupil's ability to produce a drawing that depicts the world as it is seen (although it appears to suggest this meaning) but according to the drawing's fit within a chosen symbolic order of representation. To employ a key Lacanian phrase, the word *accuracy* as used in assessment discourse is 'a signifier which represents the subject for another signifier' (Lacan 1991: 207).

Conclusion

By making reference to key Lacanian concepts I have hinted at ways in which student teachers and teacher educators may be helped to interrogate and perhaps overcome some of the difficulties and perplexities involved in the task of learning how to teach. It seems important that student teachers are able to adopt forms of discourse within which they can reflect upon their own and others' positions and experiences within the institution. I have argued that although it provides a series of helpful expectations, the Standards discourse constructs an ideal image of teaching which fails to embrace the idiosyncratic and fragile states of student teachers learning how to teach. When presented with the Standards inventory student teachers often pathologise themselves according to its demands. The Standards, in tandem with the NC Orders encapsulate a particular ideology of teaching to which student teachers and teacher educators *must* subscribe. This counteracts and suppresses critique of the ideological underpinnings of aspects of teaching such as assessment or of social structures in which institutional forms of education exist, it suppresses the task of trying to formulate a discourse-of-practice in which the practical struggle to teach effectively finds some purchase.

Questions for discussion

1   What issues does this chapter raise for understanding the student teacher's construction of him/herself as a teacher of art in relation to government requirements for teacher training?
2   Does the exploration of the human subject as a construction in language, thus denying the idea of the individual as a natural entity, offer us a purchase to interrogate the discourses in which teachers and teaching, learners and learning are conceived?

Further reading

Hammersley, M. (ed.) (1999) *Researching School Experience: Ethnographic Studies of Teaching and Learning*, London and New York: Falmer.
Moore, A. and Atkinson, D. (1998) 'Charisma, Competence and Teacher Education', *Discourse: Studies in the Cultural Politics of Education*, 19(2): 171–82.
Zizek, S. (1989) *The Sublime Object of Ideology*, London and New York: Verso.

20 Reflections on multicultural art history

Gen Doy

In this chapter, I want to think through, and encourage the discussion of, some problems and issues raised by the notion of the 'multicultural' with specific reference to researching and teaching art history and their impact in secondary schools. In so doing, I hope to suggest some ways of moving forward, rather than state hard and fast conclusions.

My impressions are that in many ways, things have improved in a large number of schools and colleges in the UK since I was at school and university in the 1950s–1970s. I grew up in a small village in Scotland and saw one Black person and, I think, one Chinese person, until I became a university student and went to live in Glasgow. Even then, no Black or Asian students were in any of the classes I took – English, French, German and history of fine art. As a white person of a vaguely Protestant upbringing in central Scotland, the most obvious targets of prejudice for someone of my background tended to be Catholics or tinkers. Fortunately I did not behave badly to the former, since I liked art and enjoyed looking at books with pictures of saints and other holy people, to the extent that my parents were worried that I might convert to Catholicism, but I, along with many others in my school, gave the occasional visiting tinker/traveller children a bad time due to my ignorance. When I consider the much more open attitudes of my own children, and the opportunities they have to make friends from a wide range of cultural and geographical backgrounds in state schools, I see a huge improvement compared to educational culture in Scotland in the post-war period. Of course there are many things which remain to be done, but it is worth pointing to the importance of such general improvements. However, these should not be taken for granted. Many steps forward are due to the attitudes and efforts of ordinary people, rather than those with state responsibility. It is important to remember that the state is not just a provider of education and healthcare, the things most people care about, but the police and the army, where it is doubtful if 'multiculturalism' has made much of an impact.

Indeed 'multiculturalism' is a vague term, and as such masks some pretty big problems. At best, it suggests a move to value various cultures equally, to take the best from a variety of cultures (while rejecting the worst?), and an avoidance of pressure to force integration of 'other' cultures into 'mainstream' culture (already the problems with the ideologically weighted terminology which is everywhere in discussions of such topics can be seen). In the middle somewhere, multiculturalism can result in a tolerance of difference, among groups of fragmented identities and smaller interest groups who have to struggle to find out what could unite them against the source of their problems. Or multiculturalism can entail a kind of woolly liberal tolerance where there is a tacit agreement among all the participants that no one will criticise any reactionary elements of any culture. At worst, multiculturalism is an avoidance of the problem of racism and imperialism, and becomes a soft option to replace a directly antiracist approach.

The artist Rasheed Araeen has written some excellent critiques of multiculturalism as a concept, and is dismissive, correctly in my view, of such fashionable postcolonial and postmodern concepts as hybridity, in-betweenness and the like. Araeen argues that the in-between space, experienced by immigrants, exiles and refugees, beloved of cultural critics such as Homi K. Bhabha, who extols its liberating potential at length in his book *The Location of Culture* (1994), is:

> A mythical space between the periphery and the centre through which the post-colonial artist must pass before he or she becomes a fully recognized historical subject. This has let the art institutions in the West 'off the hook' and provided them with a new framework – multiculturalism – by which the 'other' artist can be kept outside mainstream art history and at the same time promoted and celebrated on the basis of his or her cultural difference. In other words, multiculturalism is now a new institutional strategy of containment . . . a new marginality of multiculturalism, in which only the expressions of cultural differences are seen to be authentic.
>
> (Araeen 1999: 233)

In all of the schools my two sons have attended, pupils are obliged to do religious education. At all levels of their education, I've tried to prevent this, as we are all atheists. Responses varied from 'Well, he won't be able to go to the Christmas party then!' (infant school) to 'Do you mean you don't want your son to learn about other cultures?' (secondary school). In the latter instance, a discussion ensued which went along the lines of assuming that I was perhaps racist, because I did not want my sons to learn about other cultures (equated with faiths), which were, it was implied, not 'white'. As a result, one of my sons has ended up doing a GCSE specialising in Islam, despite his lack of interest, since he was convinced that Christianity would be even more boring. Ironically, some pupils are allowed to opt out of religious education 'on religious grounds', but not on the grounds of being non-religious! The usefulness of all this in terms of tackling racism or even fostering multiculturalism is extremely dubious. Culture is tied even more strongly to religion, a backward step in my view.

Recently I attended a seminar organised by our city council on cultural planning. Again, the framework of this was 'multicultural', and the individual talks had much of value in them. But suddenly, one of the speakers started to talk of how all the 'faith communities' in Leicester needed to be visible, to have their monuments and culture encouraged and funded by the city council and seen as part of the city and its life. I had a vision of hundreds of places of worship springing up all over the place. How atheists were to have visible culture in this scenario was not mentioned. This coupling of culture and religious faith is something I find depressing, and it seems to be on the increase after the attack on the World Trade Center in New York. Religious art exists, and obviously many impressive examples of art are religious in content, but to conflate culture and religion, and to judge culture on religious grounds, is a retrograde step and one on which teachers should encourage debate, not take for granted.

A few years ago I taught a young devout Muslim woman art history. The university was happy to see her enrol, as its staff were aware that they rarely get the chance to welcome students from Black and Asian backgrounds wanting to specialise in our subject. This student elected to study with me on a course entitled 'French art and society 1848–88'. One of the topics we looked at was Orientalism, and a key example of Orientalist painting was discussed in lectures and seminars. This was *The Slave Market* painted in the mid-1860s by the French artist J.-L. Gérôme (www.tanos.org.uk/orientalism/jlgmarche.html). This picture shows a group of Arab men in North African dress, gathered round a naked, light-skinned woman. One man puts two fingers into her mouth, perhaps to feel the state of her teeth, but this motif seems a pretext for presenting an erotic encounter between a Black man in a position of power, and a white(r) woman at his mercy. As the art historian Linda Nochlin pointed out in an article originally published in 1983, this painting and others like it seemed to be addressed to a white, male spectator in a colonial power such as France (Nochlin 1991). This spectator could enjoy the view of the naked woman and, at the same time, feel morally superior to the Arab slave traders and their inhuman and lascivious attitudes; after all, slavery had been abolished in France. Actually it was only in 1848 that slavery had been finally abolished by the French Republican government, so the situation in the painting was not as 'outdated' in terms of French culture as might be supposed. A few years after Nochlin's article, Reina Lewis (1996) wrote a book on women and Orientalism, arguing that such paintings were not just for white male spectators, and that female viewers in colonial countries could, and did, experience pleasure in viewing them, and even in painting comparable subjects. So, here was a problem to be discussed. What would the students make of it? Unfortunately I never found out what the young Muslim woman thought, because she (later) told me that she was not allowed to look at the painting due to its content. At first I thought that this was another example of cultural imperialism at work, and that white European culture had 'won' again: the 'Orientals' objectified in Orientalist painting were being prevented from discussing and criticising such works because their own culture did not permit them to look at these immoral pictures.

A few years ago I wrote a short essay discussing theory and practice in the teaching of art and visual culture history (Doy 2000b). I wanted to pay particular attention to issues of 'race', class and gender in visual culture, and I'll return to these issues later in this chapter. (I place inverted commas around 'race' because I do not accept that there is any scientific proof of the division of human beings into groups called races.) In my previous piece, I wanted to draw attention to an essay by

Walter Benjamin, 'The Author as Producer' (1934), in relation to teaching (Benjamin 1986). In his essay Benjamin discusses creative writing, and argues:

> An author who teaches writers nothing, teaches no one. What matters, therefore, is the exemplary character of production, which is able first to induce other producers to produce, and second to put an improved apparatus at their disposal. And this apparatus is better the more consumers it is able to turn into producers – that is, readers or spectators into collaborators.
>
> (Benjamin 1986: 233)

As a teacher of visual culture and art history, I would want to do something along the lines that Benjamin suggests for the revolutionary writer. Now this is not easy. It means turning consumers into producers, not producers of stuff for the same system, using the same means. This is what teaching should do, though I can't claim I manage this very often. It means enabling students to go out and do without you, and in the end, do it better, contributing to the creation of more critical and radical frameworks of creative knowledge. As I mentioned in my earlier essay, the present state of education has done much to make children, their parents and students into consumers, in a process which is completely the opposite from the one advocated by Benjamin. Many teachers have reluctantly been forced into the role of stifling what Benjamin calls the 'productive' qualities of children and young adults in their care in the interests of the National Curriculum and supposedly raising standards.

For artists, too, becoming 'productive' in Benjamin's sense of the word, means turning the viewers of your works into participants and critically aware subjects, not passive consumers. The artists' and viewers' pleasure in the work could be accompanied by a new perspective on notions of art and its institutions. This is the possibility open to the radical artist, but not all artists are, obviously. And even if they want to be, the pressures for incorporation into an art world based on 'neo-liberal multiculturalism' as Rasheed Araeen puts it, are huge. Now we do not just have a culturally exotic Other, says Araeen (2000) but a politically exotic Other. As examples he cites Chinese artists who can make fun of what happens in China, an Iranian artist living in New York can represent the condition of Iranian women as exotically alienated, and so on. Araeen continues:

> All these artists can now be *celebrated* institutionally in the West. *But the buck stops here.* Try to turn your eyes towards the ideological and institutional structures of the system, which is now so concerned with the plight and struggles of peoples in other countries, and you will see how the doors shut in your face.
>
> (Araeen 2000: 17)

One of the reasons why Araeen has not received the recognition already accorded to other Black and Asian British artists is that his works have been based on a politically critical position with regard to art institutions and ideologies. He has documented his own struggle with the Arts Council and other bodies to exhibit both his own works and the works of other Black and Asian artists (Araeen 1984).

Now clearly, part of a more 'productive' teaching process would involve doing something about the white Euro-centric content of much of the art history curriculum. However, it is not just a matter of including some more material about 'other' cultures – it is also a question of how this material is going to be taught. Since the mid-1980s or so, a great deal of progress has been made in this respect, but it remains the case that the material available and the theoretical advances in art history with regard to say, women and women's art, far outstrip those made in the field of Black and Asian artists and representations of Black and Asian people. However, more and more useful material is becoming available, for example the archive of the work of African and Asian visual artists at the University of East London, a bibliography of contemporary African, African Caribbean and Asian British art (Keen and Ward 1996), some excellent publications from the Institute of International Visual Arts (inIVA), for example the volume of theoretical texts on African art (Oguibe and Enwezor 1999) and useful Open University material (Barker 1999; King 1999). There is also a project entitled Globalising Art, Architecture and Design History (GLAADH: see www.glaadh.ac.uk) developed by art and design historians at the University of Sussex, the Open University and Middlesex University. The GLAADH website incorporates newsletters, reports, bibliographies and other useful information, for teachers wanting to develop their courses beyond the usual suspects, i.e. North American and European artists. Much of this is very helpful indeed. However, I felt a bit uneasy with the idea of 'globalisation', a term which conjures up a kind of glossy view of imperialism, as its cultural tentacles reach everywhere on earth, inviting people in poor and exploited colonies and semi-colonies to buy into a global culture based on smoking western cigarettes, wearing trainers, and designer clothes made in South Asian sweatshops. Such examples of globalisation are presented by Naomi Klein (2000) in her book *No Logo*. Debates over terminology in cultural studies and art history are common, and terms such as multiculturalism and globalisation are no exception. Ironically, while this GLAADH project sees globalisation as a way forward for art history, in economic terms globalisation is a means of the economic exploitation of colonial and semi-colonial countries (now called least developed countries), by imperialist powers and their multinational businesses. The World Bank, World Trade Organisation and International Monetary Fund and the imperialist governments push free trade and transnational capital flow as the way for poor nations to pull themselves up to 'our' levels. Increased globalisation, including the export of jobs to low-pay, non-union areas of the world economy, such as China or Mexico, has actually meant the increase of economic inequality. Imperialism's answer to this is that globalisation has not gone far enough:

> If inequality has increased in Africa, rural China and rural India they are victims of the lack of globalisation. It makes better sense to extend the scope of globalisation which means addressing the causes of their isolation.
>
> (*The Economist* 28 April 2001, quoted in Harvey 2001: 11)

Thus recent protest movements have come together in loose coalitions as an anti-globalisation movement. In my view, the idea of globalising art history has negative connotations and would be better replaced by the word 'internationalising', otherwise we risk comparing the task of including art history from other countries in the curriculum, with that of the urge to dominate other countries inherent in the economic globalisation process of the World Bank and the World Trade Organisation.

There are understandable problems with widening the curriculum though it is of course necessary. I have sometimes noticed a certain tendency to see this as a good marketing opportunity to attract so-called non-standard students. That is, since the universities have reached saturation point in the market for 'normal' students who are drawn from outside the working class and families on benefits, they need to look for students who are older, from poorer families and who are Black and/or Asian, single parents etc. What better way to attract some of these students than to put on more courses in 'their' cultures? Now of course this needs to be seen dialectically, and putting on courses in Black art is not a negative thing, but the idea that this will automatically attract Black students is a bit cynical and/or naive, and assumes that Black students will want to take 'Black' courses. Educators should consider whether the content of such courses needs to be embedded throughout the curriculum or not. I don't think there's any one answer here, and educators need to look carefully at individual contexts. A major problem for poorer students from non-standard backgrounds would be solved if all students received proper grants based on a decent industrial wage, if childcare was available at all colleges and universities, and education could become more of a pleasure rather than the uphill struggle it is for many school, college and university students in contemporary society.

Further difficulties arise in that people tend to start with what they know and move from there to less familiar material. For most art historians in Britain, this means moving from a knowledge of US and European art in order to add 'other' things to existing knowledge. Thus a framework is set up from the beginning that involves a central core of knowledge, and a surrounding periphery. It will take some time to overcome this. Also, there is just too much material for one person to assimilate and teach without becoming a kind of cultural tourist. One person simply cannot be an expert on African, Asian, and South American art. What might be a way forward here would be to structure courses around theories, approaches and methods, rather than bodies of knowledge about, say, Indian temples or contemporary African art. Even these subjects are huge. There is a lot I do not know about US or European art, which come from relatively smaller areas of the world than Africa or Asia, and I've been working on mainly European visual arts (excluding architecture) for more than thirty years! Rather than look for a globalising approach, perhaps educators can try for a critically aware anti-imperialist, antiracist, anti-exploitative approach, whether this involves looking at French Impressionism, young British artists (yBas) or Jean-Michel Basquiat. Educators need quality solutions, not quantity ones.

But . . . more problems. Given that art is, in the famous Marxist phrase, relatively autonomous (i.e. relatively detached and independent from the economics of particular societies, yet ultimately inextricably linked to these productive forces), how can educators avoid falling into the habit of 'using' art works to discuss social issues, while almost forgetting that they are art? This is something I find myself doing often unless I take care, and I want to address this issue here.

In works by, for example, Keith Piper or Roshini Kempadoo, subtle yet serious and hard-hitting embodiments of economic, political, artistic and technological engagement can be found. I have discussed works by these artists at length elsewhere (Doy 2000a), so will comment only briefly on them in this chapter. Both artists have recently used digital image construction and other computer technologies to engage with what we have seen Benjamin call 'productive' art. Kempadoo, in her website and computer-generated photography project *Sweetness and Light*, 1996–7 (http://mitpress2.mit.edu/e-journals/leonardo/gallery/gallery294/kempadoo.html) uses digital imagery tools to draw an analogy between slavery and the production of profits for the construction of English elite culture and its country houses and estates, with the exploitative development of new information technology, as well as its radical potential, and the place of female and Black workers within this context (Figure 20.1). In Kempadoo's image, a Black waitress serves the viewer with computerised visual knowledge on a silver tray, while behind her a Black woman from an earlier historical period is shown posed for an 'ethnographic' photograph which will measure and classify her along 'racial' lines. She is enclosed and framed by the stone balustrade of an English country-house garden.

Piper also sees contradictions and possibilities in art using new technologies, which can create consumers but also genuinely interactive subjects who engage positively and critically with the works. In a still, *Tagging the Other* (Figure 20.2), from Piper's CD produced to accompany a catalogue of his exhibition of *Relocating*

Figure 20.1 Sweetness and Light (1996–7), Roshini Kempadoo.

Figure 20.2 Tagging the Other (1997), Keith Piper.

the Remains (1997), from the section entitled *Unclassified*, a complex montage of imagery (and sound) includes surveillance devices, tooled-up riot police and a computer on a classical column. Immigration, uprisings and presence on streets and shopping centres are controlled and monitored by new technology, accompanied, when necessary, by old-fashioned brute force. Yet it is digital technology that enables the artist to create such powerful images to invite us to confront such situations and meanings. In particular, computer technology can be used to develop new dialogues around ethnicity and identities:

> Racial identities are rapidly evolving, partly caused by technology's role in the production of new images. Take desktop publishing and its promise and, one would hope, fulfilment in enabling a plurality of identities to be heard. On the other hand, access to tools is limited through the means of distribution. That inevitably lies with the large, moneyed institutions.
>
> (Piper in Doy 2000b: 111)

It is necessary to discuss the techniques and artistry used in these works, for this is part of their radical nature. These works are not just about their 'content'. This is clearly true for all art. Kempadoo and Piper produce intentionally political, critical works. Yet it is almost inevitable that works by Black and Asian artists will necessitate a social and political reading despite the intentions of the artist, or the lack of explicit social or political engagement of the works. For example, a portrait of a Black person may not really be seen in the same way as a portrait of a white person, and self-portraits are even more significant in this case. Because of the weight of historical marginalisation and objectification, a portrait or self-portrait by a Black artist, argues Eddie Chambers (1990), cannot avoid embodying different meanings from that of a white artist:

> A 'Black' self-portrait is nothing short of being an unequivocal statement of one's presence, one's existence, and above all, one's right to exist, one's right to struggle, in a world in which, more than ever, the white race dominates, controls, and sees itself as the pinnacle against which the pigments and efforts of all other races must be judged.
>
> (Chambers 1990: 5)

While I agree with the spirit of this, care is needed not to politicise art works against the wishes of the artists, especially those artists who appreciate recognition of their own agency. I do not mean by this that artists should always determine the social meanings of their work, but I consider that there is an issue here that historians and critics need to be sensitive to. For example Barbara Walker's painting *Attitude* (1998, 84″ × 48″) is a portrait of her daughter Daniella aged 14, which we would be wrong, I think, to read as a political work (Figure 20.3). The play of light across the face of the sitter is a sign of the different moods of young adults, the downcast eyes suggest uncertainty about appearance or an avoidance of a confrontational eye-to-eye encounter with parent or viewer. A more personal relationship between parent and child is involved here, and this should not be read as entirely positioned within 'Black' culture or debates about being Black and British.

Yet we should bear in mind that a sense of self/subjectivity has been hard won by Black and Asian people, and, on balance, it is probably not the case that postmodern rejections of the so-called autonomous, modernist subject hold a great deal of attraction for artists who, along with their forerunners, have struggled for recognition and funding in an art world based on the commodification of individual art productions. In his essay 'The Artist as a Post-colonial Subject and this Individual's Journey towards "the Centre"', Araeen makes clear that his whole trajectory as an artist and activist could never be conceptualised within postmodern frameworks which argue for the supposedly radicalising effects of the (symbolic) deaths of authors and subjects (Araeen 1999: 231). Even educational theorists who are enthusiastic about the theories of Michel Foucault and Jacques Lacan, and use them to deconstruct how educational discourses of power position both the teacher and the pupil, as well as categories of assessment, sound a note of caution. For example Dennis Atkinson (1999) argues that the sense of self, and the notion of 'self-expression' in art and art education, are constructs rather than discoveries about who we are as we participate in the symbolic order embodied in language, but follows this by adding:

> The difficulty with this constructivist understanding of subjectivity for art in

education is that if we are not careful, the human subject, or human agency, can be left out of the equation all together! If subjectivity in art practice is understood as shaped entirely by a network of discourses and practices (the social formation), then this ignores the fact that discourses and practices are operated, reviewed and changed by human agents. People do work with discourses and practices. Human subjects and their actions therefore are not only understood or conceived within discourse and practice but they also manipulate discourse and practice.

(Atkinson 1999: 17)

In looking at works by artists such as Keith Piper or Roshini Kempadoo, I am attracted by their artistic engagement with images of gender, 'race' and class as these relate to the subjectivity of both the viewed and the viewer. The interaction of these factors is complex, and admirably conveyed in examples of their multi-layered works which configure images of past, present, texts and contexts. As I write this, Dutch people are about to vote in elections in the wake of the political assassination of the right-wing populist Pim Fortuyn. Famous for his anti-immigration stance and radical campaigning for gay rights, Fortuyn rationalised his

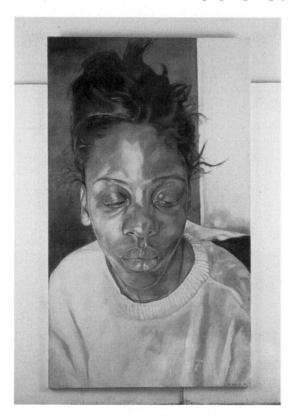

Figure 20.3 Attitude (1998), Barbara Walker.

dislike of Muslim immigrants in particular because of their attacks on gays. This is not peculiar to Muslims, however. There are doubtless many gay people from Muslim backgrounds, and also many other varieties of religious belief that condemn gays, such as Jehovah's Witnesses. What has puzzled some commentators is that the acting leader of Pim Fortuyn's party after the latter's death was a black Dutch immigrant, Joao Varela, from Cape Verde, a former Portuguese colony off the coast of Africa. He ran away from his parents and seven brothers and sisters because 'The situation in which we lived made it very difficult for me to make any progress' (Black and Thornton 2002: 3). He became a tennis champion and then a marketing analyst for the cosmetics company L'Oréal. Varela backs curbs on immigration, and in this he is not alone among immigrant communities, many of whom are fearful that more immigrants will destabilise their often precarious situations in 'host' countries. Yet is it really so unbelievable that there can be Black and gay racists and fascists? In the light of the failure of social democratic and labour parties in Europe to push forward towards greater social equality by political and economic means, many people have looked towards far right populism and nationalism for action. Postmodern theories of fragmentation, rejection of subjectivity and agency, dismissal of the notion of ideology in favour of 'discourse' or 'performativity', and the rubbishing of so called totalising master narratives, offer little in terms of understanding the political interplay of class, gender, 'race' and sexuality within capitalist societies. As John Roberts (1993) argues, discussing images of class in photography:

> The construction of gender-relations, sexuality and race as fictionalised categories of human difference are no less subject to negation than to positive appropriation. But working-class identity as it is constructed in tension with relations of gender, sexuality and race cannot take its place simply as one identity amongst many. For being working-class or not determines *how*, and *under what conditions*, the individual experiences themselves as a 'man' or a 'woman' or as 'gay' or 'black'. There is a sense then in which gender and sexual identity and racial identity are experienced in uneven ways – that is with different degrees of intensity and pressure – depending on a person's class location.
>
> (Roberts 1993: 5)

If teachers in schools want to look at art by Black, South Asian, Chinese or any other artists including European and North American ones, it is not enough to be multicultural or inclusive. Working from the same basis as Araeen or Roberts, I would suggest that they introduce a political dimension to their analysis and teaching. This does not mean forcing political analyses on to works which really are not political, but trying to have, and to foster, a political understanding of all works whether they are political, ideological or determined not to be either. And, as Roberts says, it is not enough to look at Blackness, femininity, or sexuality in isolation from class as it exists within global capitalism. This goes a long way to explaining why it is not so surprising that gays can be fascists, or a Black immigrant can be the leader of a racist political group, or why people should not really make any distinction between economic migrants and refugees. If globalisation is so good for everyone, and capital can travel across national boundaries, why don't people have the same rights? Should things have rights that people do not have?

Questions for discussion

1   What issues are raised by considering religion in relation to (a) the teaching of art history and (b) making value judgements about art?
2   What do you understand by the term 'multiculturalism' and how might it be usefully related to (a) teaching art history and (b) making and exhibiting art works?

Further reading

Doy, G. (2000a) *Black Visual Culture: Modernity and Postmodernity*, London and New York: I. B. Tauris.
—— (2000b) 'Frameworks of Theory and Practice: Looking at Class, "race" and Gender in Visual Culture History', in J. Swift and J. Swift (eds) *Disciplines, Fields and Change in Art Education, vol. 2, Aesthetics and Art Histories*, Birmingham: Department of Art, University of Central England, ARTicle Press.
King, C. (ed.) (1999) *Views of Difference: Different Views of Art*, New Haven, CT and London: Yale University Press and Open University Press.

References

Abbs, P. (ed.) (1987) *Living Powers: The Arts in Education*, London: Falmer.
—— (1989) *Aa is for Aesthetic: Essays on Creative and Aesthetic Education*, London: Falmer.
—— (1994) *Educational Imperative: Defence of Socratic and Aesthetic Learning*, London: Falmer.
—— (1996) *The Polemics of Imagination: Selected Essays on Art, Culture and Society*, London: Skoob.
ACHiS (2002) *ACHiS – Regions of Silence: In-Between Discourses*, unpublished research reports, London: Institute of Education, University of London.
Addison, N. (2001) 'Tried and Tested: Resourceful Art Histories in the Secondary School', *engage*, 8 (Spring): 15–21.
Addison, N. and Burgess, L. (eds) (2000) *Learning to Teach Art and Design in the Secondary School*, London: RoutledgeFalmer.
Advisory Group on Citizenship (1998) *Education for Citizenship and the Teaching of Democracy in Schools: Final Report of the Advisory Group on Citizenship*, London: Qualifications and Curriculum Authority and DfEE.
Allen, D. (1994) 'Teaching Visual Literacy: Some Reflections on the Term', *Journal of Art and Design Education*, 13(2): 133–44.
Allen, D. and Sefton-Green, J. (1999) 'Assessment and Evaluation in Creative Media', paper presented to 'Creative Media' conference, Institute of Education, University of London.
Allen, F. (2002) 'Museums and Social Inclusion: The GLLAM Report', *engage, 11, Inclusion under pressure*.
Allison, B. (1981) 'Identify the Core in Art and Design', *Journal of Art and Design Education*, 1(1): 59–66.
Anderson, D. (1997) *A Common Wealth: Museums and Learning in the UK*, London: Department of National Heritage.
Araeen, R. (1984) *Making Myself Visible*, London: Kala Press.
—— (1999) 'The Artist as a Post-colonial Subject and this Individual's Journey towards "the Centre"', in C. King (ed.) *Views of Difference: Different Views of Art*, New Haven, CT and London: Yale University Press and the Open University.
—— (2000) 'A New Beginning: Beyond Postcolonial Cultural Theory and Identity Politics', *Third Text*, 50 (Spring): 3–20.
Atkinson, D. (1998) 'The Production of the Pupil as a Subject in the Art Curriculum', *Journal of Curriculum Studies*, 30(1): 27–42.
—— (1999) *A Critical Reading of the National Curriculum for Art in the Light of Contemporary Theorisations of Subjectivity*, Broadside 2, Birmingham: Department of Art, University of Central England, ARTicle Press.

—— (2000) 'Assessment in Educational Practice: Forming Pedagogised Identities in the Art Curriculum', *International Journal of Art and Design Education*, 20(1): 96–108.

Auster, P. (1989) *Moon Palace*, London: Faber and Faber.

Austin, J. L. (1966) *How to Do Things with Words*, London: Oxford University Press.

Badiou, A. (2001) *Ethics: An Essay on the Understanding of Evil*, London: Verso.

Baker, H. Jr (1994) 'Critical Memory and the Black Public Sphere', *Public Culture*, 7(1): 3–33.

Bal, M. and Bryson, N. (1998) 'Semiotics and Art History: A Discussion of Context and Senders', in D. Preziosi (ed.) *The Art of Art History: A Critical Anthology*, Oxford: Oxford University Press.

Ballengee-Morris, C. and Stuhr, P. (2001) 'Multicultural Art and Visual Cultural Education in a Changing World', *Art Education*, 54(4): 6–12.

Barker, E. (ed.) (1999) *Contemporary Cultures of Display*, New Haven, CT and London: Yale University Press and the Open University.

Barone, T. and Eisner, E. W. (1997) 'Arts Based Educational Research', in R. Jaeger (ed.) *Complimentary Methods of Educational Research*, New York: Macmillan.

Barrett, T. (2000) 'About Art Interpretation for Art Education', *Studies in Art Education*, 42(1): 5–19.

Baudrillard, J. (1989) *America*, trans. C. Turner, London: Verso.

Bauman, Z. (1998) *Work, Consumerism, and the New Poor*, Philadelphia, PA: Open University Press.

—— (2001a) *The Individualized Society*, Cambridge: Polity.

—— (2001b) 'The Journey Never Ends: Zygmunt Bauman Talks with Peter Beilharz', in P. Beilharz (ed.) *The Bauman Reader*, Malden, MA: Basil Blackwell.

Beck, U. (1992) *Risk Society*, trans. M. Ritter, Thousand Oaks, CA: Sage.

Becker, C. (1994a) *The Subversive Imagination: Artists, Society and Social Responsibility*, New York: Routledge.

—— (1994b) 'The Education of Young Artists', in H. A. Giroux and P. McLaren (eds) *Between Borders: Pedagogy and the Politics of Cultural Studies*, New York: Routledge.

—— (1996) 'The Education of Young Artists', in L. Dawtrey, T. Jackson, M. Masterson and P. Meecham (eds) *Critical Studies and Modern Art*, Buckingham: Open University Press.

Benjamin, W. (1970) 'The Storyteller', in *Illuminations*, ed. H. Arendt, trans. H. Zorn, London: Jonathan Cape.

—— ([1934] 1986) 'The Author as Producer', in *Reflections: Essays, Aphorisms, Auto-biographical Writings*, New York: Schocken.

Bennett, T. (1998a) *Culture: A Reformer's Science*, Thousand Oaks, CA: Sage.

—— (1998b) 'Cultural Studies: A Reluctant Discipline', *Cultural Studies*, 12(4): 528–45.

Berger, P. (1991) 'Aporias of Modern Aesthetics', in A. Benjamin and P. Osborn (eds) *Thinking Beyond Traditional Aesthetics*, London: Institute of Contemporary Arts.

Bernstein, B. (2000) *Pedagogy, Symbolic Control and Identity*, Oxford: Rowan and Littlefield.

Besançon, A. (2000) *The Forbidden Image: An Intellectual History of Iconoclasm*, trans. J. M. Todd, Chicago: University of Chicago Press.

Betjeman, J. (1934) quoted in *London Evening Standard*, 22 May.

Betterton, R. (1996) *Intimate Distances: Women, Artists and the Body*, London: Routledge.

Bhabha, H. K. (1994) *The Location of Culture*, London: Routledge.

Binch, N. (1994) 'The Implications of the National Curriculum Orders for Art', *Journal of Art & Design Education*, 13(2): 117–31.

Binch, N. and Robinson, L. (1994) *Resourcing and Assessing Art, Craft and Design: Critical*

Studies in Art at Key Stage 4, Corsham, UK: National Society for Education in Art and Design.

Black, I. and Thornton, G. (2002) 'The New Face of Rightwing Politics in Holland', *Guardian*, 10 May.

Bloom, B. (1999) 'The Reign of Narcissism', in K. McShine (ed.) *Museum as Muse*, New York: Museum of Modern Art.

Bloom, H. (1994) *The Western Canon: The Books and School of the Ages*, New York: Harcourt Brace.

Boggs, C. (2000) *The End of Politics: Corporate Power and the Decline of the Public Sphere*, New York: Guilford Press.

Boime, A. (1990) *The Art of Exclusion*, London: Thames and Hudson

Bordo, S. (1990) 'Reading the Slender Body', in N. Mirzoeff (ed.) (1998) *The Visual Culture Reader*, London: Routledge.

Boughton, D. (1995) 'Six Myths of National Curriculum Reforms in Art Education', *Journal of Art & Design Education*, 14(2): 139–51.

—— (1997) 'Reconsidering Issues of Assessment and Achievement Standards in Art Education', *Studies in Art Education*, 38(4): 199–213.

Bourdieu, P. (1977) *Reproduction in Education, Society and Culture*, London: Sage.

—— (1984) *Distinction: A Social Critique of the Judgement of Taste*, trans. R. Nice, London: Routledge & Kegan Paul. (From *La Distinction*, Paris: Editions de Minuit, 1979.)

—— (1993) *The Field of Cultural Production*, Cambridge: Polity.

Bowie, D. (1991) *Lacan*, London: Fontana.

Brenkman, J. (1995) 'Race Publics: Civil Illiberalism, or Race after Reagan', *Transition*, 5(2): 4–36.

—— (2000) 'Extreme Criticism', in J. Butler, J. Guillary and K. Thomas (eds) *What's Left of Theory*, New York: Routledge.

Brighton, A. (1994) 'Art Education and the Scrutineers', in P. Hetherington (ed.) *Artists in the 1990s: Their Education and Values*, London: Wimbledon School of Art in association with Tate Gallery.

Britzman, D. (1997) 'Towards a Polymorphous Perverse Curriculum', in H. Giroux and P. Shannon (eds) *Education and Cultural Studies: Toward a Performative Practice*, New York: Routledge.

Bryson, N. (1981) *Word and Image*, Cambridge: Cambridge University Press.

Buckingham, D. (1998) *Teaching Popular Culture: Beyond Radical Pedagogy*, London: UCL Press.

—— (2000) *Making of Citizens, Young People News and Politics*, London: Routledge.

Bullock, A. (1975) *A Language for Life* (Bullock Report), London: HMSO.

Burgess, L. (1995) 'Human Resources: Artists, Craftspeople, Designers', in R. Prentice (ed.) *Teaching Art and Design: Addressing Issues and Identifying Directions*, London: Cassell.

Burgess, L. and Addison, N. (2000) 'Contemporary Art in Schools: Why Bother?', in R. Hickman (ed.) *Art Education 11–18: Meaning, Purpose and Direction*, London: Continuum.

Butler, J. (1993) 'Engendered/Endangering: Schematic Racism and White Paranoia', in R. Gooding-Williams (ed.) *Reading Rodney King/Reading Urban Uprising*, New York and London: Routledge.

—— (1997) *The Psychic Life of Power: Theories in Subjection*, Stanford, CA: Stanford University Press.

Carson, F. and Pajaczkowska, C. (eds) (2000) *Feminist Visual Culture*, Edinburgh: Edinburgh University Press.

Castoriadis, C. (1991) *Philosophy, Politics, Autonomy: Essays in Political Philosophy*, New York: Oxford University Press.

—— (1996) 'Institutions and Autonomy', in P. Osborne (ed.) *A Critical Sense*, New York: Routledge.

—— (1997) 'Culture in a Democratic Society', in D. A. Curtis (ed.) *The Castoriadis Reader*, Malden, MA: Basil Blackwell.

Central Advisory Council for Education (CACE) (1967) *Children and their Primary Schools* (Plowden Report), London: HMSO.

Chalmers, G. (1995) 'Reflections on the Past: Windows to the Future', *Australian Art Education*, 19(1): 7–17.

—— (1996) *Celebrating Pluralism: Art, Education and Cultural Diversity*, Los Angeles: Getty Education Institute for the Arts.

Chambers, E. (1990) *Let the Canvas Come to Life with Dark Faces*, exhibition catalogue, Coventry: Herbert Museum and Art Gallery.

Claxton, G. (1997) *Hare Brain, Tortoise Mind*, London: Fourth Estate.

Clement, R. (1986) *The Art Teacher's Handbook*, London: Hutchinson.

Clifford, J. (1988) *The Predicament of Culture: Twentieth Century Ethnography, Literature, and Art*, Cambridge, MA: Harvard University Press.

Cole, M. and Engestrom, Y. (1993) 'A Cultural–Historical Approach to Distributed Cognition', in G. Salomon (ed.) *Distributed Cognition: Psychological and Educational Considerations*, New York: Cambridge University Press.

Cornwell, J. (2001) 'Learning the Hard Way', *Sunday Times Magazine*, 9 September: 22–7.

Corrin, L. (1994) 'Artists Look at Museums', in F. Wilson (ed.) *Mining the Museum: An Installation*, Baltimore, MD and New York: Contemporary and New Press.

Creed, B. (1986) 'Horror and the Monstrous Feminine: An Imaginary Abjection', *Screen*, 27(1): 44–70.

—— (1993) *The Monstrous Feminine: Film, Feminism, Psychoanalysis*, London: Routledge.

Cronbach, L. J. (1975) 'Beyond the Two Disciplines of Scientific Psychology', *American Psychologist*, 30(2): 116–27.

Csikszentmihalyi, M. (1996) *Creativity*, New York: HarperCollins.

Cussans, J. (1993) 'Incessant Texts to Corporal Disintegration', in N. Cummings (ed.) *Reading Things*, London: Chance.

Damisch, H. (1975) 'Semiotics and Iconography', in D. Preziosi (ed.) (1998) *The Art of Art History: A Critical Anthology*, Oxford and New York: Oxford University Press.

Danet, B. (2001) *Cyberplay: Communicating Online, New Technology/New Cultures*, Oxford: Oxford International Publishers.

Davies, T. (1995) *Playing the System*, Birmingham: University of Central England.

—— (2000a) 'Postgraduate Teacher Education (Art & Design); "Wising-up" or "Dumbing-down"?' *Journal of Art and Design Education*, 19(3): 332–42.

—— (2000b) *Cultural Identity, Digital Media and Art*, Birmingham: BIAD, University of Central England and Cascade.

Davies, T. and Worrall, P. (2001) *BIAD Art and Design Education*, Slide/Digital Archive. Birmingham: School of Art and Design Education, Birmingham Institute of Art and Design.

Davies, T., Pimentel, L. and Worrall, P. (1999) *Electric Studio: New Practice in ICT Art and Design*, Norwich: Anglia Multimedia.

Dawtrey, L., Jackson, T., Masterson, M. and Meecham, P. (eds) (1996) *Critical Studies and Modern Art*, Buckingham: Open University Press.

Debord, G. (1977) *Society of the Spectacle*, Detroit, MI: Black and Red.

Department for Culture, Media and Sport (DCMS) (2001a) *Libraries, Museums, Galleries and Archives for All: Co-operating Across the Sectors to Tackle Social Problems*, London: DCMS.

—— (2001b) *Culture and Creativity: The Next Ten Years*, London: DCMS.

Department for Education (DfE) (1995) *Art in the National Curriculum*, London: HMSO.

Department for Education and Employment (DfEE) (1998) *Circular 4/98: Teaching: High Status, High Standards*, London: DfEE.

—— (1999a) *New Opportunities Fund (NOF) ICT Training Initiative: Funding and Certification for All UK Teachers*, London: DfEE.

—— (1999b) *The National Curriculum for England: Art & design*, London: Stationery Office and QCA.

—— (1999c) *The National Curriculum Handbook for Secondary Teachers in England Key Stages 3 and 4*. London: DfEE.

—— (2000) *National Curriculum for Art and design* (revised for September 2000), London: DfEE.

—— (2001) *Key Stage 3 National Strategy: Literacy across the curriculum*, London: DfEE.

Department for Education and Skills (DfES) (2001a) *White Paper: Culture and Creativity: The Next Ten Years*, London: DfES.

—— (2001b) *Teacher Workload (DFES 2001: Study conducted by Pricewaterhouse Coopers*. Available: http://www.dfes.gov.uk/pns/pnattach/20010326/1.htm (11 April 2002).

—— (2001c) *White Paper, Achieving Success*, Available: http://www.dfes.gov.uk/achievingsuccess/ (11 April 2002).

—— (2001d) *Press Notice: Information and Communications Technology in Schools in England*. Available: http://www.dfes.gov.uk/statistics/DB/SFR/s0284/index.html (4 September 2001).

Department of Education and Science (DES) (1991) *National Curriculum: Art for Ages 5 to 14*, London: HMSO.

Derrida, J. (2000) 'Intellectual Courage: An Interview', *Culture Machine*, 2, online. Available: http://culturemachine.tees.ac.uk/articles/art_derr.htm (29 March 2002).

Dewey, J. (1934) *Art as Experience*, New York: Minton, Balch.

Dirlik, A. (2000) *Postmodernity's Histories: The Past as Legacy and Project*, Lanham, MD: Rowman and Littlefield.

Dodd, J. and Sandell, R. (2001) *Including Museums: Perspectives on Museums, Galleries and Social Inclusion*, Leicester: Research Centre for Museum and Galleries, University of Leicester.

Douglas, M. (1966) *Purity and Danger: An Analysis of the Concepts of Pollution and Taboo*, London: Ark Paperbacks (1984).

—— (1991) *Purity and Danger: An Analysis of the Concepts of Pollution and Taboo*, London and New York: Routledge.

Doy, G. (2000a) *Black Visual Culture: Modernity and Postmodernity*, London and New York: I. B. Tauris.

—— (2000b) 'Frameworks of Theory and Practice: Looking at Class, "Race" and Gender in Visual Culture History', in J. Swift and J. Swift (eds) *Disciplines, Fields and Change in Art Education, vol. 2, Aesthetics and Art Histories*, Birmingham: Department of Art, University of Central England, ARTicle Press.

Duncum, P. (2000) 'Deconstructing Media Images of Postmodern Childhood', in D. Fehr, K. Fehr and K. Keifer-Boyd (eds) *Real-World Readings in Art Education: What your Professor Never Told You*, London: Falmer.

Eagleton, T. (1990) *The Ideology of the Aesthetic*, Oxford: Blackwell.

Efland, A. (1976) 'School Art's Style of Functional Analysis', *Studies in Art Education*, 17(2): 32–41.

—— (1990) *A History of Art Education*, New York: Teachers College Press.

Eisner, E. W. (1965) 'Children's Creativity in Art: A Study of Types', *American Educational Research Journal*, 2(3): 125–36.

—— (1972) *Educating Artistic Vision*, New York: Macmillan.

—— (1985) *The Educational Imagination*, New York: Macmillan.

—— (1988) 'The Primacy of Experience and the Politics of Method', *Educational Researcher*, 17(5): 15–20.

—— (1993) 'Forms of Understanding and the Future of Educational Research', *Educational Researcher*, 22(7): 5–11.

—— (1994) *Cognition and Curriculum Reconsidered*, 2nd edn, New York: Teachers College Press.

—— (1998a) *The Kind of Schools We Need*, Portsmouth, NH: Heinemann.

—— (1998b) 'Does Experience in the Arts Boost Academic Achievement?', *Journal of Art and Design Education*, 17(1): 51–60.

Elliott, J. (2000) 'Towards a Synoptic Vision of Educational Change', in H. Altrichter and J. Elliott (eds) *Images of Educational Change*, Buckingham: Open University Press.

Emin, T. (2000) 'I Need Art like I Need God', in W. Furlong, P. Gould and P. Hetherington (eds) *The Dynamics of Now: Issues in Art and Education*, London: Wimbledon School of Art in association with Tate Publications.

Espada, M. (2000) 'Viva Vieques!', *The Progressive*, 29 (28 July): 9.

Evans, D. (1996) *An Introductory Dictionary of Lacanian Psychoanalysis*, London and New York: Routledge.

Falk, J. and Dierking, L. (1992) *The Museum Experience*, Washington, DC: Whaleback.

Ferge, Z. (2000) 'What are the State Functions that Neoliberalism Wants to Eliminate?', in A. Anton, M. Fisk and N. Holmstrom (eds) *In Defense of Public Goods*, Boulder, CO: Westview.

Feyerabend, P. K. (1995) 'Science, History of the Philosophy of', in T. Honderich (ed.) *The Oxford Companion to Philosophy*, Oxford: Oxford University Press.

Field, D. (1970) *Change in Art Education*, London and New York: Routledge and Kegan Paul.

Foster, H. (ed.) (1985) *Postmodern Culture*, London: Pluto.

—— (1996) *The Return of the Real*, New York: MIT Press.

Foucault, M. (1977) *Discipline and Punish: The Birth of the Prison*, Harmondsworth: Penguin.

Frascina, F. and Harris, J. (1992) *Art in Modern Culture*, London: Phaidon.

Fraser, N. (1990) 'Rethinking the Public Sphere: A Contribution to the Critique of Actually Existing Democracy', *Social Text*, 25(26): 56–80.

Frayling, C. (2001) 'Building Bridges', *Arcady, the Newsletter of the Arts & Humanities Research Board*, 4(Winter): 2.

Freedman, K. (1995) 'Educational Change within Structures of History, Culture and Scientific Discourse', in R. W. Neperud (ed.) *Context, Content, and Community in Art Education*, New York: Teachers College Press.

—— (1997) 'Curriculum Inside and Outside School: Representations of Fine Art in Popular Culture', *Journal of Art and Design Education*, 16(2): 137–46.

Freedman, K. and Wood, J. (1999) 'Reconsidering Critical Response: Student judgements of Purpose, Interpretation, and Relationship in Visual Culture', *Studies in Art Education*, 40(2): 128–42.

Gardner, H. (1991) *The Unschooled Mind: How Children Think and How Schools should Teach*, New York: Basic Books.

—— (1993) *Creating Minds*, New York: Basic Books.

Geertz, C. (2000) *Local Knowledge: Further Essays in Interpretive Anthropology*, New York: Basic Books.

Geras, N. (1999) 'Minimum Utopia: Ten Theses', in L. Panitch and S. Gindin (eds) *Necessary and Unnecessary Utopias*, New York: Monthly Review Press.

Gere, C. (2001) 'The Canon and the Network Society', *engage*, 8 (Spring): 57–60.

Giroux, H. A. (1994) 'Benetton's "World without Borders": Buying Social Change', in C. Becker (ed.) *The Subversive Imagination: Artists, Society and Social Responsibility*, New York: Routledge.

—— (2001) *Public Spaces, Private Lives: Beyond the Culture of Cynicism*, Lanham, MD: Rowman and Littlefield.

Giroux, H. A. and McLaren, P. (eds) (1994) *Between Borders*, London: Routledge.

Giroux, H. A. and Simon, R. I. (1989) *Popular Culture: Schooling and Everyday Life*, New York: Bergin and Garvey.

Gitlin, T. (1997) 'The Anti-political Populism of Cultural Studies', in M. Ferguson and P. Golding (eds) *Cultural Studies in Question*, Thousand Oaks, CA: Sage.

Graham, G. (1997) *Philosophy of the Arts: An Introduction to Aesthetics*, London: Routledge.

Gramsci, A. (1971a) *Selections from the Prison Notebooks*, London: Lawrence & Wishart.

—— (1971b) *The Prison Notebooks: Selections*, trans. Q. Horare and G. Howell Smith, New York: International Publishers.

Greenberg, C. (1992) 'Avant-garde and Kitsch', in C. Harrison and P. Wood (eds) *Art in Theory 1900–1990*, Oxford: Blackwell.

Greene, M. (1995) *Releasing the Imagination: Essays on Education, the Arts and Social Change*, San Francisco, CA: Jossey-Bass.

Grossberg, L. (1994), 'Introduction: Bringing It All Back Home', in H. A. Giroux and P. McLaren (eds) *Between Borders*, London: Routledge.

Group for Large Local Authority Museums (GLLAM) (2000) *Museums and Social Inclusion: The GLLAM Report*, Leicester: Research Centre for Museum and Galleries, University of Leicester.

Guba, G. (1978) 'Toward a Methodology of Naturalistic Inquiry in Educational Evaluation', *CSE Monograph Series in Evaluation* 8, Los Angeles: Center for the Study of Evaluation, University of California.

Guilliano, E. M. (2001) *The Installment Plan*, Baltimore, MD: Baltimore City Paper.

Hall, J. (2000) 'The Spiritual in Art', in R. Hickman (ed.) *Art Education 11–18: Meaning, Purpose & Direction*, London: Cassell.

Hall, S. (1977) 'Culture, the Media and the "Ideological Effect"', in J. Curran, M. Gurevitch and J. Wollacott (eds) *Mass Communication and Society*, London: Edward Arnold for the Open University.

—— (1997a) 'Encoding, Decoding', in S. During (ed.) *Cultural Studies Reader*, London: Routledge.

—— (ed.) (1997b) *Representations: Cultural Representations and Signifying Practices*, London: Sage in association with Open University Press.

Hammersley, M. (ed.) (1999) *Researching School Experience: Ethnographic Studies of Teaching and Learning*, London and New York: Falmer.

Harland, J., Kinder, K., Lord, P., Stott, A., Schagen, I., Haynes, J. *et al.* (2000) *Arts Education in Secondary Schools: Effects and Effectiveness*, Slough: National Foundation for Educational Research.

Harvey, K. (2001) 'Is Globalisation Good for You?', *Workers Power*, global supplement, July.

Hebdidge, R. (1996) 'On Image and Identity', in J. Thompson (ed.) *Towards a Theory of the Image*, Maastricht: Jan Van Eyck Academy.

Heim, M. (2000) 'The Cyberspace Dialectic', in P. Lunenfeld (ed.) *The Digital Dialectic: New Essays on New Media*, Cambridge, MA and London: MIT Press.

Hein, G. (1998) *Learning in the Museum*, London: Routledge.

Heumann Gurian, E. (1999) 'Thinking about my Museum Journey', in B. Pitman (ed.) *Presence of Mind*, Washington, DC: American Association of Museums.

Hickman, R. (1999) 'Representational Art and Islam: A Case for Further Investigation', in D. Boughton and R. Mason (eds) *Beyond Multicultural Art Education: International Perspectives*, New York and Berlin: Waxmann.

Higonnet, A. (1998) *Pictures of Innocence: The History and Crisis of Ideal Childhood*, London: Thames and Hudson.

Hodge, R. and Kress, G. (1993) *Social Semiotics*, Ithaca, NY: Cornell University Press.

Hollands, H. (2001) 'From School to Art College', *engage*, 8(Spring): 51–6.

hooks, b. (1994) *Teaching to Transgress*, New York and London: Routledge.

—— (1995) *Art on my Mind: Visual Politics*, New York: New Press.

Hughes, A. (1998) 'Reconceptualising the Art Curriculum', *Journal of Art and Design Education*, 17(1): 41–9.

—— (1999) 'Art and Intention in Schools: Towards a New Paradigm', *Journal of Art and Design*, 18(1): 129–34.

Hume, D. (1874) *A Treatise on Human Nature*, edited by T. H. Green and T. H. Grose, London: Longmans, Green.

Hunter, I. (1994) *Rethinking the School: Subjectivity, Bureaucracy, Criticism*, New York: St Martin's Press.

Hutchinson, M. (1998) 'Of Monsterology', in D. McCorquodale, N. Siderfin and J. Stallabrass (eds) *Occupational Hazard: Critical Writing on Recent British Art*, London: Black Dog.

Isaak, J. A. (1996) *Feminism and Contemporary Art: The Revolutionary Power of Women's Laughter*, London: Routledge.

Ishaq, I. (2001) http://www.imf.org/external/pubs/ft/fandd/2001/09/ishaq.htm, International Child Art Foundation website, Washington, DC.

Itten, J. (1965) 'The Foundation Course at the Bauhaus', in G. Kepes (ed.) *Education of Vision*, New York: George Braziller.

Jackson, P. (1968) *Life in Classrooms*, New York: Rinehart & Winston.

—— (1998) *John Dewey and the Lessons of Art*, New Haven, CT: Yale University Press.

Jacoby, R. (1999) *The End of Utopia*, New York: Basic Books.

Jameson, F. (1990) *Signatures of the Visible*, New York and London: Routledge.

Jay, M. (1993) *Downcast Eyes: The Denigration of Vision in Twentieth Century French Thought*, Berkeley, CA: University of California Press.

Jones, A. (1993) 'Postfeminism, Feminist Pleasures and Embodied Theories of Art', in D. Preziosi (ed.) (1998) *The Art of Art History: A Critical Anthology*, Oxford: Oxford University Press.

Jones, P. (1998) 'Art', in Ofsted, *The Arts Inspected*, Oxford: Ofsted and Heinemann.

Keen, M. and Ward, E. (1996) *Recordings: A Select Bibliography of Contemporary African, Afro-Caribbean and Asian British Art*, London: Institute of International Visual Arts and Chelsea College of Art and Design.

Kincheloe, J. L. and Steinberg, S. R. (1993) 'A Tentative Description of Post-formal Thinking: The Critical Confrontation with Cognitive Theory, *Harvard Educational Review*, 63(3): 296–320.

King, C. (ed.) (1999) *Views of Difference: Different Views of Art*, New Haven, CT and London: Yale University Press and Open University Press.

Klein, N. (2000) *No Logo*, London: Flamingo.

Kohn, M. (2001) 'The Mauling of Public Space', *Dissent*, Spring: 71–7.

Kress, G. (1995) *Writing the Future: English and the Making of a Culture of Innovation*, Sheffield: National Association for the Teaching of English.

Kress, G. and van Leeuwen, T. (1996) *Reading Images*, London and New York: Routledge.

—— (2001) *Multimodal Discourse: The Modes and Media of Contemporary Communication*, London: Arnold.

Kress, G., Jewitt, C., Ogborn, J. and Tsatsarelis, C. (2001) *Multimodal Teaching and Learning: The Rhetorics of the Science Classroom*, London and New York: Continuum.

Kristeva, J. (1982) *Powers of Horror: An Essay on Abjection*, New York: Columbia University Press.

Lacan, J. (1977) *Ecrits: A Selection*, London: Routledge.

—— (1988) *The Seminar Book 1: Freud's Papers on Technique 1953–54*, trans. J. Forrester, New York: Norton.

—— (1991) *Four Fundamental Concepts of Psychoanalysis*, Harmondsworth: Penguin.

Lash, S. (1990) *Sociology of Postmodernism*, London: Routledge.

Leader, D. (2002) *Stealing the Mona Lisa: What Art Stops us from Seeing*, London: Faber and Faber.

Lewis, R. (1996) *Gendering Orientalism: Race, Femininity and Representation*, London and New York: Routledge.

Library and Information Commission (2000) *Empowering the Learning Community*, London: Library and Information Commission.

Lowenfeld, V. (1947) *Creative and Mental Growth*, New York: Macmillan.

Lunenfeld, P (ed.) (2000) *The Digital Dialectic: New Essays on New Media*, Cambridge, MA and London: MIT Press.

McChesney, R. W. (1999) *Rich Media, Poor Democracy: Communication Politics in Dubious Times*, New York: New Press.

McDermott, R. and Hervé, V. with Goldman, S., Naddeo, M. and Rizzo-Tolk, R. (1998) *Successful Failure: The School America Builds*, Boulder, CO and Oxford: Westview.

MacDonald, S. (1999) 'The Trouble with Post-Modernism', *Journal of Art and Design Education*, 18(1): 15–22.

McShine, K. (1999) *Museum as Muse*, New York: Museum of Modern Art.

Marcuse, H. (1979) *The Aesthetic Dimension: Toward a Critique of Marxist Aesthetics*, London: Macmillan.

Marwick, A. (1998) *The Sixties*, Oxford: Oxford University Press.

Mason, R. (2000) 'The Meaning of Craft', in R. Hickman (ed.) *Art Education 11–18: Meaning, Purpose & Direction*, London: Cassell.

Meecham, P. and Sheldon, J. (2000) *Modern Art: A Critical Introduction*, London: Routledge.

Meskimmon, M. (1996a) 'The Monstrous and the Grotesque', *Make*, 72: 6–11.

—— (1996b) *The Art of Reflection: Women Artists' Self-portraiture in the 20th Century*, London: Scarlet Press.

Mirzeoff, N. (1995) *Bodyscape: Art Modernity and the Ideal Figure*, London: Routledge.

—— (1999) *An Introduction to Visual Culture*, London: Routledge.

Moore, A. and Atkinson, D. (1998) 'Charisma, Competence and Teacher Education,' in *Discourse: Studies in the Cultural Politics of Education*, 19(2): 171–82.

National Advisory Committee on Creative and Cultural Education (NACCCE) (1999) *All Our Futures: Creativity, Culture and Education*, London: Department for Education and Employment.

Newman, A. and McLean, F. (2000) 'Museums as Agents of Social Change', *Museums Professional Group Transactions*, 32: 10–15.

Nochlin, L. (1991) 'The Imaginary Orient', in *The Politics of Vision: Essays on Nineteenth-Century Art and Society*, London: Thames and Hudson.

Ofsted (1998) *The Arts Inspected: Good Teaching in Art, Dance, Drama and Music*, Oxford: Ofsted and Heinemann.

Oguibe, O. and Enwezor, O. (eds) (1999) *Reading the Contemporary: African Art from Theory to the Marketplace*, London: Institute of International Visual Arts.

Olson, G. A. and Worsham, L. (1998) 'Staging the Politics of Difference: Homi Bhabha's Critical Literacy', *JAC*, 18: 3–35.

—— (1999) 'Rethinking Political Community: Chantal Mouffe's Liberal Socialism', *JAC*, 19: 163–99.

—— (2000) 'Changing the Subject: Judith Butler's Politics of Radical Signification', *JAC*, 20: 727–65.

Orava, J. (2001) 'Online Tools: Interactive Learning Environment', lecture presentation, *Conference Visivel e o Invisivel na Arte Atual*, Escola de Belas Artes da UFMG, Centro de Experimentacao e Informacao de Art, Belo Horizonte, Brazil, 17–21 September 2001.

Pancratz, D. (1993) *Multiculturalism and Public Arts Policy*, Westport, CT: Bergin and Garvey.

Panofsky, E. (1968) *Idea: A Concept of Art Theory*, Columbia, SC: South Carolina University Press.

Pereira, L. (1999) Unpublished manuscript.

Perkins, D. (1994) *The Intelligent Eye: Learning to Think by Looking at Art*, Santa Monica, CA: Getty.

Persky, H. R., Sandene, B. A. and Askew, J. M. (1999) *The NAEP 1997 Arts Report Card: Eighth Grade Findings from the National Assessment of Educational Progress*, Washington, DC: Office of Educational Research and Improvement, US Department of Education.

Peters, G. (2001) 'Against Integration: Distinguishing Art Theory and Aesthetics', *Journal of Art & Design Education*, 20(2): 180–94.

Pimentel, L. (2001) 'The Teaching of Art and Contemporary Technologies: From the Subjective to the Multicultural', lecture presentation, *Conference Visivel e o Invisivel na Arte Atual*, Escola de Belas Artes da UFMG, Centro de Experimentacao e Informacao de Art, Belo Horizonte, Brazil, 17–21 September.

Plato (1957) *The Republic*, edited by J. Ferguson, London: Methuen.

Pollard, A. (2002) 'Research in Primary Education', lecture, Institute of Education, University of London, 25 February.

Pollard, A. and Trigg, P. (1997) *Reflective Teaching in the Secondary School*, London: Cassell.

Pollock, G. (1988), *Vision and Difference: Femininity, Feminism and Histories of Art*, London and New York: Routledge.

Pope, D. (1998) 'Doing School: "Successful Students" Experiences of the High School Curriculum (Academic Success)', *DAI*, 60,08A: 2785–3081

Powell, A., Farrar, D. and Cohen, D. (1985) *The Shopping Mall High School*, Boston, MA: Houghton Mifflin.

Prawat, R. S. (1989) 'Promoting Access to Knowledge, Strategy, and Disposition in Students: A Research Synthesis', *Review of Educational Research*, 59(1): 1–41.

Prentice, R. (1999) 'Art: Visual Thinking', in J. Riley and R. Prentice (eds) *The Curriculum for 7–11 Year Olds*, London: Paul Chapman.

Prentice, R. and Dyson, T. (2000) 'Art and Design: Developments and Dislocations', in A. Kent (ed.) *School Subject Teaching: The History and Future of the Curriculum*, London: Kogan Page.

Preziosi, D. (1989) *Rethinking Art History: Meditations on a Coy Science*, New Haven, CT and London: Yale University Press.

—— (ed.) (1998) *The Art of Art History: A Critical Anthology*, Oxford and New York: Oxford University Press.

Price, E. (1982) 'National Criteria for a Single System of Examining at 16+ with Reference to Art & Design', *Journal of Art & Design Education*, 1(3): 397–407.

Putnam, J. (2001) *Art and Artifact: The Museum as Medium*, London: Thames and Hudson.

Qualifications and Curriculum Authority (QCA) (1995) *Art in the National Curriculum*, Suffolk: DfEE.

—— (1997) *Education Bill 1997*, London: The Stationery Office.

—— (1998) *Education for Citizenship and the Teaching of Democracy in Schools*, London: DfEE.

—— (2001) *National Curriculum: Art and Design, Key Stage 3, Programmes of Study*, London: QCA.

QCA and DfEE (1999) *Citizenship: The National Curriculum for England*, London: QCA and DfEE.

Reid, L. A. (1986) *Ways of Understanding and Education*, London: Institute of Education, University of London.

Re:source, (2001) *A Learning and Access Standard for Museums, Libraries and Archives*. London: Re:source (Council for Museums, Archives and Libraries).

Richardson, M. and Stevens, M. (1999) *John Soane Architect*, London: Royal Academy of Arts.

Richmond, S. (1998) 'In Praise of Practice: A Defence of Art Making in Education', *Journal of Aesthetic Education*, 32(2): 11–20.

Riley, J. (1999) 'Thinking to Learn: Learning to Think', in J. Riley and R. Prentice (eds) *The Curriculum for 7–11 Year Olds*, London: Paul Chapman.

Roberts, J. (1993) *Renegotiations: Class, Modernity and Photography*, exhibition catalogue, Norwich: Norwich Gallery, Norfolk Institute of Art and Design.

Robins, C. and Woollard, V. (2001) *Creative Connections: Teaching and Learning in Museums and Galleries*, report of the DfES funded research project run in partnership between Institute of Education, University of London and the Victoria & Albert Museum.

Rogers, R. (1998) *The Disappearing Arts?*, London: Royal Society of Arts.

Rose, G. (2001) *Visual Methodologies*, London: Sage.

Rosenthal, M. (1987) *Constable*, London: Thames and Hudson.

Ross, M. (1983) *The Arts: A Way of Knowing*, London: Pergamon Press.

—— (ed.) (1986) *Assessment in Arts Education: A Necessary Discipline or a Loss of Happiness?* Oxford: Pergamon.

—— (1995) 'National Curriculum art and Music', *Journal of Art and Design Education*, 14(3): 210–6.

Royal Society of Arts (RSA) (1999) *Opening Minds: Education for the 21st Century. Final Report of the RSA Project: Redefining the curriculum/by Valerie Bayliss*, London: RSA.

Ruskin, J. (2000) *Modern Painters*, edited and abridged by D. Barrie, London: Pilkington Press.

Salmon, P. (1985) *Living in Time*, London: J. M. Dent.

—— (1995) 'Experiential Learning', in R. Prentice (ed.) *Teaching Art and Design*, London: Cassell.

School Curriculum and Assessment Authority (SCAA) (1996) *Promoting Continuity between Key Stage 2 and Key Stage 3*, London: SCAA.

Schostak, J. (2000) 'Developing under Developing Circumstances: The Personal and Social Development of Students and the Process of Schooling', in H. Altrichter and J. Elliott (eds) *Images of Educational Change*, Buckingham: Open University Press.

Schwab, J. (1969) 'The Practical: A Language for Curriculum', *School Review*, 78: 1–24.

Scottish Consultative Council on the Curriculum (SCCC) (1996) *Teaching for Effective Learning: A Paper for Discussion and Development*, Dundee: SCCC.

Scottish Museums Council (2000) *Museums and Social Justice: How Galleries and Museums can Work for their Whole Communities*, Edinburgh: Scottish Museums Council.

Secondary Examinations Council (SEC) (1986) *Report of the Working Party: Art & Design Draft Grade Criteria*, London: SEC.

Siegesmund, R. (1998) 'Why Do We Teach Art Today?', *Studies in Art Education*, 39(3): 197–213.

Sizer, T. (1992) *Horace's Compromise*, Boston, MA: Houghton Mifflin.

Smith, C. (1998) *Creative Britain*, London: Faber and Faber.

Smith, L. (1968) *The Complexities of an Urban Classroom*, New York: Holt, Rinehart & Winston.

Smith, R. A. (ed.) (1987) *Discipline-Based Art Education: Origins, Meaning and Development*, Urbana, IL: University of Illinois Press.

Snow, C. P. and Collini, S. (1993) *The Two Cultures*, Cambridge: Cambridge University Press.

Solso, R. (1994) *Cognition and the Visual Arts*, Cambridge, MA: MIT Press.

—— (1997) *Mind and Brain Sciences in the 21st Century*, Cambridge, MA: MIT Press.

Spours, K. and Hodgson, A. (eds) (1997) *Dearing and Beyond: 14–19 Qualifications Frameworks and Systems*, London: Kogan Page.

—— (1999) *New Labour's New Educational Agenda Issues and Policies for Education and Training from 14+*, London: Kogan Page.

Stake, R. (1975) *Evaluating the Arts in Education: A Responsive Approach*, Columbus, OH: Merrill.

—— (1985) 'Case Study', in J. Nisbet, J. Megarry and S. Nisbet (eds) *World Yearbook of Education 1985: Research Policy and Practice*, London: Kogan Page.

Stallabrass, J. (1999) *High Art Lite*, London: Verso.

Steers, J. (2001) 'Orthodoxy or Globalisation', lecture, Institute of Education, University of London, 19 November.

Street, B. (1993) 'The New Literacy Studies: Implications for Education and Pedagogy', *Changing English*, 1(1): 113–26.

Student interviews (2001) *Video Recording of the Sir John Soane Intervention Project by PGCE Students*, London: Institute of Education, University of London.

Suchin, P. (1998) 'After a Fashion: Regress as Progress in Contemporary British Art', in D. McCorquodale, N. Siderfin and J. Stallabrass (eds) *Occupational Hazard: Critical Writing on Recent British Art*, London: Black Dog.

Swift, J. and Steers, J. (1999) 'A Manifesto for Art in Schools', *Journal of Art and Design Education*, 18(1): 7–14.

Tallack, M. (2000) 'Critical Studies: Values at the Heart of Art Education?', in R. Hickman (ed.) *Art Education 11–18: Meaning, Purpose and Direction*, London: Continuum.

Tate, N. (1997) Author's notes of his keynote address as SCAA chief executive to SCAA conference 'Curriculum, Culture and Society', Kensington Hilton, London, 7 February, 1996.

Taubin, A. (1996) 'Douglas Gordon', in *Spellbound: Art and Film Catalogue*, London: Hayward Gallery and British Film Institute.

Taylor, R. (1986) *Educating for Art: Critical Response and Development*, London: Longman.

Teacher Training Agency (TTA) (1999) 'The Use of Information and Communications Technology', in *Subject Teaching Identification of Training Needs: Secondary Art*, London: TTA.

—— (2000a) *Skills Tests: Initial Teacher Training, Qualified Teacher Status*, London: TTA.

—— (2000b) *Supporting Assessment for the Award of Qualified Teacher Status (Art and Design – Secondary)*, London: TTA.

—— (2001) *Standards for the Award of Qualified Teacher Status*, London: TTA.

Terry, L. (1997) 'The Hard Road to Renewal', *Arena Journal*, 8: 39–58.

Thistlewood, D. (1989) *Critical Studies in Art and Design Education*, London: Longman.

—— (ed.) (1992) *Histories of Art and Design Education: Cole to Coldstream*, London: Longman and NSEAD.

—— (1993) 'Herbert Read: An Appreciation', *Journal of Art & Design Education*, 12(2).

Thompson, E. P. (1975) *Whigs and Hunters: The Origin of the Black Act*, London: Allen Lane.

Thompson, J. (1991) 'Campus Camp', in P. Hetherington (ed.) (1994) 'Artists in the 1990s: Their Education and Values', *Issues in Art Education*, 1, London: Tate Gallery Publications.

Ua-Anant, M. (1987) 'A System for Analysing and Evaluating Thai Art Curriculum Content', *Journal of Multi-Cultural and Cross-Cultural Research in Art Education*, 5(1): 67–73.

Unger, R. (1998) *Democracy Realized: The Progressive Alternative*, London: Verso.

Unger, R. and West, C. (1998) *The Future of American Progressivism*, Boston, MA: Beacon Press.

Usher, R. and Edwards, R. (1994) *Postmodernism and Education*, London: Routledge.

Vergo, P. (ed.) (1989) *The New Museology*, London: Reaktion.

Virilio, P. (1997) *Open Sky*, London and New York: Verso.

Vygotsky, L. S. (1978) *Mind in Society*, edited by M. Cole, V. John-Steiner, S. Scribner and E. Souberman. Cambridge, MA: Harvard University Press.

Walker, J. A. (1999) *Art and Outrage: Provocation, Controversy and the Visual Arts*, London: Pluto.

Walker, J. A. and Chaplin, S. (1997) *Visual Culture: An Introduction*, Manchester: Manchester University Press.

Wallis, B. (ed.) (1995) *Blasted Allegories: An Anthology of Writings by Contemporary Artists*, New York: New Museum of Contemporary Art.

Warner, M. (1994) *Managing Monsters: Six Myths of our Time*, London: Vintage.

Williams, E. (1998) 'Suffering for One's Art', *Guardian Higher, Guardian*, 17 March.

Williams, J. (1997) 'Edward Said's Romance of the Amateur Intellectual', in H. Giroux and P. Shannon (eds) *Education and Cultural Studies: Toward a Performative Practice*, London: Routledge.

Williams, R. (1965) *The Long Revolution*, Harmondsworth: Pelican.

Withers, R. (2000) 'How can Students Critically Engage with Representations of Contemporary Art when their Views are Largely Determined by the Media', paper presented to 'Looking Over the Overlooked: Local Resources and Art History', Association of Art Historians and Tate Education Conference, Tate Britain, London, 30 June.

Witkin, R. (1974) *The Intelligence of Feeling*, London: Heinemann.

Wolin, S. (2000) 'Political Theory: From Vocation to Invocation', in J. Frank and J. Tambornino (eds) *Vocations of Political Theory*, Minneapolis, MN: University of Minnesota Press.

Worrall, P. and Davies, T. (1997) *IT Works in Schools*, Birmingham: BIAD, University of Central England and Cascade.

Yeboah, D. A. (2002) 'Enhancing Transition from Early Childhood Phase to Primary Education: Evidence from the Research Literature', *Early Years International Journal of Research and Development*, 22(1): 51–68.

Zizek, S. (1989) *The Sublime Object of Ideology*, London and New York: Verso.

—— (1991) *Looking Awry: An introduction to Jacques Lacan through Popular Culture*, Cambridge, MA and London: MIT Press.

—— (1997) *The Plague of Fantasies*, London and New York: Verso.

—— (ed.) (1998) *Cogito and the Unconscious*, Durham, NC: Duke University Press.

Index